On Blatchington Hill

History of a
Downland Village

On Blatchington Hill

History of a
Downland Village

by
Rodney Castleden

Rodney Castleden.

- Blatchington Press -

to Brendon Franks,
local historian, for his generous support and help
at every stage in the writing of this book

Front cover: Blatchington Street in 1850, a watercolour
reconstruction by Rodney Castleden.
Back cover: photograph of Blatchington Hill in 1914,
the rectory just visible on the skyline, Blatchington Pond
in the bottom right-hand corner.

Published in 2011
by Blatchington Press
Rookery Cottage, Blatchington Hill,
Seaford, East Sussex BN25 2AJ
Copyright Text & Line Drawings © Rodney Castleden 2011

ISBN: 978-1-4478-5768-6

Contents

Acknowledgements

A major resource for this book has been the wonderful collection of artefacts and documents at the Seaford Museum. Without the resources of the museum, the level of detail that has been achieved in this book would not have been possible. I must thank all the staff and volunteers at the Museum who have helped me, most especially Sue Sutton, the Archivist, and Kay Turvey, who runs the Museum.

Many of the images have come from the Museum archives and I am grateful to the Museum for letting me reproduce them. I am also grateful to Richard Hill for letting me use his excellent photographs of the three date plaques on his property, and to Rosemary Holland for allowing me to reproduce images from her comprehensive collection of archive photos.

Local historian Kevin Gordon has helped by patiently answering my questions, and supplying me with information. Another local historian, Ben Franks, has been generous in sharing his own researches into Blatchington's history, freely handing over large quantities of data and being ready to spend time proof-reading and discussing the many problems of interpretation. I am very grateful indeed to Ben for the unstinting work that he has been prepared to put into this book and the interest he has shown in its production.

Many Blatchington residents were ready to share their reminiscences of the village during the last few decades, and frequently lent me their property deeds to research. I was repeatedly surprised at how much their deeds revealed about the history of the village as a whole. It was useful to be shown round some of the houses, including their cellars, and see at first-hand how they had evolved, in some cases, over three hundred years; I do appreciate the surrender of privacy that this involved.

In particular I would like to thank Michael and Anne Ford-Smith, Jean Mote, Pat Wright, John and Jo Eastlake, Yvonne and Andy Casey, Geoff and Pauline Cheetham, Richard and Linda Hill, Susan and Frank Drader, Charles Pearsall-Horner, Peter and Barbara Withers, Norma Good, Tim and Kate Kay, Olivia Coffey, Laurie and Rosemary Holland, Bob Moore and Elizabeth Roberts. Carol Chamberlain, one-time secretary at Blatchington Court School, and Valerie Naylor, wife of Mr Ray Naylor who was Headmaster of Blatchington Court School, gave me some interesting insights into life at Blatchington Court.

On Blatchington Hill

Introduction

This is the story of a Downland village that for a millennium amounted to little more than a single street. Today its former existence as a village has been almost forgotten, as the last hundred years have seen it swamped by the outgrowth of Seaford, to the extent that many see it as no more than a district of the town. But until that happened East Blatchington was a village with a separate and independent existence, a village with a strong identity of its own, and a history of its own too. It developed as a straggle of cottages, barns, sheds and ponds along Blatchington Street, which is now Blatchington Hill and the southern half of Firle Road. A street. Just one street that started as a country lane, the Greenway, passing across the fields, over the Downs and into the Weald.

Today, both the village and its parish are known as East Blatchington. In the past it was often just Blatchington, or Bletchington. An 1877 conveyance refers to the place as 'Blatchington otherwise Bletchington', recognizing that both spellings and pronunciations were in use. And we can drop the 'East' if we wish. There is a West Blatchington, but it is unconnected and a long way off, north of Hove; both Blatchingtons are in the diocese of Chichester and it may be that diocesan administration sometimes required a distinction between West and East Blatchington.

There was a single reference to Blachyngton Peverel in the manor court book for 1540. The Peverel suffix was added in acknowledgement of the family who were lords of the manor here in the middle ages. 'Blecchinton' was held in 1161 by Robert Peverel. In 1364 the same family evidently owned Alfrynston Peverel and Exceate Peverel. In an Exchequer document dated 1121, Blatchington becomes 'Blacinctona', which looks like an attempt to latinize the name or a relic of the ancient Anglo-Saxon -*tūna* ending. In this book I tend to use whatever version of the name, whatever spelling, appears in the documents of the time.

Too often parish histories are swamped by accounts of the principal family. This happens partly because the gentry were major property owners; they drew up deeds, conveyances and wills, signed contracts, left themselves grand memorials in the parish church and left a trail of documents and inscriptions for historians to follow. It also happens partly because they were upper class and therefore have attracted the interest of snobs and social climbers. By contrast, the ordinary people of the parish, often poor and illiterate, left the barest of traces, a meagre spoor of baptisms, marriages and burials in the parish register. Like any other village historian, I have been limited by the information available to me, but I have tried to avoid a disproportionate emphasis on the gentry.

Talking to present-day residents has given many leads, and several different interpretations of the events of the recent past and the remoter past as well. Evaluating what people say is difficult, especially when what they say is hearsay, and several removes from the historical reality, whatever that may have been. There is a neat example of this in one of Blatchington's village characters, the mid-eighteenth century miller William Coombs, who firmly believed that the windmill in Firle Road (then Mill Road) had been in his family since the time of Henry VIII. The documents show otherwise, and ultimately it is the documents that this book will follow. William Coombs, like many of the rest of us, carried within his head and heart his own version of village history, of the history of his family, and these personal myths have their own place and value. It is not the place of historians to blow away treasured myths, but rather to tell an alternative and perhaps equally exciting story that is firmly based on documents, photographs, surviving architecture and archaeology.

A fascinating survey of the Cuckmere valley was undertaken in 2010, and the consultants who carried it out commented that the results were among the best they had ever achieved. Electrical currents were sent through the ground to find out the shape of the solid rock surface beneath the floodplain. The geomorphologists who carried out the research interpreted the instrumental data, and were fairly sure they had found the bedrock, thirty metres down, its surface eroded by the many channels of an ancient Cuckmere River over 10,000 years ago. But they had to drill down in at least one place, to be sure that that really was what they had found. They were proved right. The technique is called 'ground-truthing', and it is an essential part of research in geomorphology or archaeology. With local history it is the same. The stories handed down by oral tradition have to be corroborated, ground-truthed.

One source that is tantalizing in this respect is a description of the village as it was in about 1900. It was written in heavy black ink in a handwriting style that suggests an elderly person who had been educated in the Edwardian period; the content shows that the writer knew the village well and wrote the reminiscence in about 1970. There is neither name nor date attached to it, so I refer to it in the notes & sources lists at the ends of chapters as 'UU' – unsigned, undated. There are some clues buried within it, such as the reference to 'my aunt's watercolour' of The Star House. This suggests that the author might be a nephew of the Miss de St Croix who was showing people her watercolours of the village in the 1920s. To an extent this is corroborated by the comment that the writer had taken out the stalls in the stable at The Gables in 1962; The Gables had been the home of the two de St Croix sisters.

One passage towards the end of the notes reads, 'When did the mill go. . . before 1890s – not shown on E.AX painting of the cottage.' The typist who transcribed the notes added at the end in frustration, 'Who/what is E.AX? Who was his aunt who painted the watercolour?' These are the leading questions, and they turn out to be closely linked. The cryptic 'E.AX' is the all-important key. X is shorthand for 'Cross', or more specifically 'St Croix', St Cross in French, and it can be imagined that family members in private fell back on a simple X, to save themselves the trouble of repeatedly writing 'de St Croix'. 'E.AX' was Miss **Ethel Augusta** de St **Croix**, who was the watercolourist and whose full name appears on the 1898 conveyance for the purchase of The Gables. That should make identifying the author easy, but Ethel had eleven nephews. Four died before 1950 and therefore can be ruled out. Of the remaining eight, the one who fits best is Francis William de St Croix, who was born in 1901 and was the owner though not the occupier of the Gables from 1942 to 1970. As owner, he might well have removed stall partitions from the stable in 1962, perhaps with the idea of turning it into a garage or workshop for the use of his tenants.

This is a working hypothesis, and without definite proof it is safer to leave the document as 'UU'. It is part-reminiscence, part-hearsay. No doubt much of the detail is accurate. But there are moments where UU does not stand up to ground-truthing. Blatchington Court, it says, was bought by Robert Lambe, the last squire, in about 1899 and he probably bought the estate at the same time. But we have Robert Lambe's own record that he bought the estate in 1877, and almost certainly (on the evidence of other documents) the house with it. He let the house from 1877 onwards, as the previous owner had done, and only moved into it - he said so himself - in 1900. So the more reliable corroborative document tells a different story from UU. If UU was, as I believe, written by Francis de St Croix, he was describing events that took place before he was born, and therefore could not have witnessed. There are some other inaccuracies in UU, which means that we cannot rely on it when we come upon statements that we cannot test or corroborate.

This is too long to spend discussing the authorship and value of one document, but it does stand for many other such situations and illustrates how careful we have to be in using documents.

I had a hunch when starting the research that the key to this history of Blatchington (which I believe has not been attempted on this scale before) was going to be house history, or rather sets of house histories, and this unusual approach has proved to be very fruitful. I have been helped enormously in this by residents who have allowed me to study the title deeds of their properties, as these contain fine factual detail and sometimes key elements of village history. Individually fascinating, put together, they have proved to be an invaluable resource.

There are also official public records, which I have drawn upon to support the history of the modern period. There was no census before 1801. There was no formal requirement for parishes to keep written records before the sixteenth century, apart from the manor courts. Even when compulsory recording of baptisms, marriages and burials was ordered, there was resistance to it from a semi-literate community. The government had to legislate repeatedly before reliable and systematic recording got under way, and even then it was restricted to noting the bare bones of village life. The Blatchington records are of a high quality, beginning in 1563 and going on until the present, with only one break - the year 1618, for some reason. But before 1563, the lives of most people in Blatchington went completely unrecorded.

When reading *Montaillou*, the wonderfully detailed re-creation of life in a fourteenth century French village, one becomes acutely aware of all the richness of the lost medieval world, a world to which we have only restricted access at Blatchington. But Montaillou was only so carefully recorded because it was a hotbed of heresy, and an inquisitor compiled a detailed dossier on all the interrogations of villagers. Only under these extraordinary circumstances do we hear what ordinary people of the past actually thought, and what they said in conversation.

Nearly every settlement carries within it traces of its past, some more than others, and it is easy when walking up Blatchington Hill to see how it would have been two or three hundred years ago. The road would have been in the same place, and the footway running beside it at a higher level too; so would the flanking flint walls. The trees have come and gone, and come again; some of the houses would have been there, some not. We all sense that. We all carry within our minds, quite unconsciously, the idea of the *cadastre*, the pre-existing pattern of settlement that it is still possible to perceive, behind, within and beneath the modern settlement. On Blatchington Hill, now more or less at the geometric centre of Seaford's built-up area, it is still possible to see old Blatchington, the ghost of the ancient settlement. But how many ancient settlements are we able to see and carry in our imaginations? Perhaps that is something that varies with individuals.

This book is intended for the general reader, so intimidating footnotes and numbered endnotes have been left out. To enable readers to pursue particular ideas I have added a list of the principal sources at the end of each chapter, and a comprehensive alphabetical list of references at the end of the book. So 'Lower 1851' at end of this chapter can be traced in the References: 'Lower, M. A. 1851 *The Chronicle of Battel Abbey, 1066-1176*. London: John Russell Smith [publisher].' I hope this gives readers what they need.

We all have historical preferences: periods, events or themes in which we have a particular interest. I don't doubt that that will be the case with this history of Blatchington, and some readers will skip chapters on centuries that do not interest them. Yet there is a special reason for looking at the story whole. The very beginning of Chapter 1 shows how events widely separated in time connect with each other - and with us. The village is a product of all the centuries of its existence. Its life is a continuous narrative, a little like the life of any one of us, and a biography with some decades missing is likely to make an unsatisfying read.

It has been difficult to know what to leave out. How can we tell what may be significant and what may be incidental to the life of a village, when the story is far from over? When Mark Antony Lower wrote his introduction to the Battle Abbey Chronicle, he undertook 'to hand down, collected into a book, whatever we have been able to learn worthy of the remembrance of aftercoming times.' That seems to me a good test of what should be included. What follows is what I have been able to learn, and I hope the reader will think that what is in this book is worthy of the remembrance of aftercoming times. Above all, I hope the book will give the reader a sharper sense of the special personality of the place - its identity.

Notes & sources

Account of Castle Guard Rents (list of knights' fees, 1364-5)
Ladurie 1978 (Montaillou)
Lambe c.1914 (moved into Blatchington Court in 1900)
Lower 1851
UU

Chapter 1
The Prehistoric Hill

A pagan past uncovered

The earth-fast paving stones came up reluctantly, one by one, each piece of the past grinding against the other and yelping as it was prised up with a pick. The dark soil underneath had not seen daylight for five hundred years, not since the tower was built. Robert Dennis watched as the floor of the tower was transformed. A week ago it had been a medieval pavement, part of the worn fabric of his church; now, this December day in 1860, it had become an anonymous ten-foot square of ageless pagan earth.

The workmen were to lay new slabs, but not on this damp earth. They started digging out the topsoil; they would spread sand to give a dry footing for the new floor. They started digging in the centre: it was easier to swing a pick there. Almost at once a piece of coarse pottery was exposed. Robert told the men to be careful. Whatever it was, he wanted it whole. Eventually it was completely exposed – a large urn capable of holding half a bushel, standing upright and complete, with charred human bones inside. In the soil round the urn were ashes and pieces of burnt wood.

Then, two steps away, in the south-east corner of the tower, another urn was found on its side.

Cremation burials from the time of the Roman occupation in the second century AD. A funeral ceremony had taken place here, with a pyre to burn the corpse. Afterwards, people had gathered the charred bones and ashes and placed them in a jar, then buried the jar in a shallow grave. And more than once. So, a full thousand years before any of the existing fabric of the church was built, this was a place where people brought their dead and took their leave of them. Long before this was a Christian burial ground, it was a *pagan* burial ground.

Was it a coincidence that the church was built on this spot? Or was there folk memory and continuity of religious observance at an ancient sacred site? Like many other Victorian rectors, Robert Dennis was an antiquarian, interested in the history of his church, and he wrote a short note about the discovery for the Sussex Archaeological Society's journal.

But nagging questions remained, and still remain. Where were the people from, whose bones were cremated on the site of the church? They must have lived nearby, in round thatched wooden

huts that stood where now the flint and brick cottages of Blatchington village stand.

A prehistoric Blatchington

The view down Blatchington Hill from beside the church points
directly towards the western slope of Seaford Head, as if that was
once the road's destination, even if it isn't any longer. At the time
of the Roman occupation at least the slopes to the north and west
of the old hillfort on Seaford Head were still occupied. Pottery
dating from the second century AD, the same date as the cremation
burials at Blatchington, has been found in the upper fill of the fort's
enclosing ditches. There was a large encampment on the site of
Fitzgerald Avenue, which overlooked the mouth of the Ouse.

Was Blatchington Hill perhaps a fragment of a Roman or
Romano-British road leading to or from this encampment?

A road probably ran inland from the camp to reach the Weald,
and one possible route kept to the high ground, first striking east to
the site of South Hill Barn, then north following the line still
followed by Chyngton Lane, continuing northwards along what is
now the eastern edge of Seaford's built-up area to join The Comp,
the long track that heads for the col in the chalk escarpment at Bo-
Peep. This route was proposed by that great pioneering expert on
Roman roads, Ivan Margary: it was his Road No 144.

An alternative, more direct, route for the southernmost section
is currently favoured by archaeologists. Instead of going east from
the hillfort before going north and then north-west, it strikes
directly north across the golf course, across what is now the
junction of Arundel Road and Chyngton Road, across the Downs
Centre. This route too would have joined The Comp track.

The Romans' interest in the area may have been the mouth of
the Ouse, a useful harbour. In 1927 a Romano-British bronze
figurine was found in the old river bed of the Ouse at Seaford. The
figurine was of Harpocrates, who was portrayed as a boy with his
index finger to his lips, to indicate childhood but later taken to
mean silence. Harpocrates came into his own in the first centuries
BC and AD, with the vogue for mystery cults. At that time
Harpocrates figurines were made for house shrines right across
the Roman Empire. The figure was a good luck charm, probably
lost accidentally, dropped into the river while a ship was being
loaded or unloaded, then covered by the shingle. This happened at
the same time that people, probably the local people, were cremat-

Harpocrates

ing their dead at Blatchington.

Blatchington Hill, Firle Road and their continuation across the golf course was a likely early route up into the Downs from the waterfront. This opens the possibility that Blatchington's village street constitutes a very old road route indeed. It would certainly go some way towards explaining the location of the Romano-British burials found at the site of the church. A Romano-British hamlet may have grown up on the roadside in the second century, and formed the nucleus of the later village. The medieval village of Chyngton had a late iron age or Romano-British predecessor: Blatchington may have had a prehistoric predecessor too.

Traces of another Romano-British road have been found in East Blatchington parish, running 200 metres to the north of Belgrave

Road and more or less parallel to it. It has been traced from the Buckle by-pass and Kingsway across Tudor Close, heading towards Alces Place on Firle Road.

The main economic activity of the locals at East Blatchington during the Roman occupation would have been mixed farming (arable and livestock). The mixed farmers were the ones who cremated their dead on the downland slope where St Peter's tower would one day be built, over a thousand years into the future.

The river mouth had been a focus of activity for a long time. Neolithic axe heads have been found all over the area, but nearly always singly and found where they were accidentally dropped five thousand years ago. An exception is Seaford, where *fifteen* axe-heads were found all together in one place. They were discovered in 1986 under the roadway in front of 34 Upper High Street. This is the largest find of stone axes in southern England. Neolithic stone axe traders paddled from bay to bay, collecting and delivering consignments of axes on the shores of natural harbours for distribution. These flint axes are probably a consignment of locally-crafted axes buried in a pit close to the mouth of the Ouse, ready to be exchanged for goods landed by coastwise traders when they paddled into the river mouth harbour. The axes were for some reason never collected, but the cache does suggest that the mouth of the Ouse was being used as a harbour as long ago as 3000 BC.

No-one seems to have been living on the site of Blatchington village in the neolithic, though they were living in the parish, and not far away. There was a farmstead in Princess Drive just to the west of Firle Road. There was also a settlement in the middle of the eastern half of the golf course, where many neolithic and bronze age flints have been found. 5000 years ago, people were living close to the village, and at least hunting, foraging and collecting firewood across the area where the village of East Blatchington later grew up.

It is rare for the remains of prehistoric houses to survive, so we should not expect to find them on Blatchington Hill. In any case, if the later village developed on the site of a prehistoric village, any early remains will have been destroyed in the course of successive rebuildings.

Saxon & early medieval Blatchington

After the Romans left there was a shift in economy and land use in the South Downs generally. Some of the land that previously been under the plough was abandoned, left to degenerate into scrub and woodland. Elsewhere the cultivation of crops gave way to livestock grazing. There was a scaling-down of the previous economy, though no wrenching change.

We have no direct evidence that anyone was living at Blatchington in the period AD 500-1000, apart from the name of the place, which is pure Anglo-Saxon. Settlements with names ending in *–ington* are fairly early, second only to the *–ing* settlements. So it is likely that Blatchington was founded early. It may have been occupied as an Anglo-Saxon settlement as early as the sixth century.

Direct evidence for Anglo-Saxon settlement generally is hard to find, and discoveries like the recent finds at Bishopstone, a mile away, are exceptional. There was a possibility that the piece of land at the centre of Blatchington village and now occupied by Hogplot might have yielded some evidence of Anglo-Saxon settlement. A report by archaeologist Chris Butler recommended further invest-igation, but the opportunity was missed.

The medieval village almost certainly had a Saxon predecessor on the same site. A document from AD 788 mentions the river entering the sea at a place called 'Safforda'. This could refer to Seaford already existing as a settlement, but the name may refer to the shingle spit that made a natural causeway across from Newhaven's Castle Hill almost to Seaford Head, literally a sea-ford.

The area is one of historic importance in the story of Anglo-Saxon colonization. The small block of chalk Downland between the Ouse and the Cuckmere has the highest density of early Saxon settlements in Sussex, with five out of the six known early Saxon cemeteries, all dating from the fifth century. This stretch of the Downs, with Blatchington halfway across it, must have been the heartland of Aelle's kingdom of the South Saxons.

The name of the village may come from an original name something like Blaeca's tun, the farm of Blaeca, perhaps pronounced 'Bletcha'.

Blatchington is not mentioned as such in the Domesday survey: nor is Seaford. Along with Chyngton and Sutton they came under the minster church of Bishopstone, but the Edwardian rector of Blatchington, Arthur Richardson, noticed that in the Domesday Book for Sussex there was a coastal place called 'Bechingetone' which does not match any other known settlement, so perhaps Blatchington, which often in earlier days was 'Bletchington', was after all recorded in the Domesday survey as Bechingetone.

A Saxon chapel probably stood on the site of the present structure of St Peter's church, but nothing is known about it for certain. The following chapter explores the story of the fabric of the church as we now see it, and the chapter after that circles back, to return to the puzzle of its hidden earlier history. Meanwhile, there is a strange free-standing anecdote about St Peter's church in Arthur Mee's *Sussex*, written in 1937, and which says a lot about Blatchington's history. Mee mentions cryptically that 'the Norman font was found buried in the churchyard.' We don't know where this font is today, and no photo or drawing of it has survived. It seems that we have lost a piece of Romanesque sculpture. It is odd that this is the only documentary evidence we have of a significant find and it is hard to know what to make of it. There are many episodes in Blatchington's past that, in a similar way, teeter on the edge of history.

Notes & Sources

Anon 1963
Bell 1978 (Bishopstone)
Cooper 1879 (Romano-British urns)
Dennis 1861b (Romano-British urns)
Gardner 2003 (post-Roman economy)
Garwood 1985
Grinsell 1931(bronze age Sussex)
Nicklin & Godfrey-Faussett 1935 (place names)
Page 1905 (photographs of cinerary urns, facing p. 322)
Tattersall 1927 (Harpocrates)
Vincent 2000 (Roman roads)

Chapter 2
Blatchington in the Middle Ages

St Peter's Church

The parish church of St Peter the Apostle is central to the geography and history of the village. For centuries a major focus of village life, it is the one building that has survived all the social, political and religious vicissitudes of the last thousand years. It has been built, rebuilt, added to, modified and restored, yet preserving within its fabric traces of each episode of its history.

The oldest elements of St Peter's identified so far date from the twelfth century – parts of the nave – but there will have been earlier buildings on the site, perhaps a timber chapel that was rebuilt in stone in the early 1100s. The building was extensively reshaped in the thirteenth century, at the time when the tower was constructed.

The early twelfth century church was a simple box with a pitched roof, the present nave, with no western tower and probably without a chancel. The altar stood close to the east wall of the church, where the chancel arch is now. Once the chancel had been added in the thirteenth century, the altar was moved eastwards to occupy a similar position against the chancel's east wall. When the wall plaster was stripped off in 2010, the broken interior half of a piscina, a ritual stone wash basin, was found embedded in the south wall close to the east end of the nave. The exposed and intact piscina is located immediately to the right of the altar. The newly discovered second piscina might at first look like positive evidence that the church originally ended at the east end of the nave and the twelfth century altar stood against this east wall, right next to the piscina. But it is built into the ?1350 wall that fills the ?1300 arch, and therefore cannot have existed before 1350. Perhaps some medieval services were taken further forward than the fixed altar, as they often are today, and a second piscina was needed for these.

The chancel is surprisingly large and roomy for a church and village of this size. Before the Napoleonic Wars it is unlikely that there were ever more than about a hundred people living at Blatchington, generating little income, and for hundreds of years the rector was personally responsible for the church's upkeep.

A peculiarity of the nave's construction is the marked thickening of the walls at the eastern end. This is thought to show

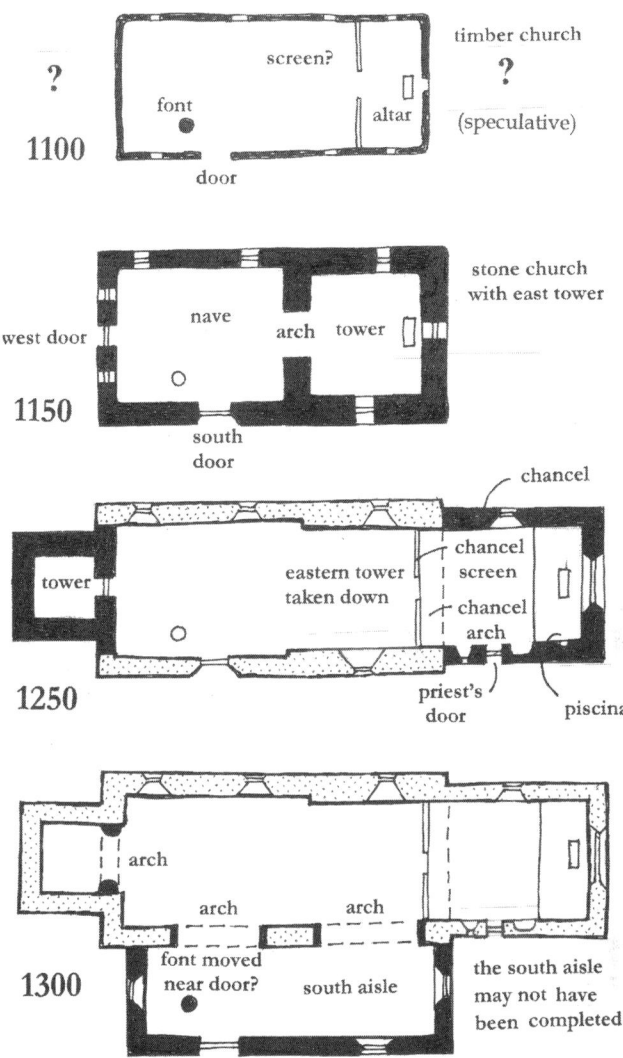

Development of the medieval church (sketch-plans)

that the eastern end was designed to support the weight of a tower. The normal place for the tower in an English church is the *west* end of the nave. Sussex has a number of variations from this, including several churches with the tower at the east end, where nave meets chancel. It might look like a transitional design, a step towards a cross plan, with the tower at the crossing, as at Alfriston, which has a central tower and a pair of transepts. But the tower over the east end of the nave is not necessarily a preliminary to a cross shape, and at Blatchington transepts were never attempted.

St Peter's church is one of a group of only eleven Sussex churches to have been fitted with a tower at the east end, and St Peter's eastern tower was later removed. The old tower was 6 metres (19 feet) square inside and 8.5 metres (28 feet) square outside, to judge from the surviving walls of the nave. It is possible that, in spite of its metre-thick walls, it fell down around 1200, or became unsafe and its upper walls had to be taken down.

Another risky structure was attempted - the addition of a south aisle. Building the south aisle structure against the south wall of the nave was not a problem, but piercing the rubble walls of the nave to make large openings for access weakened the wall dangerously. Two wide arches were cut into the wall, one 4 metres across through the south wall of the nave, the other 5 metres across through what had been the south wall of the tower. It may have been this that undermined the tower and necessitated its demolition. The poor engineering of these shallow arches is apparent even now in the exterior wall. The voussoirs of the large eastern arch in particular sag weakly, and it is easy to imagine medieval masons working fast to rebuild the wall, trying to fill the arch aperture up again before the whole wall collapsed. The new south aisle was made, presumably, to cater for a growing population. After the Black Death this enlargement was no longer necessary, but the new arches were unsafe anyway, so the south aisle was taken down and the arches were filled in.

It is odd that the two arches were of different sizes. The wide chancel arch was knocked through the east wall of the old tower at the same time. The remodelling of the church was risky. The base of the square tower had a gap already on its west side, where the nave passed underneath it. Now two more sides were knocked out, the south and east. It is surprising that the entire building did not fall down. It is easy to see how the mistake came about. If the south wall had been continuous and uninterrupted, three piercings for arches rather than two might have been made and these smaller arches would have been structurally stronger. But the south wall was in two distinct sections, nave and tower, possibly at that time separated by an arch on the site of the old tower's west wall. That meant that three arches were not possible, two a more obvious option. Four small arches would also have been possible, and they would have been safer than two large arches. Four were perhaps considered and rejected because, at only 2 metres wide, they might have looked rather fussy - but they would have been stronger.

The nave still has the old tie-beams from this post-eastern-tower period, three of them, equidistant, each bearing a central king-post to support the ridge and sprouting four curving braces to take the weight of the nave roof; three stylized trees with five branches perch on the tie-beams, holding up the roof. Looked at in another way, each of them was like an upside-down version of the base of a post-mill, like the windmill that stood, even then, on the open windswept Downs above the village, its other landmark.

The interior of the medieval church was plastered and probably painted. There is no firm evidence that there were mural paintings, but any that survived into the nineteenth century would have been destroyed in the 1859-60 restoration. Arthur Richardson, who was rector in the late nineteenth century, thought that there *had* been traces of wall paintings. It may be that they were little more than the ghosts of paintings, like the ones in Southease church, and that the rector who organized the restoration, Robert Dennis, did not think them worth preserving in that state.

The fabric of the church is an interesting conglomeration of unshaped local rocks, the only shaped stones being the quoins or corner-stones and the masonry round the window apertures. Most of the wall stone is local flint, but there are also substantial quantities of a distinctive orange-brown rock that is rich in iron. It has been suggested that this might be erratic material brought in from far outside the local area, but it is just as local as the flint. It comes from the Reading Beds. This rock layer can be seen outcropping halfway up the cliffs at Newhaven, an orange sand-stone rich in iron, with ancient beach flints strongly cemented into it. This very hard rock is an excellent choice of building stone. The layer of rock continues on the eastern side of the Ouse valley, unseen beneath the soil up Firle Road, and from there across to Sutton and Chyngton. Weathered blocks of it are dug up from the subsoil round the church itself. The same mix of local rocks can be seen in the flint walls round the churchyard and down Blatchington Hill.

The last change to the church in the middle ages was the building of a small but beautifully proportioned tower at the west end. This was 16 feet (5½ yards) across, a medieval dimension that we will keep finding in the village: an ox-goad's length (a perch), used for cottages and cultivation strips. Some think the tower was made in the late thirteenth or early fourteenth century, though the shape of it, together with its string courses, is typically Norman and

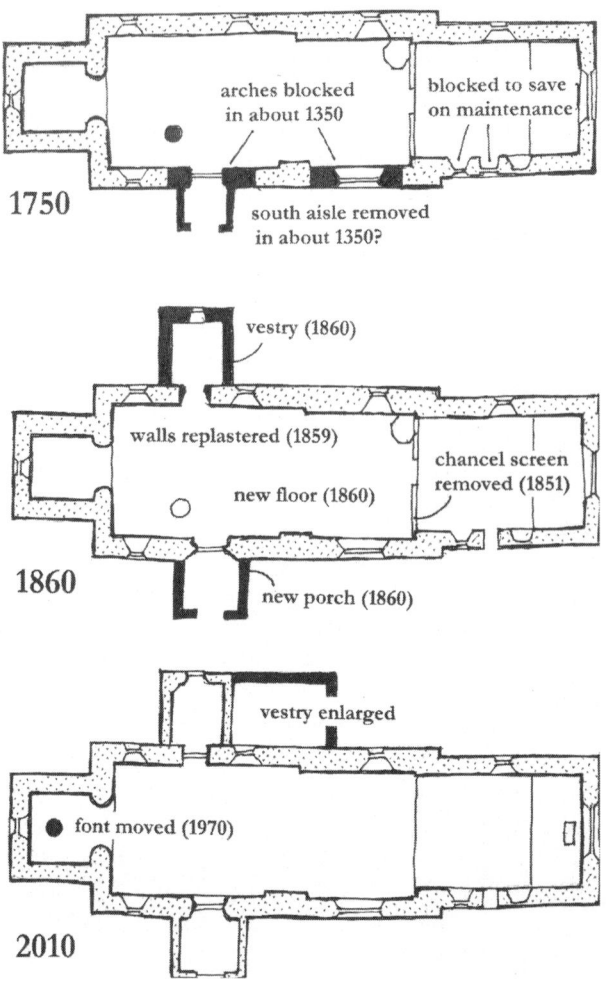

The post-medieval development of St Peter's church (sketch-plans)

that suggests that it might be older. The tower perhaps stands across the original west end of the nave, which may account for the absence of a Norman west door. In the exterior face of the nave wall just south of the tower there are two shaped stones, laid end to end as if to make a string course, though there is no equivalent on the north side of the tower. These asymmetrically placed, but carefully crafted, stones look like one half, the right-hand half, of

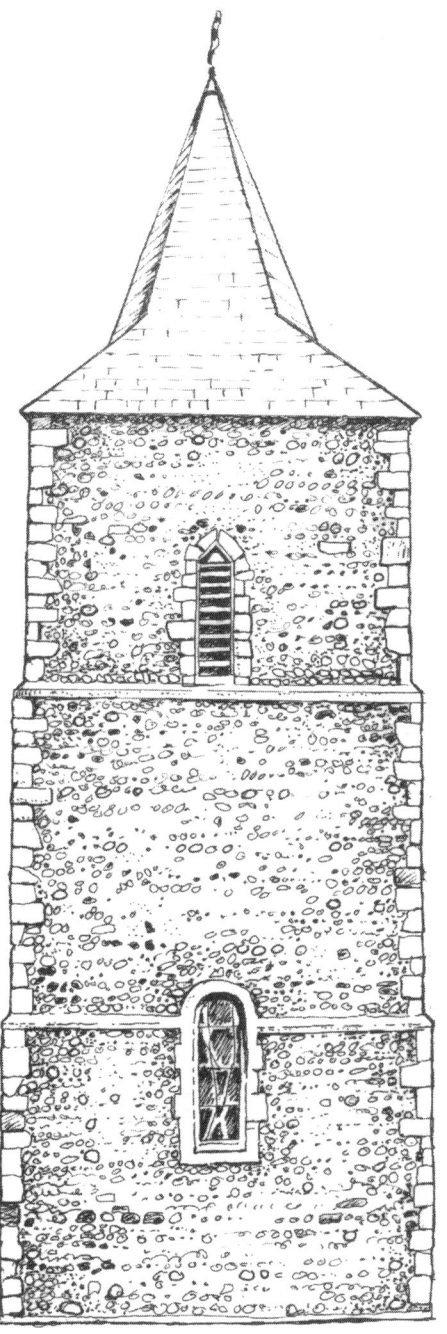

The church tower: the west wall.

a recycled stone window frame. The window aperture would have been a metre high and 30 cm wide with a semi-circular top, a typical Saxon or Norman window. This may indicate that the entire original Norman west wall of the nave was taken down and the materials reused as the tower was built.

The possible site of the original west door, in the centre of the east wall of the tower, has been opened up to make an arch, and this in turn has been rebuilt in modern times. The effect is fresh, harmonious and pleasant, but it is unfortunate that the medieval west door has disappeared.

A curiosity of the church is that the chancel was built on in the thirteenth century, and yet the small priest's door in its south wall seems to be older. This apparently Norman door may have been borrowed from another part of the church during the rebuilding: a rescue. And one thought is that this is the original west door of the church, moved when the tower was built.

Early drawings show that the priest's door was for a long time blocked up, presumably to save on maintenance. The same was true of the lower half of the east window and the westerly of the two lancets in the south wall of the chancel. All of these were reinstated at the time of the mid-nineteenth century restoration organized by Robert Dennis.

Another curiosity is that Blatchington was a chantry. A chantry was a chapel with an endowment to support a priest from the stipends of Masses for the dead, incomes normally paid to the King's treasury. In about 1547 Henry Foulks was commissioned to make a survey of all chantries in Sussex. One of these chantries was at Blatchington, and to support it the parish was allowed to keep back two shillings a year. The chantry was probably of long standing, which may explain why in such a small parish provision was being made for two priests, when really it needed only one. And this is why in the south wall of the chancel there are two thirteenth century seats: one for the rector, one for the chantry priest.

Both the vestry and the substantial and well-designed porch were added in the middle of the nineteenth century as part of the Revd Robert Dennis's church restoration programme in 1860. Some of the replacement rainwater goods bear the date. Earlier in Robert Dennis's time, in 1851, the chancel screen was taken out. The church was restored again in 1960, when the old pews were taken out. In 1966 the pulpit and choir stalls were taken out to create extra seating space. The existing font was removed to make space for two more pews. The tower was turned into a baptistry, and a marble floor put in to show off the new font, installed in 1970 in memory of the churchwarden, Robert Hall.

Lepers - the medieval hospital

In the middle ages the valley leading south-westwards from the pond, followed then as now by Blatchington Road, was open country. The bottom of the valley marked the parish boundary. In this no-man's-land, midway between the parish churches of Seaford and Blatchington, stood the medieval Hospital of St James. It was a natural choice of site for an isolation hospital, halfway between two settlements.

In the second half of the nineteenth century this was still open country, empty apart from a long building, the Workhouse, the Workhouse Master's cottage and a short run of terrace houses. The Workhouse building is still there, as the St James Centre, though now surrounded and hidden by later housing, and it was built directly on the site of the medieval hospital. Twyn House, the original dwelling of the Workhouse master, is also still standing, and probably stands on the site of the hospital master's house.

The leper hospital that stood on the site of the Workhouse was endowed in the twelfth century by Roger de Fraxineto, who was described in 1147 as 'the King's Constable'. He gave ten acres of land between Seaford and East Blatchington, specifically in order that a chapel and hospital could be constructed. It is often said that the hospital was founded at this time, but the wording of Roger's grant makes clear that the lepers already had a dwelling there; he was, in 1160, giving them the land they were already occupying. How long the leper colony had been in existence before 1160 is not known.

But the choice of location was unfavourable. The original grant of land mentions marshland to west and east of the leper colony. The hospital site is on a low-lying valley floor sloping down towards The Salts, then a marshy embayment on the landward side of the Ouse estuary. During storm surges, seawater must have invaded The Salts and swept up the valley towards the hospital and beyond.

Leprosy was widespread in the twelfth century. Doubtless some lepers were soldiers who had picked up the disease while crusading in the Holy Land. A few were allowed to beg by the roadside, but had to sound a wooden clapper to warn people off, and their alms dish had to be placed on the far side of the road. Lepers were not

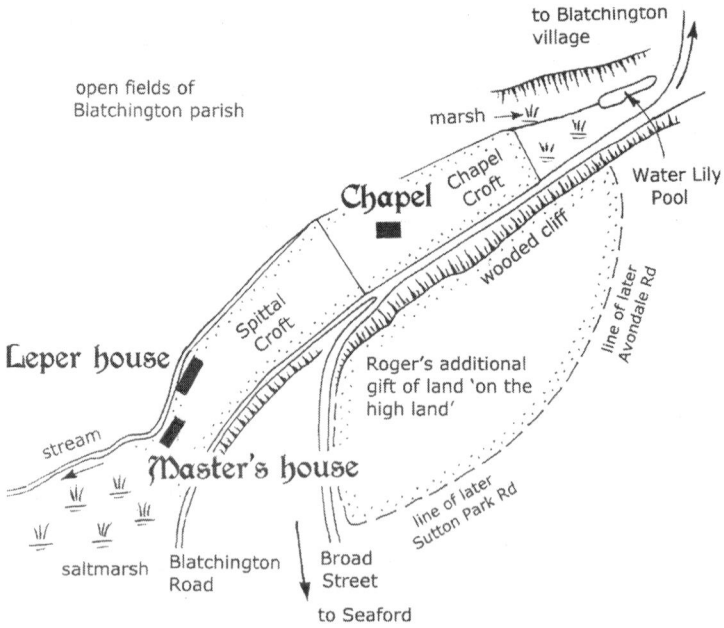

The geography of the Hospital of St James

only suffering from a disease, they were outcasts. Their doubled sufferings were exceptional and because of the medieval Christian preoccupation with suffering it was fashionable for the rich to give them money.

The allocation of space for the Hospital of St James sounds generous, and no doubt Roger de Fraxineto wanted his gift to sound generous. The complex had to include houses for the staff who were to run the hospital, gardens, kitchens and a chapel, as well as infirmary accommodation for the sick; a burial ground was needed too. The boundaries and plot names on old maps show a long narrow enclosure to the south-west for the hospital, running from Twyn House across to the footpath on the west side of the Trek Club and a smaller enclosure to the north-east for the chapel. The chapel enclosure, which included what is now the Trek Club, Mendall Auto Services and the wasteland to the east, may at around two acres seem unnecessarily large for a hospital chapel; but the enclosure for the chapel probably included a burial ground for the lepers. The site of the chapel was a place known in the middle ages as Burgham or Bargham.

A map dating from 1772 shows two walled enclosures, Spittal Croft and Chapel Croft, one enclosure for the hospital, one for the chapel. The north-eastern boundary of the chapel enclosure is still marked by a flint wall beside Chichester Road, which may have begun as a farm track skirting the boundary wall. The parish boundary dog-legs so that the two enclosures are in Seaford parish.

But there is no doubt, as Mark Antony Lower wrote in 1860, about the site of the hospital and its chapel. The entire complex lay to the southwest of the bowling club. The two acres of the Chapel Croft ran from Chichester Drive to the twitten west of the Trek Club. The remaining eight acres of the gift ran from there southwestwards as far as the site of the railway station, which in the middle ages would have been the inland edge of the Salts. The allocated land was described as lying between marshes to west and east, no doubt the saltmarsh to the west and the waterlogged ground round the two ponds to the east.

The newly-built chapel was consecrated by Bishop Hilary of Chichester in the middle of the twelfth century. The grant of land for the hospital and its chapel dating from the 1160s has survived.

'Grant by Roger de Fraxineto to the lepers dwelling next Seaford of the land upon which they dwell, and the marsh which could be enclosed towards the west and all the marsh towards the east as far as the pit [or well], except so much upon which the priest who served in their church might build if he wished,

A leper hospital chapel. This is the chapel at the Hospital of St Bartholomew, built at Oxford in 1126 and rebuilt in 1329. (Engraving from Ingram's Memorials of Oxford, *1837)*

and an acre near their house and one-and-a-half acres above the pit [or perhaps well], which land was called Gore [Garam]. . .'

'Gore' is an old word for a small triangular plot, though this helps little in identifying its location.

Roger granted to the chaplain of the lepers the strip of land above the chapel, between Blatchington Road and what is now Avondale Road:

'7 acres of land lying together on the high land next the way from Blachington to Sutton against the south side of the chapel of the lepers.' This was granted, *'with all other land granted to him [the chaplain], viz. 10 acres, on the day the church was consecrated by Bishop Hilary. Albreda his wife and Beatrice his daughter concurred'.*

Some have seen this as describing some other location, because Blatchington Road does not lead from Blatchington to Sutton as the charter says, but rather from Seaford to Blatchington and Sutton. But the location does match the description if we read it as 'from Blatchington *parish* to Sutton' rather than 'from Blatchington *village*'. The open fields of Blatchington parish ran right down to

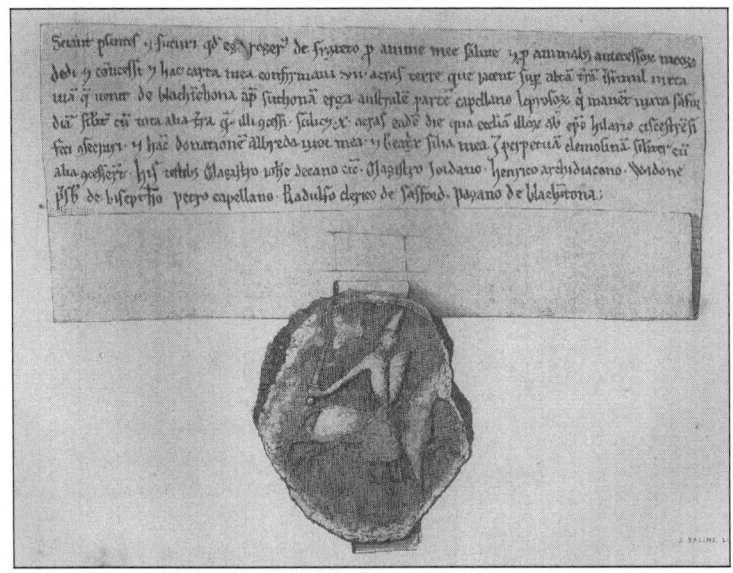

Part of the leper hospital charter.
The name Pagano de Blachingtona can be seen on the last line.

the bottom of the valley where the hospital lay. The junction of Chichester Road with Blatchington Road lies in the parish of Blatchington – stones marking the southern boundary of the parish are lost among the trees on the steep slope to the south of the road. The stretch of Blatchington Road running past the Bowls Club is therefore in Blatchington parish, so the road running north-eastwards from there could be said to be 'the way from Blachington to Sutton'. The 7 acres described in the charter could not be on the high land to the south of Sutton Drove, as they would not then be 'on the south side of the chapel of the lepers'.

Roger's gift of land was formally witnessed at the consecration ceremony. All the important churchmen of the area were present, along with the most important laymen. Roger was elderly – by 1166 he would be dead – and concerned about the future of his hospital, arranging for his wife Albreda and his daughter Beatrix to provide 'perpetual alms' after his death.

Roger and his family made their gift at the altar of St James in the presence of the assembled witnesses: Hilary, Bishop of Chichester, Master John, Dean of Chichester, Master Jordan and Master Henry, the Archdeacons, Master Joseph, Guy the priest of Bishopstone, Peter the chaplain of Seaford, Robert de Denton, Adam de Puningis [Poynings], Bartholomew de Querceto, Pagan of Blachington and many other clergymen and laymen. Among the laymen was Robert Peverel, lord of the manor at Blatchington.

The chapel fell into ruins and was demolished long ago, but we can get an idea of what it looked like from other leper hospitals. In 1126 a very similar hospital was founded at Oxford, and in a similar location, in Cowley Marsh, in open country between the city of Oxford and the neighbouring village of Cowley. It was on the margins of three parishes: St Clements, Cowley and Headington. An asylum was later built immediately to the north of the hospital, to house the outcasts of another time. An engraving of St Bartholomew's Chapel shows the likely scale and style of the chapel at the Hospital of St James. The leper house can be seen in the background. The chaplain's house was a separate building standing a short distance away to the west (left).

Roger and Albreda's daughter Beatrix married Simon, son of Simon. They had a daughter, Cicely, who married William de Averenches, lord of the barony of Fulkestan. Simon and Beatrix gave William the manor of Sutton, which included the Hospital of St James, as a marriage gift. They had a son, also called William. William de Averenches senior died. When the younger William was imprisoned by King John, Cicely, desperate to free her son, sold the manor of Sutton to the monastery of Robertsbridge for the sum of 700 silver marks. In 1215 she used this money to have her son William released from prison.

From 1215 onwards, the affairs of the Hospital of St James were administered from Robertsbridge. In 1523, Bishop Sherburn of Chichester founded a prebendal stall in Chichester Cathedral for the Hospital of St James together with 'the free chapel of Bargham'. At that time, the hospital was described as 'lying vacant and of so small rents [yielding such low income] that no one could take it.' Yet on 4 July the next year the Warden, Thomas Garrard, succeeded in letting the hospital site to Nicholas Tufton and John Seman. It was a 99-year lease and the rent was to be 20 shillings. The warden had the permission of the Bishop, Dean and Chapter of Chichester and the Convent of Robertsbridge.

In October 1533, the Abbey of Robertsbridge granted John Seman of Seaford a new lease on the hospital and the ten acres of land called Spittelland. This time it was a 40-year lease. The rent was to be £3 16s 8d and he was to pay annually ten pounds to the Dean and Chapter of Chichester. Thomas Garrard was to be the last Master of the St James Hospital. After the Dissolution, John Seman became liable for the payment of a pension of 20 shillings a year to Thomas Garrard – for life.

It is not known how John Seman used the site from 1534 onwards, but we catch occasional sight of him in documents. In his Will of 1541, William Best of Seaford left small bequests to John Ockenden and John Seman, whom he described as his 'overseers'. Although it is not certain how the Hospital was used after the Dissolution, there are clues from other comparable sites. In Chichester the Hospital of St James & St Mary Magdalene went through a continuous transition from medieval leper hospital to post-medieval almshouse. The same may well have happened at the Hospital of St James in Blatchington Road, especially since there had already been references in the late middle ages to the inmates as 'the poor' rather than 'the lepers'.

The changes in ownership are complicated but traceable. After John Seman, the proprietor was Thomas Taylour of Seaford. In 1565 Thomas Taylour surrendered a lease on the Hospital of St James to Sir Henry Sidney of Penshurst. The property passed from Sir Henry to Sir Robert Sidney and he in turn sold it, along with the manor of Blatchington, the manor of Sutton-Sandore and a clutch of other manors, to Sir Thomas Sherley of Wiston for £2000 in 1589. Specifically mentioned are 'the site of the hospital, chapel or chantry of St James in the co. of Sussex and all houses &c. belonging also 10 acres *called Spittellands thereto belonging and all other the messuages, granges &c. of the said Sir Robert Sydney in Sandore and Sutton, Seaford, Beddingham and Bletchington'.*

In March 1593, Sir Thomas Sherley sold off these manors to a number of individuals. *'The site of the hospital, chapel or chantry of St James in Seaford and the chantry lands in Eberton; also 10 acres of land called Spittlelands belonging to the said chapel or chantry of St James'* were passed on to Edward Lewknor of Kingston Bowsey and his brother Thomas. They in turn sold to William Farnefoulde of Newtimber.

In 1603 the hospital site was mentioned in connection with casual 'squatter' agriculture taking place there. A Mr Segar was told that he *'shall not hensforth plow or sow the spittle land without the consent of Mr Bayliff and his brethren generally, under paine of £10'.*

In January 1626, the Hospital was sold by William Farnefoulde to Sir Benjamin Pellatt of Bolney. The property was described as *'the site of the hospital, chapel, or chantry of St James near Seaford, and of 10 acres of land called Spittal lands thereto belonging'.* The site was to be for the use of Sir Benjamin for life and then for the use of his granddaughters and co-heirs, Anne, Katherine and Rose Pellatt. The following year there was a legal dispute between Sir Benjamin Pellatt and Thomas Elfick; the problem was confusion over the 'intermixed' lands of the two landowners in Sutton Sandore. In September 1646, the overseers of the poor in Seaford were directed by the court to go to Jevington to view the land currently occupied by Ralph Edwards, 'belonging to the poor of this town'. This implies that there may have been thought of shipping Seaford's poor out to Jevington. At the same time the Spittal Croft was let for 40 shillings a year. There were further sales and transactions during the next hundred years, and the hospital site slipped from view, as the buildings fell into ever more anonymous ruins.

The disintegrating ruins of the medieval leper hospital were still standing until 1780, when they were cleared. Then, immediately afterwards, the Seaford parish Poorhouse was built on the site. The master and his assistant lived in Twyn House and Twyn Cottage respectively. The inmates lived in the long building in the yard at the back, which still stands and is occupied by the St James's Trust. The inmates of the workhouse were moved to Eastbourne in about 1810, and at that time Twyn House and Twyn Cottage were turned over to ordinary domestic use. It was probably then that the eighteenth century flint walls with brick quoins were rendered over with incised lines to imitate masonry, and the bay windows were added. Nineteenth century gentrification.

The Seaford Volunteers Association was founded in 1990 to create facilities for the elderly and disabled. When the Volunteers decided to take on the Poorhouse buildings, they were in a poor state. Now eighteen different community and disabled groups use the centre.

The Hospital of St James is a fascinating example of a long-continued tradition. In the twelfth century the site was a charitable foundation, a colony-refuge for the sick, the needy, the poor and the social outcasts. After the Dissolution of the Monasteries, religious foundations such as this were abolished. Yet the need to shelter the poor, the sick, the disabled and the needy was still there, so it probably continued as an almshouse. The site went on and its work went on. It became the parish Poorhouse or Workhouse, another colony-refuge. When workhouses too became politically incorrect, it became the St James Centre.

Notes & sources

André et al 1900 (wall paintings)

Date of charter. Lower argues for 1172-73; he says it is the one year when 'Master John' de Greeneford was Dean of Chichester, but John was Dean from 1150. The charter says Roger was present and according to the Red Book of the Exchequer he had died by 1166. The charter also has Bishop Hilary present, and he died in 1169. All this suggests to me that the charter dates from before 1166, most likely 1160-65.

Godfrey 1940 (eastern tower)

Guide to Seaford 1910

Leper hospital. False traditions have been circulated about the leper hospital's location and extent. One found its way into print in a St Peter's Church Guide; 'local tradition has it that a leper hospital was halfway down Blatchington Hill, probably where the old house Sanctuary stood.' But Sanctuary is not an old house: it was built in 1923. Sale details for Sanctuary mention 'remains of an old ivy-clad Priory wall'. There is no evidence of a Priory here or anywhere else in the parish, but the priory tradition may have suggested to some that the site was connected with the hospital. These traditions regarding Sanctuary, combined with the genuine, document-based, evidence for the leper hospital on the St James's site, have led some to suppose that the leper colony was very large, stretching from Station Approach all the way to the Old Rectory. This cannot be true as the maximum grant of land was only 17 acres.

Lower 1860 (leper hospital)

National Archive: Sutton and Seaford. Documents SAS-M/1/331, 352, 354, 355, 356, 357, 358, 366, 367, 370, 372. (Hospital of St James)

Page 1905.

Chapter 3
In Bishopstone's shadow

Under the minster

Often the earliest recognizable mention of an English village is to be found in the 1086 Domesday Survey, but Blatchington's history is not so easily come by. The village does not appear in Domesday, even though it must have existed at that time. The village lay in Flexborough Hundred but the way this hundred was recorded in Domesday has baffled experts. The survey tells us a little about Tarring Neville ('Toringes'), South Heighton ('Estone') and at least two places called Firle ('Ferles'), one of which is probably Frog Firle, but it leaves Norton, Bishopstone, Blatchington, Sutton and Seaford unmentioned. Elsewhere in Domesday we read, 'In Flexberge hundred, the Bishop of Cicestre holds in demesne Biscopestone. In the time of King Edward it was assessed for 25 hides [around 3,000 acres] and now likewise.'

The account of Flexborough hundred gives the names of the landholders both before and after the Conquest. In the 1080s Tarring was held in demesne by Count Robert of Mortain, the Norman overlord of the Rape of Pevensey, while before the Conquest 'Azor held it of Earl Godwin', the father of King Harold. One of the Firles was held post-Conquest by the Abbot of Grestain (in Normandy) of Count Robert, while before the Conquest King Harold's queen, Edith, was the landholder. South Heighton was held by William, while before the Conquest 'Gundulf held it of King Edward [the Confessor]'. The Anglo-Saxon landholders were frequently displaced, though not always. One of the landholders at Firle in King Edward's time, when he held land of Earl Godwin, was the Saxon thegn Heming; he still held his land twenty years later, but from a Norman overlord.

The Domesday survey treated Blatchington as part of the episcopal estate of Bishopstone. Norton was the North Farm of the estate, Sutton was the South Farm, and Blatchington, between the two, would have been firmly embedded in the middle of the Bishopstone estate in the eleventh century.

At the centre of a royal or ecclesiastical estate like Bishopstone was a minster. This church had a resident monastic community of

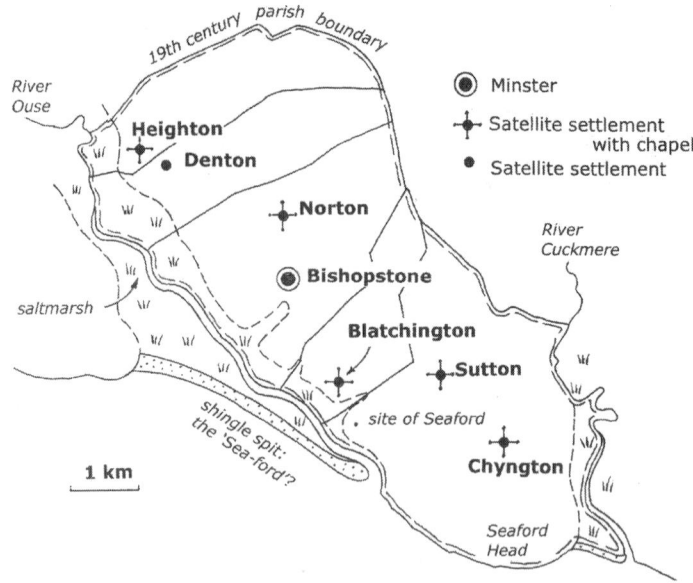

The Bishop of Selsey's estate at Bishopstone in 800

clergy who served a group of dependent chapels within its jurisdiction. The dependent chapels had no *right* of burial or baptism, so if burials or baptisms took place in them a payment had to be made to the mother church at Bishopstone.

This *parochia*, or super-parish, included the later parishes of South Heighton, Denton, Bishopstone, East Blatchington and Sutton. It is known for certain that there was a dependent chapel at South Heighton, and there were probably dependent chapels at Blatchington, Chyngton and Sutton too. The nineteenth century antiquarian, William Figg, was convinced that there was a chapel at Norton, while others think Norton was too close to Bishopstone for a chapel to have been necessary, but in the map above I have followed Figg's suggestion.

The dependent chapels were the forerunners of the medieval churches, which were most likely built on the same sites. Blatchington church probably began as a dependent chapel in the eighth century. The Bishopstone estate had been given to Abbot Plegheard, who in turn had given it to the Bishop of Selsey. In an ownership dispute resolved at the Synod of Clofesho in 825, the estate was given a curious shorthand tag, the number XXV, which seems to have stood for its 25 hides.

So, in the eight, ninth and tenth centuries, Blatchington was close to the centre of an estate belonging to the Bishops of Selsey. It existed as a small Saxon farming village huddled round a modest chapel, dependent upon and dominated by the episcopal minster at Bishopstone a mile away to the north-west. The chapel is likely to have stood on the site of the present church.

Handing on

In 1161 Robert Peverel owned the land at Blatchington, and it remained in his family for over two hundred years after that. The lordship of the manor passed from Robert to Walter, then to Thomas, who held 'a third part of a knight's fee in his manor of Blecchinton'. The lordship passed from Thomas to his son Robert and then to his grandson Andrew, who succeeded to the lordship in 1227. In the Fine Roll of 11 Henry III (Oct 1226-Oct 1227), we are told, 'Concerning the fine of Andrew Peverel. Andrew Peverel has made the fine with the king by 15 marks for his relief of the lands which Robert Peverel, his father, held of the king in chief in Burton and Blatchington, which fall to Andrew by hereditary right.' The court, held at Guildford, seems to have been making allowance for the fact that Andrew had difficulty in paying the fine (or fee) for accepting his inheritance. After him, three more Andrew Peverels inherited the lordship, the last of them born in 1318 and dying in 1375-76 without a male heir. At that time the advowson of the church, the appointment of the rector which was in the gift of the lord of the manor, was assessed at 26 marks.

Whether any of the Peverels lived at Blatchington is open to question. They each owned several lordships, Walter holding as many as eleven knight's fees, so they were more likely than not absentee lords.

In 1375, the parish and the lordship of the manor passed to John Brocas, who was a distant relative of Sir Andrew Peverel; Sir Andrew was John's mother's mother's uncle. Brocas was born in 1351, became lord of the manor of Blatchington in 1376 and died in 1379.

After that the fate of the lordship becomes harder to trace. The lord of the manor in 1411 was Richard Weyvils (or Wyvill), who was described as having 'manors, lands. . . viz. manor of Radmyld [at Eastbourne] £10; manor of Blachyngton, with lands called Knollond, £20; and an annuity from the lordship of Lewes, £20'. It seems that in the fifteenth century Blatchington was for some time in the hands of the West family and then the de la Warr family, who kept it until 1554. Later the lordship of the manor passed to the Jefferays, who subsequently moved to Chiddingly. The parish was repeatedly handed on and this handing-on of the manor from family to family was to continue in later centuries too.

In the 1460s economic recession, tenants refused to go on holding land at the old, high rents. They gave it up rather than continue to pay their lords rents that they could not afford; that forced lords to reduce rents. Thomas Seman was a tenant farmer at Blatchington. He occupied a grange, an outlying farmhouse belonging to a feudal lord. Thomas found that he could not afford the rent demanded, so he relinquished the grange with its nine acres, on which he was expected to pay an annual rent of eleven shillings and ninepence. This left the lord with no rent at all for some time. As he could find no takers at the high rent, he eventually had to let it out for six shillings, half the original rent.

A thirteenth century rector of Hailsham came from Bletchington. He was Master Robert de Blechynton and he was rector at Hailsham from about 1230 until about 1295. He was mentioned in 1286 and described as 'rector ab antiquo'. In 1501 another villager, Matthew Blachington, was a canon at Michelham Priory; in 1521 he was a sacrist there.

Rebels - rebellion and non-payment of rent

We tend to think of the peasants as being the rebels and malcontents in the middle ages, with flare-ups like the great revolts of 1381 and 1450 as culminations of long periods of smouldering resentment. But sometimes the rebels were priests. Bishop Thomas Rushoke (1385-88) excommunicated seventeen of his clerics for non-payment of subsidy — all on the same day, 21 December 1386. One of them was William Courtays, Rector of Blachyngton by Seford.

The 1450 Peasants Revolt in Sussex was fuelled as much by social and economic problems as by political grievances. The picture currently emerging is that the 1450 revolt was more like the 1381 revolt than historians previously believed. In Sussex, the artisans and other young men who joined the rebels had suffered, along with their families, from the mid-century recession - and they resented the burden of demands from their lords. Some of the rebels certainly called for a new king who knew better how to rule. Some called for the destruction of all lords.

At least one farmer from Blatchington joined the Jack Cade rebellion in 1450. He was 'William Jefferay of Blachyngton, husbondman' and he was pardoned. It was customary to execute the ring-leaders in rebellions, to make an example of them, but pardon the followers. Perhaps the leniency was pragmatic, to avoid depleting the workforce.

Murder - a stabbing on Blatchington Hill

In 1378, there were French raids at various places along the Channel coast, while at Canterbury Cathedral, masons began work on the fine new nave. At Blatchington, in March that year, a murder was committed. It happened on Blatchington Hill, not in one of the cottages, but out in the road. It was a street fight between two men, in which one stabbed the other to death. It is not known what the fight was about, or which of the men provoked the other, but we know their names and the exact time of the murder because the details were recorded at the inquest conducted by the County Coroner, William Cade, the very next day.

The victim was John Crokebek, a local man who 'owned' or worked a plot of land in Seaford. A property deal in 1366 or 1367 mentions 3 rods of land abutting in the 'west on the land of the heir of John Draneke, who now is John Crokebek.'

The inquest was held on 15 March 1378 and the village is named as 'East Blachyngton by Sefford'. It was held in the presence of 'trusty and lawful jurors of Flaxebergh Hundred', though they are left unnamed. The murder happened 'at the hour of vespers', the evening service, on 14 March. This would be 5 or 5.30pm. Whether the implication is that the two men were on their way to church to take part in Vespers, or should have been, is unclear. Maybe it was just a way of describing the time of day.

The coroner's report reads:

'At the hour of vespers on 14 March Philip atte Hale the elder of East Blatchington, a tithing of Flexborough hundred, assaulted John Crokebek with a baslard in the king's highway in the township of East Blatchington, but John seized and held the baslard. Philip then drew his knife called 'twytel', struck John in the chest with it and thus killed him.'

The description is short but vivid. A baslard was a long dagger that was worn suspended from a girdle. It was not considered proper for priests to carry it. A reference in the time of Henry VI suggests that by then it was regarded as mainly a *northern* weapon, and by implication barbarous. Philip was out on Blatchington Hill armed not only with his baslard but with a smaller knife as well.

The coroner noted Philip's pet name for his knife, 'Twytel'. To twittle is to tell tales, prattle, blab. This is a glimpse of an ancient tradition. Kings and princes in the dark ages gave their swords names: Arthur's Excalibur is a legendary example, but it represents a common practice in sixth century Britain. King Rhydderch of Clyde, for instance, named his sword Dyrnwyn. Like Excalibur, it was believed to possess special magical qualities; when drawn from its sheath, Dyrnwyn flamed like fire. So Philip atte Hale, with his Twytel, came near the end of a long tradition of named weapons.

What happened next is perhaps the most extraordinary part of the story. We might expect to read that Philip was thrown into the lock-up in Seaford High Street for the night, tried by the Bailiff and hanged the next day. The middle ages were a time of quick, rough justice, we tend to assume. But as we have already seen, one villager was let off – even for treason. Philip was imprisoned, but he was not hanged.

If the crime had been committed just a few hundred yards to the south, in the parish of Seaford, then Philip would have fallen into the town's justice system. He would have been tried by the Bailiff and Jurats of Seaford, almost certainly condemned to death, and hanging would have followed. But Blatchington parish, though *by* Seaford, was not *of* Seaford. The case had to be referred up – and out.

The case was sent to Chancery on a writ dated 12 November 1379. This represents a long delay – 20 months – during which time Philip was in prison. He was still not brought to trial. After a delay of another five months, on 16 April 1380 the case was sent from Chancery to King's Bench, presumably because this was clearly a criminal case. It is hard to understand why the case was delayed in this way, especially since from the facts that we have there seems to be no question about Philip's guilt.

The Marshalsea Prison in Southwark was in use from at least as early as 1329 until its closure in 1842, and a brick wall in Angel Court is all that remains of it today. In its final phase it was a debtors' prison, but earlier it was used to incarcerate those who had been convicted by the Marshalsea Court. In the fourteenth century King's Bench used a special writ to imprison in the Marshalsea a defendant in a civil suit on a bogus criminal charge, which was then dropped when the court was ready to try the original one; it was a ploy that acted as a kind of remand system.

Many prisoners did not emerge alive from the Marshalsea, which Philip probably knew. If he stayed in the Marshalsea he would eventually be hanged and, while the case was pending, when the opportunity arose, he broke out. Somehow, Philip managed to escape. He was outlawed, sentenced in his absence to a life of rootless wandering. Many outlaws fled for refuge to the forests, which was at least as safe as trying to leave the country. The sentence of outlawry, an ancient punishment dating from Anglo-Saxon times, put Philip outside the law's protection. In common law, a writ of outlawry made the pronouncement *Caput gerat lupinum* ('Let his be a wolf's head'). In the eyes of the law the person concerned was a beast that could be killed on sight – by anyone – just as if he were a wild animal.

Nobody knows where Philip atte Hale went after his escape from the Marshalsea, but he would not have returned to Blatchington. Nothing more was heard of him.

It is possible that he committed an earlier murder, at sea off Shoreham, 25 years before the Blatchington murder. Two captured pirates were pardoned on condition that they 'abjure the realm'. The pirates embarked at Shoreham for Normandy, but they were thrown overboard by six other men. The six were charged with murder, but on the Earl of Arundel's supplication they were pardoned. Among the six was Philip atte Hale.

There is no way of knowing whether the Philip atte Hale who murdered two pirates in 1353 is the same Philip who committed murder in Blatchington in 1378, but he might be and, if he is, he got away with three murders.

Country life in the middle ages

Medieval Blatchington had a complex social and economic structure. It had its lord of the manor and its villagers, but they interacted with the lord of another manor - Alciston - and a kind of tension existed between the two lords. And there were claims from elsewhere too.

John Brocas, born in 1351, belonged to a Gascon family that had become established in England in the reign of Edward II. He acquired the manor of Shopwyck near Chichester, and he also inherited lands at Blatchington, Ripe, Selmeston, Exceat and other places. He was in debt in 1376, the year before he was called up to help repulse the French landing at Rottingdean in 1377. After John Brocas died in 1379, it was noted that he held '50 acres of land and pasture for 300 ewes at Exceat' and 'a messuage and a dovecot at

Blatchington in the Rape of Pevensey'. A stranger in Rottingdean held a property with a dovecot (almost certainly the manor house) at Blatchington, and with it the lordship of the manor.

A system of farming that deployed three open fields was the norm across much of England. It was in use at Blatchington, but in a more ambitious and progressive way than in most other places.

By the thirteenth century, this part of the South Downs had a reputation for advanced agricultural techniques, and for producing good wool and fine fleeces. One reason for this was a segregation of the lord's fields from the peasants' common fields and the lord's pasture from the grazing lands of the small farmer. This segregation allowed the lord of the manor to experiment with new techniques that would lead to greater profitability, while the conservative peasants simply continued at a subsistence level. Blatchington was a typical Eastern Downland settlement, with all the peasant farmers living in a nucleated village. This gave the lord of the manor greater control in laying out and allocating the agricultural lands: indeed greater control over the villagers in every way. But there was also an important environmental reason.

The thin chalk soils needed replenishing to sustain high corn yields. Peasant farmers with only a few sheep were unable to manure their arable strips adequately, though the records show that some villagers owned surprisingly large numbers. At Blatchington in the fifteenth century, Richard French had 200, and Thomas Jeffrey had 300 sheep. Putting the sheep into a common fold, along with the sheep of the other villagers, created a big enough flock to have a major fertilizing effect, if guided round the fields by an expert shepherd. Blatchington had a common flock of perhaps 1000 sheep, which could dung in rotation each of the villagers' strips of land in the common fields. The shepherd expertly controlled the grazing with constantly shifting arrangements of hurdles supported by stakes; he was one of the key figures in the village economy.

It was only by introducing the common sheep-fold that peasant farmers were able to survive in the chalk Downland landscape. It was a system that worked well, and lasted 300-400 years, until brought to an end by the consolidation of land holdings that began in about 1500. The common sheep-fold kept the soil fertile and the corn yield high. Yields of wheat and especially barley were at least 50% higher in the Eastern Downs than they were in the Western Downs. The Tudor Bishop Hugh Latimer commented, 'Plough-lands must have sheep; yea, they must have sheep to dung their ground for the bearing of corn; for if they have none to fat the ground, they shall have but bare corn and thin.'

Operating the common sheep-fold worked best with all the small farmers living in the village. But the villagers paid a high price for the benefits of this system. They had to endure something close to hereditary serfdom, heavy obligations in terms of work for the lord, and they had to accept imposed farming routines. The system was economically one of the most efficient in the kingdom, but it was politically and socially oppressive, putting community above individuals. Even so, Blatchington kept to the common flock system until at least the middle of the seventeenth century.

The lord of the manor presided over village life from his manor house. In the 1790s, when Blatchington Court was on the market, it was described as 'newly built'. There are plenty of references to lords of the manor before that time, and some of them lived at Blatchington. Documents tell us that someone bought Blatchington manor house in 1717, so we know that a manor house existed before the one that was built in the 1780s. That earlier manor house may have been a late seventeenth century building made of flint and brick, like some of the cottages still standing on Blatchington Hill, or a much older structure, perhaps a timber frame hall house dating from the fifteenth century. Neither picture nor description of it survives. If it was a hall house, it may have looked something like my speculative reconstruction on the following page, and it probably stood on the same footprint as the new mansion built in the 1780s. The messuage with dovecote owned by John Brocas in the 1370s may have been an even earlier manor house, preceding the one demolished in the 1780s.

As in other medieval villages, there were two peasant classes. The villeins were peasants who were tenants with perhaps 15 acres of arable, enough to be self-supporting. The bordars or cottars were lesser tenants who worked smaller areas that were not sufficient to sustain them and their families; as a result they had to work for wages on the lord's demesne, and the time they spent ploughing, hoeing and harvesting the lord's land meant less time spent on their own.

Free tenure in the later middle ages was the equivalent of modern freehold tenure, ownership in the fullest sense, which gave security of tenure. Unfree (copyhold) tenure was property held 'at the will of the lord', but it gave some guarantee of safety against an unfriendly lord, as it was tenure according to the ancient custom of the manor. The conditions might vary from manor to manor, but they were written down and copies held by the copyholder:

Blatchington Court – a lost hall house?

individual lords did not have the power to change them. At Rottingdean and Ditchling, for example, the widow of a copyholder was
entitled to inherit the whole of her husband's copyhold lands for
life, while a widow at Rotherfield had no such entitlement.
Blatchington had its own peculiar ancient custom, shared by a
number of other Sussex manors, and known as Borough English.
This meant that the customary descent of a copyhold property was
to the *youngest* son. No-one knows when or why this custom
originated, though it may have been designed to safeguard the
interests of the son likely to be the most disadvantaged by his
father's death.

A standard individual peasant land holding at Blatchington,
called a 'wist' in these parts, was 11 acres. A man might hold
between one and two wists, but others held only part of a wist; at
Blatchington, on average one person held a little under one wist, a
low land allocation by comparison with other places; in Newhaven
and Brighton, for instance, the size of the wist was 12-16 acres. The
apparent severity of the land allocation at Blatchington, 11 acres,
was offset by the productivity of the land; because of the common
sheep-fold system, the yield of the land was higher. Each wist was
split up into strips of arable land scattered about amongst a number
of open arable fields, and the standard strip size was suitable for
one night's dunging by the common flock.

In the middle ages, Blatchington operated a three-field system.
On the Tithe Map the block of three furlongs to the east of
Blatchington Hill and Firle Road, Bowdean, Middle and Home
Furlongs, looks like a surviving Anglo-Saxon open field and, sure

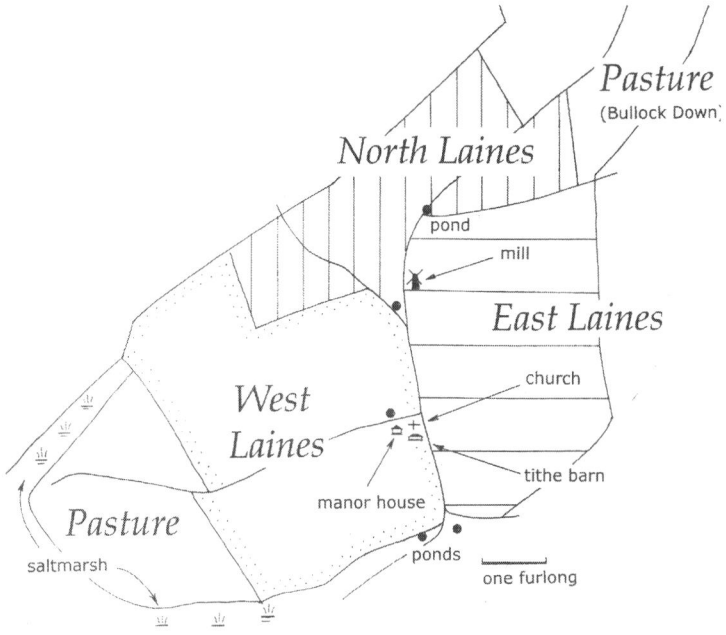

The three open fields
(reconstructed from the Tithe map of 1843, William Figg's map of 1818)

enough, in the middle ages it was known as the Eastleyne. It was organized in a systematic way using standard measurements, the perch (5½ yards), chain (4 perches) and furlong (10 chains or 40 perches). A standard strip was 4 perches by 40 perches, 22 yards by 220 yards, its 4840 square yards making one acre, the area of land that could be ploughed by an ox team in a day.

The cultivated strips ran away east and west from Blatchington Street, roughly at right angles to the street, for 220 yards (40 perches). They terminated at north-south headlands, balks of grass making boundary markers, from which two further sets of strips were struck to east and west for another 220 yards, where another pair of headlands was laid out, and so on. The three sets of strips to the east of the village made the East Laines. The four sets to the west made the West Laines. Each block of parallel strips was called a furlong: 'Home Furlong' was the block next to the village.

Strips were ploughed clockwise, which turned the soil in towards the middle of the strip, so that it became a low ridge. The furrows on each side served as useful visible boundaries.

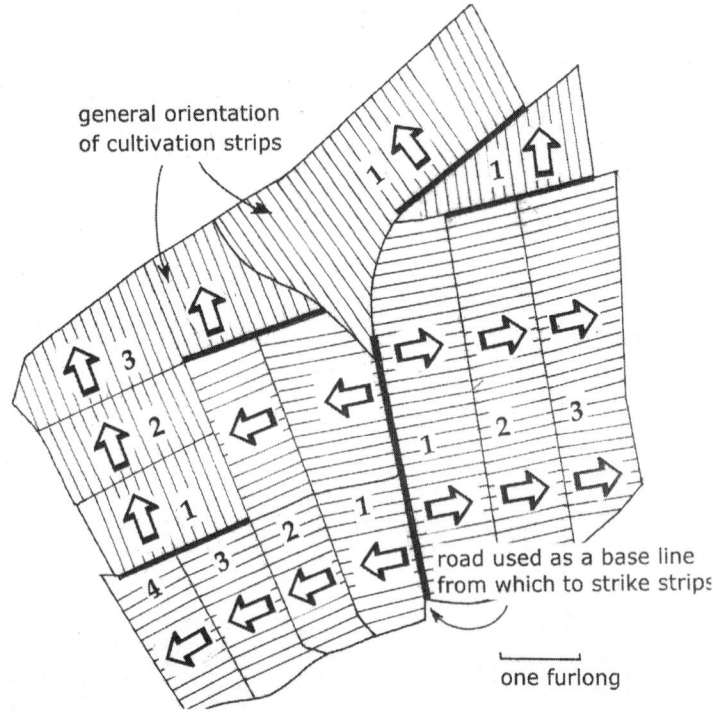

general orientation
of cultivation strips

road used as a base line
from which to strike strips

one furlong

How the three open fields may have been laid out with strips, starting from the village street. Each block of parallel strips was known as a furlong; only later did the furlong become a unit of linear measurement. This map shows how the blocks of strips at Blatchington were commonly a furlong (220 yards) wide.

The village ends of several of the strips were enclosed with fences or walls to make house-and-garden plots. The Star Inn and Widows' Cottages were built in one such enclosure, the inn's north wall and the cottages' south wall marking the edges of a strip 4 perches wide, 40 perches long; this is shown on William Figg's 1818 map. Both buildings were 15 feet wide, the builder's idea of a 'short' perch. Perhaps the houses were built in plots marked out by the strips, or it may be that the houses and their gardens and paddocks were there first and their boundaries were simply extended out across the fields. Because the houses have been replaced several times over it is now impossible to tell.

The strips running northwest at right angles to the northern part of Firle Road, the North Laines, only made a single run of 40 perches or so before reaching the parish boundary. To the southwest and northeast of the three large arable fields lay pasture.

The pasture on the higher ground is not called Tenantry Down on the 1843 Tithe Map. This could indicate that the tenantry had by custom been required to graze their sheep on the arable land and

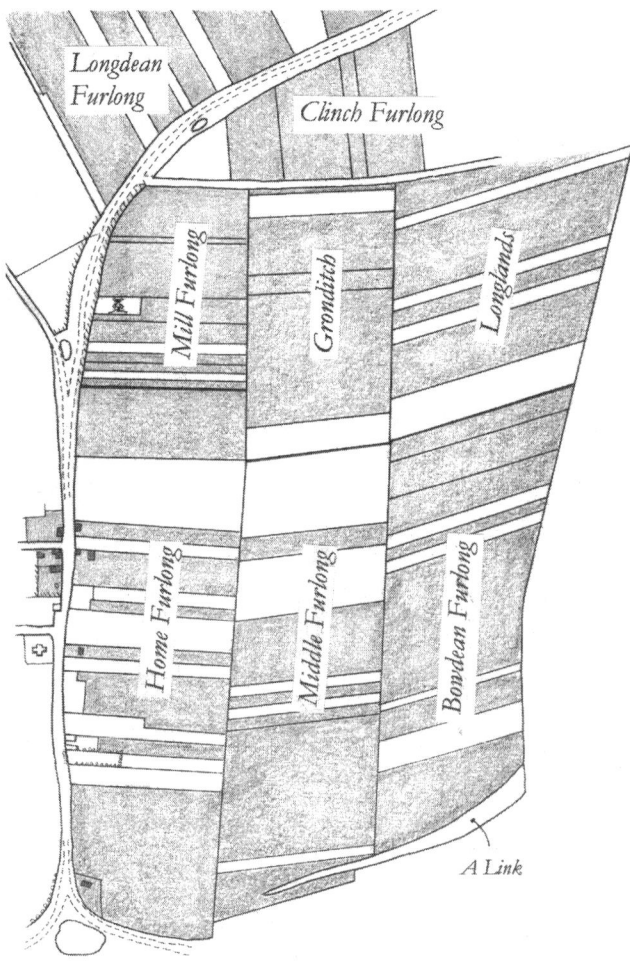

The North and East Laines in 1818 (from William Figg's map). All the land marked grey and all the buildings marked dark grey belonged to the manor of Alciston. Exchanges had by this time been made among the land-holders in order to consolidate some of the medieval strip holdings.

that this patch of higher downland was in the middle ages reserved for the *lord's* flock. In the 1840s Upper, Middle and Lower Hill Pieces were arable, and only the 150-acre Sheep Down was used for pasture, but in the middle ages all four of these plots were probably used for grazing the lord's flock: certainly they were pasture in 1818. The 1818 Deed of Covenant between Lord Gage and John King stated that Bullock Down was the Tenantry Down at that time, but it may be that enclosure meant that villagers could no longer be allowed to fold their sheep in the common flock, on the common fields, as they had been in earlier centuries. The Tenantry Down asserted in 1818 may have been a recent creation.

By the middle of the seventeenth century some of the common rights had disappeared because of enclosure. The demesne arable and sheepdown in many parishes had been enclosed. But there is no evidence to suggest enclosure, dismemberment of the tenantry sheepdown and dispersal of the common flock at Blatchington. In fact the common flock is known to have existed there at least as late as the 1640s.

The cottage gardens, paddocks and yards in the village were flint-walled, as many still are. Most of the old plot names have long gone, though 'Hog Plot', shown on an old map, has been revived as the name of a new property on the site at the corner of Firle Road and Belgrave Road.

The agricultural land surrounding these enclosed plots was unwalled, unfenced, unhedged. In the sixteenth century, this medieval prairie landscape still survived and writers described it as 'champion', recalling the landscapes of Champagne in France. The open sheep pastures were called 'downs' and the open arable lands were called 'laines'; they were separated from each other by headlands, strips of unploughed grass. The handful of walled enclosures were known as 'fields' or 'crofts'. On the southern edge of the parish there were two crofts, the flint-walled enclosures defining the lands belonging to the leper hospital and its chapel. Hedgerows were rare: most of the crofts were flint-walled and the rest of the parish was open to the wind.

A survey was made in 1433 of the holdings at Blatchington held by 15 Alciston tenants, and the three open fields are named as Eastleyne, Westleyne and Northleyne. By the time the Tithe Map was drawn up in 1843, these had been divided and given other names, though 'West Laines' (part of the original Westleyne) survived. Some of the names of smaller plots in use in 1843 may have been in use in the middle ages too. In between times, still other names were evidently in use for the surviving medieval strips or consolidated groups of strips. In the manor court book for 1693, we read of Thomas Elphick surrendering two tenements to the use of Ann Barnham of Selmeston. One was a barn and 24 acres called Tarres. The other was a 20-acre plot called Percival Dibbs, then occupied by John Dippery. Five years earlier, in 1688, Thomas Elphick surrendered the same two plots, under slightly different names – Tarrie and Percival Dibble.

The open field system of farming was still operating in the late eighteenth century in Blatchington, with the lands belonging to individual farmers scattered in several pieces among the different open fields. When the property (dwelling and outbuildings) now known as Alces Place was sold copyhold in 1774, it was offered together with 'four acres of valuable arable land lying in three pieces dispersed in the common laynes of Blatchington'. This well describes the medieval system of land ownership and management.

In 1433, the largest land holding in Blatchington was 39.5 acres and the average holding was 11 acres. The way the parish economy worked was complicated by the way manors crossed parish boundaries. In the reign of Edward I, for instance, there were 17 tenants in Alciston manor who held a total of four hides (176 acres) in East Blatchington parish. Tenants holding land at Alciston and also holding land at Blatchington included five families; the Semans, the Chopyns, the Jeffreys, the Frenches and the Hollibones. These were families who would still be in Blatchington two hundred years later.

This connection with Alciston opens the door on a major complication in the way Blatchington was managed in the middle ages. In addition to being a feudal manor with a number of holdings in Blatchington, Alciston was a satellite of Battle Abbey. The abbey was founded by William the Conqueror in fulfilment of a vow made before the Battle of Hastings, and he endowed it with several manors scattered about the southern counties to provide it with revenue. To sustain it, he also gave a *banlieu*, a circular estate three miles in diameter surrounding the abbey. Lullington and Alciston were among the manors given to Battle Abbey, and there was a subsidiary grange at Blatchington. This grange may have been Blatchington House, which in 1818 was the major property in the village to be under Alciston manor. The way the various land transactions operated suggests that to some extent Blatchington was managed through Alciston. It is possibe that the unusually large barn at Alciston may have been designed to hold some of the corn and wool produced at Blatchington as well as that from Alciston.

Blatchington was not an entirely freestanding feudal manor; there was an element of control from Battle Abbey via Alciston. There is a tendency to think of the manor as coinciding with the parish, but it was not so simple. The lord of the manor of Alciston held lands in Blatchington; similarly, the lord of the manor of Blatchington held lands elsewhere. In a survey of 1589, the manor of Blatchington is described as lying in the parishes of Sutton, Seaford, Blatchington and Beddingham.

In 1276 there were 17 holdings at Blatchington that were in the hands of tenants at Alciston. The names of the Alciston tenants are listed, along with their holdings, which were in units of half-hides; two were holdings of half a hide, nine were of one wist, and six were of half a wist. Each half hide contained 2 wists, so the 17 Alciston holdings at Blatchington added up to 16 wists, or exactly four hides. The 1276 rents were very evenly and fairly imposed, at 13s 4d for half a hide, 6s 8d for a wist and 3s 4d for half a wist. An exception was made for two tenants, who only paid 3s, but they paid a thousand herrings as rent in lieu. There was also a charge on all the other tenants in common, a charge of 11d for the repair of the lord's sheepcote. The total of rent paid by the Alciston tenants at Blatchington was £5 6s 0d.

More information about the Alciston land-holders at Blatchington comes from a later document, a Rental of the Manor of Alciston dated 1433. By then the number of tenants had fallen from 17 to 12, but the aggregate of their holdings came once again to 16 wists. This later document allows us to calculate the total acreage of the Alciston strips that were scattered across the three open fields: 185 acres. The 1433 rent was slightly lower than the 1276 rent.

A minor road runs south-west from Alciston, turning into a footpath as it mounts the lower slopes of the South Downs escarpment. Then it slants diagonally westwards, climbing the steep upper slope beneath Bostal Hill to reach the col at Bo-peep. The Greenway track that ran from Alciston over the Downs and south towards Bullock Down, at last becoming Firle Road, was an important commercial link between Alciston and its land holdings at Blatchington. The Greenway must have been well used.

Today it is a highway only as far north as the golf club, and a footpath the rest of the way, but it was a road over the Downs as recently as the nineteenth century. In 1905 William Banks of Southover wrote an affidavit, in which he confirmed its long use as a road.

1) I was 83 in December last.
2) I well know the road leading from Blatchington to Alciston and Firle and have known same since I was a child.
3) When I was a child I frequently drove with my mother and friends over the road to Firle Beacon for Picnics. This was during the time when my father kept the Old Tree Inn at Seaford (1826-1833).
4) I often walked over the road when a child as well as in more recent years and have seen others using the Road and I have always understood that the road was a Public Road.
5) I can remember when a child driving over the road with a man to obtain Lime from the Bo-Peep kilns and this was when the Malthouse was being built for Mr Brooker at Seaford (1830-32).

In the 1880s, Robet Lambe promised to repair the road up to Firle Beacon. As late as 1910 the Greenway to Firle Beacon and Alciston was still a public right of way but by then there was 'only a cart road over it, for the repair of which no-one is responsible. Carriages have, therefore, in order to avoid the ruts, to be driven a greater part of the way over the greensward of the Downs.'

The large flocks of Alciston with Lullington totalled 3,000 sheep, kept mainly for their wool. The total clip amounted to over 2,000 fleeces and up to 10 sacks of wool each year, and both fleeces and wool were of high quality. Alciston was the centre; all the wool from the subsidiary Abbey estates was collected there, including, we may speculate, the wool from Blatchington, brought over the Greenway.

Control from Battle Abbey put Blatchington into a premier league of progressive agriculture. The village was subjected to innovation from its monastic masters, and this was how its high level of productivity in sheep and corn was achieved. Chalk Downland soils are frequently only 15 cm deep, but at Blatchington they are up to four times deeper.

Whether the individual villagers gained enormously from these agricultural benefits is uncertain. When we look at the fourteenth century returns for the Sussex Subsidy, very few Blatchington villagers were sufficiently well off to pay tax. There were seven tax-payers at Bishopstone in 1332 and eight at South Heighton, but only three at Blachington. One of those was Alice de Peverel. The others were Philip Gerveys and William Godegrom.

In 1773, Gilbert White commented that in the Eastern Downs the sheep were 'hornless with black faces with a tuft of white wool on their foreheads, and speckled and spotted legs'. There was a shift from the old long-legged sheep on the Western Downs to the improved Southdown breed of the Eastern Downs. Nineteenth century Downland farmers claimed that their Southdowners had 'a pedigree older than the peerage' and they were probably right. The parent stock of the Southdown breed were bred over a long period in the Eastern Downs, and the great improvements made by breeders in the eighteenth century were built upon significant earlier improvements made way back in the middle ages.

The Black Death

In 1340, on the eve of the Black Death, commissioners were appointed by Parliament to levy taxes. The assessment for tax was based on an inquiry into the state of agricultural production in that year. The levy was to be the ninth lamb, the ninth fleece and the ninth sheaf, and it would be collected within two years. In March and April 1341, the commissioners were in Lewes to receive the returns from the parishes. Most places were worth less in 1340 than in 1292.

Some coastal and near-coastal parishes at that time were being attacked by 'the Normans', meaning pirates; Friston and East Dean were attacked in this way. In many coastal parishes like Blatchington, the loss in value was due to loss of farmland to erosion by the sea. At Blachington *juxta mare* (Blatchington by the sea), it was noted that 'four virgates were not sown on account of the inability of the tenants' to find seed to sow. A pattern of land lying uncultivated for no recorded reason was fairly common, but at Blachyngton the chronicler attempted to explain. 'On the third part of the lands the wheat did not grow because of the drought and the warmth of the weather.' The bad weather had killed sheep and caused the crops to fail. Meanwhile agricultural production at other parishes was even worse - 'annihilated'. And this was a few years *before* the Black Death, the truly annihilating disaster.

The impact of the Black Death was very severe. There was huge loss of life from this plague that arrived from the sea, and ports like Seaford suffered first. The mortality peaked slightly later to the north of the Downs, away from the coast. At Alciston, no deaths were reported at the January court, 24 at the April court, 39 in the June court, 15 in the August court, and none in the September and October courts. So the mortality peaked at Alciston in May and June 1349. At Blatchington 14 deaths were reported at the April court, 5 at the June court, 1 at the August court. So at Blatchington the mortality peaked in the spring, reflecting the coastal location of the parish.

There is no sure way of knowing how many people died at Blatchington in the Black Death. The rental of 1336 lists 105 tenants at Alciston, Telton, Lullington, Alfriston, East Blatchington and Hellingly. The post-plague rental of 1349 lists 78 tenants as having died in those parishes. So 78 out of 105 people may have died in that area, about three-quarters, but, if population had increased between 1336 and the outbreak of the plague 13 years later, that might be reduced to two-thirds. But there is other evidence that at Alciston the proportion may have been more like one-third. Of 31 tenants listed in 1336, ten are recorded as having died in 1349. Other areas were harder hit. 16 wists of land were owned by Battle Abbey at Blatchington in the time of Edward I, and these were held by 19 people. The court rolls show that 10.5 of these wists were made vacant by the deaths of 10 out of 19 people. This implies close to a 50 percent death rate and shows that the coastal location was worse hit than inland locations.

The Alciston court rolls show the deaths of 24 tenants in the weeks running up to the April 1349 court. These tenants were the heads of families, but other family members must also have perished. At the next court, in June 1349, it was noted that 16 of the holdings of the deceased tenants were still in the lord's hands 'because no-one came after them following the death of the tenants, nor did anyone put in a claim for them'. Here is the evidence that many more people had died than just those mentioned in the records. The tenant, the head of the household, has died, but where are the younger brothers, the sons, the nephews? Where are the wives? The implication, because they have not come forward to claim, is that they too are dead. Whole families were wiped out, as can be seen from the disappearance of their names from the manorial records. All of these dead, it must be assumed, were buried in the little churchyard at St Peter's. The number of deaths and consequent burials over the course of at least eight centuries means that the dead must lie several deep across the whole of the churchyard.

Work for the lord, and work for Battle Abbey, required a significant number of tenants to carry it out. At Alciston itself there were *famuli*, the regular servants who carryied out some of the tasks: ploughing, harrowing, driving, carting, shepherding, etc. There were also customary workers, who by custom and obligation carried out tasks like threshing, winnowing, carrying, ditching, breaking clods, mowing grass, gathering hay, etc. And there were hired workers; there would have been a high proportion of cottars, peasants with tiny holdings that gave them too little to live on, so that they had to work as wage labourers for the lord.

The Black Death and the depopulation it caused transformed life in Blatchington. The villagers would have been overworked even before the Black Death. The lords recognized that their villagers could not cope; hours of work were increased, but so also were wages. Men formerly paid seven shillings a year were now paid ten. When the wage levels of the 1490s are compared with those of the 1360s, ploughmen received 50% more, cowherds 80% more, and shepherds' wages were almost doubled.

There were critical seasonal labour shortages. At harvest time, it became necessary to bring extra labour and expertise in from outside for five weeks, and this went on from 1350 right through the next two centuries and more. It happened at Blatchington, and at Alciston and Lullington too. In 1580, John French of Blatchington gave instructions for the payment and lodging of the temporary hands who needed to be recruited for the harvest. The incomers were accommodated wherever there was available space, even in attics. At Alciston, the big barn was used; it was fitted with an external staircase at the southern end to provide access to the accommodation. Wealden labourers were often used because harvest time came earlier on the warm, south-facing slopes of the Downs than in the Weald.

Wealden village girls had a reputation for being unfaithful while their men were away 'at harvest in the downes'. There were other social problems too. Normally the itinerant labourers were paid in corn allowance, which they took home with them by the cart-load. But when the price of corn was low this payment in kind was less satisfactory. In 1463 and 1464, years of low corn prices, the migrant labourers were strong enough to make extra demands. They went on strike until there was an agreement to supply generous board 'at the lord's table' instead of the corn allowance.

The economic and social shifts that followed in the wake of the Black Death brought about a gradual change in the status of villein tenants generally in England. They came to be valued more. By the sixteenth century, the courts were intervening to protect their tenure and there was increasing acknowledgement that custom should have a secure place in law. This was when copyhold tenure became established, and it marked a significant reduction in the power of successive lords.

Survival in the middle ages was by no means guaranteed. Blatchington survived the Black Death, but it might easily not have done so. The three nearest villages to the east virtually disappeared, shrinking to the point where they became economically non-viable. Sutton-next-Seaford, Chyngton (or Chinting) and Exceat villages were each reduced to a single farm in the aftermath of the plague. Blatchington was lucky not to share their fate; it survived the crisis by the skin of its teeth.

Notes & Sources

Banks 1905 (Greenway as road)
Blaauw 1839.
Brandon 1998.
Brent 1968 (Alciston in the middle ages)
Budgen 1944 (wists)
Budgen 1946 (acreage)
Burleigh 1973 (lost plague villages)
Combes 2002 (Bishopstone minster).
Consolidation of land holdings. Probably similar to what happened in Seaford, where 'medieval' strips mapped in 1759 were exchanged so that by 1772 large areas were in the hands of a few land-holders.
Cooper 1866 (Jack Cade rebellion)
Corner 1853 (Borough English)
Custumal of Alciston Manor
Deed of Covenant 1818 (Viscount Gage and John King)
ESRO: QR/EW/72/120
Feoffment from Juliana West to Hugh at Rede. 17 Mar 1366/67 ESRO: GLY/1640/1645 (John Crokebek)
Fine Roll C60/25, 11 Henry III 1226-1227 (Arrangements for payment of Andrew Peverel's fine)
Gardner 2003 (economy and landscape)
Gray 1915 (field systems)
Halliwell 1904 (baslard)
Holden 1963
Hudson 1907 (tax assessment)
Hunnisett 1957 (John Crokebek murder)
Jefferay, the Blatchington rebel, married in 1452, and he and his wife acquired 6 acres of land that year. The rebellion took place in May-June 1450. Cade must have furnished the complete muster rolls during the negotiations, as the pardons were issued promptly on 7 July, and they listed hundreds of names and occupations. Other rebels from nearby included Richard Fyncho of Heighton and William Herston of Bishopstone, who were constables for the Hundred of Flexborough, and Richard Carpenter, who was bailiff of Seaford; Robert Poynings of Sutton was Cade's 'carver and sword bearer'.
King's Bench Controlment Roll 32, m.45. (1378 murder)
Mate 1992. (rebellion)
Odam 1999 (electioneering)

Open-field system. This was for a long time assumed to be a medieval creation but, where dated, it has proved to be Anglo-Saxon. Cultivation strips have been found preserved under a motte-and-bailey castle, proof of a pre-Norman date.

Page 1905

Rental of the Manor of Alciston (1433). (ESRO Deeds G. 45/13)

Robinson 1822 (origin of Borough English)

Roll of a Subsidy levied 13th Henry IV

Salzman 1901 (Robert de Blechynton)

Salzman 1942 (excommunicated priests)

Searle 1963 (Battle Abbey)

Sussex Weekly Advertiser for 5 September 1774

Tate 1949 (enclosure in Sussex)

Chapter 4
Tudor & Stuart Blatchington

The lord of the manor

The ordinary people of the Tudor village were subject to the authority of the Crown and the laws of England. But they were also subject to two other authorities. There was the lord of the manor, whose steward might employ villagers or discipline them through a constable or beadle. There was also the rector, who exerted power over villagers both directly and by way of his vestry and church-wardens; he might also employ a parish clerk and a sexton. Everyday life in Blatchington depended to a great extent on the character of these local powers. We know the names of the lords of the manor and the rectors and a little about what they did; we also know the names and property dealings of many of the villagers; but we know very little about the personalities of the people involved.

Manor court books allow disjointed glimpses, no more, of what went on. They record that in 1524-25 one of the Blatchington villagers, Richard French, was the copyholder of a piece of land halfway up Firle Road, at the northern edge of the village. 'Richard French produces copy containing one acre of land called Mill acre with a certain windmill built there in Blachyngton date 24 September 15 Henry VIII and rent yearly 11s.' Another note, four years later, tells that 'Juliana Giles produces copy of John Giles, her husband, containing one cottage 6 acres of land in the tenure of William Reynold dated 21 April 19 Henry VIII rent 5s.'

On 21 March 1534, John and Juliana Giles swapped cottages with another couple in the village, John and Alice Holybone. John and Alice 'surrendered a tenement (tenancy of a house) with 16 acres of land sometime of John Wrigger at rent 17 shillings and 9 pence to the use of John Gyles.' At the same time John Gyles surrendered a cottage and 6 acres in the tenure of William Reynolds rent 6 shillings to the use of John and Alice Holybone. It looks as if the Gileses were becoming richer, the Holybones poorer. John Holybone (or Hollibone) would die and be buried at Blatchington in December 1566; Alice, his widow, seems to have moved away as there is no record of her burial or remarriage at St Peter's. John and Juliana Giles are also absent from the Blatchington parish register; they disappear.

At the same court in the spring of 1534, a day was given to John Bene (Bean), Edward Baker, William Colvyld (Colvill) and John

Sir John Gage

Gyles 'to repair their tenements and cottages where necessary'. It is hard to tell whether this was a generous and considerate act or a thinly veiled public admonition for allowing their houses to fall into disrepair.

In the 1530s Thomas Alce sold to Sir John Gage a messuage (dwelling and outbuildings) that had in the past belonged to or been occupied by Nicholas Alce. The messuage was sold along with 67 acres of land. Sir John (1479-1557) was an important figure, Vice Chamberlain of the Council to Henry VIII, Captain of the Guard and Chancellor of the Duchy of Lancaster. Later he would be Queen Mary's Chamberlain, Constable of the Tower, and so Princess Elizabeth's gaoler.

Because Sir John was acquiring land copyhold at Blatchington, land holden of the lord of the manor of Blatchington, in spite of his grand titles, he was obliged to do fealty to the lord of Blatchington – and the lord of Blatchington could *compel* him to come and do it. The record of the sale is followed by the comment, 'The Bedell is to distrain Sir John Gage to be at the next court to do fealty and other services.' The service (heriot) required of Sir John Gage was then specified exactly; it was to be 'a mare price 13s 4d.'

The beadle was a minor and local law-enforcer, a parish official whose job it was to keep order in church and administer punishments for minor offences. He would whip boys who misbehaved. On this occasion he was to act as a messenger of the court, delivering what amounted to a summons – to a dauntingly powerful man.

The arrangement with Sir John Gage was changed in 1540, as a rental record from that year shows. 'A barn and 56 acres of land with appurtenances' in Blatchington were exchanged with the lord of Blatchington for lands that were all in Exceat. But the Gages were to re-assert manorial rights at Blatchington. In the middle ages, the Gages as lords of the manor of Alciston had exerted considerable control over Blatchington, and some of the lands at Blatchington were still holden of the Gages in the sixteenth century. In the Alciston court book for 1540 we are told that at a court of James Gage Esq 'There came Richard Frenche and the Rector of the Church of Blachyngton and do fealty and attorn [do homage] to the lord [Gage] by payment of 1d.' James Gage was one of Sir John's sons, presumably here deputizing for his father. The fealty might be token, but it was still fealty, and it is interesting to see that even the Rector was subject to it. This was a matter that would not be sorted out until the late nineteenth century, when copyhold lands were enfranchised: changed by agreement, plot by plot, to freehold.

There was a great deal of collecting and exchanging of manors among the gentry in the wake of the Dissolution of the monasteries. The sixteenth century became an era of property speculation and manors changed hands fairly frequently.

The law and its enforcement could appear oppressive and arbitrary. In the reign of Elizabeth, one man in Seaford was formally charged with opening his windows without permission. But this was evidently someone who had blocked up windows in order to avoid paying window tax, and later re-opened them without declaring his action; it was a case of tax evasion. Some of the authoritarian control was necessary. The citizens of Seaford were evidently dumping rubbish all over the place, in front of houses and in the streets; they were charged with throwing dead dogs, pigs and even horses into the highway. Punishments were laid down centrally and often it was the stocks or pillory for men or the cucking stool for women. Although the cucking stool is sometimes portrayed as a quaint and picturesque old custom, the ducking was usually into foul water of some kind. Seaford had its gallows and pillory at the southern end of Broad Street; Blatchington had its stocks on the west side of Blatchington Hill, perhaps in what is now the front garden of Sanctuary.

The rental record for 1540 names some of the free tenants at Blatchington. One was John Baker, who held one tenement with 9 acres and a second with 23 acres. Richard French was mentioned in relation to the windmill and its one acre, and also as 'farmer of demesne lands'. There were thirteen other tenants, who included Isabel Gyles. In 1548 Thomas Mason, who was rector for only two years, is recorded to have held a quarter of an acre of land 'near the parsonage'.

The name of French the mill-owner crops up again a generation later, and perhaps the John French who appears in the 1559 will of Thomas Gratwyke of Seaford is Richard French's son. Gratwyke's will says, 'John French of Blatchington to take possession of my lands.' John French was twice-married. By his first wife Elizabeth he had two children, Ellyn, born in 1564, and John, born the following year. When Elizabeth died in 1569, John French married Margaret Robbyns in the same year; together they produced Moses, born in 1570; another son, Joseph, died in infancy in 1575. John French himself died in 1580.

Why John French was left land by Thomas Gratwyke is not known. The Gratwicks were a high-profile family in Seaford, a town noted for family feuds in the sixteenth and seventeenth centuries. The Gratwicks were one factional family, the Elphicks another. Richard Elphick, who was born in Blatchington in 1579, was described in a Deposition Book in 1611 as a yeoman 'of Alciston'. At some point he had walked over the Greenway. In 1621, Edward Gratwick asserted that he and Thomas Elphick had been quietly living in amity, but that this changed when he, Gratwick, had been chosen Jurat. The poor of Seaford had appealed to him to restore certain common land to them, and Elphick, who had kept them for himself, resented this and resisted.

A century-and-a-half later, in 1775, there was a riot in Seaford when Thomas Woolgar and others physically forced the Senior Jurat out of his chair at the Town Hall. We can assume that Blatchington did not escape the Seaford power struggles, when some of the families involved – the Elphicks, for instance - lived at Blatchington. In 1622, Offington Elphick was a yeoman of Blatchington, where he had been living for 13 years, though he had been born at Alciston in 1591. Richard Elphick was born at Blatchington in 1579, moved to Alciston, where he was a yeoman, then at the age of 40, in 1618, moved to Seaford, another Greenway migrant. The factional families moved back and forth, no doubt taking their quarrels with them.

When the site of the Well House was cleared and the foundation trenches were dug out, the remains of an older building came to light: a cottage half the length of the present Well House and standing on its rear central third. It had thick flint walls. All round it were found clay pipes. Behind the garage was the well which gives the modern house its name. Halfway down the back garden an Elizabethan shilling was found. Minted in 1560-61 at the Tower of London, it shows the crowned bust of the young Queen Elizabeth I facing left. The Latin text round the portrait reads 'Elizabeth by the grace of God Queen of England France and Ireland'. The mintmark on the reverse is identifiable as a bird. There was only one bird mintmark, the martlet, and that was used only at the Tower of London in 1560-61, which gives us the date of the coin. The queen was then 27 or 28 and had been on the throne for 2 or 3 years. The coin had been clipped twice - clipping was quite common, even though punishable by torture and death - before it was dropped in the back garden of the cottage, a considerable loss to its Tudor owner.

Elizabethan shilling found at the Well House

There is a fleeting mention of Blatchington in a 1563 report on the state of the Elizabethan diocese. 'Blachington: parsonage no curat.' This implies that the parish of Blatchington was either too small to justify having a curate or too poor to afford one.

In 1603, the absentee lords of the manor, the Gages, sold the lordship to John Gilbert. On 3 January 1604, John Gilbert held his first court as the new lord of Blatchington. The court book makes it clear that the lordship was previously shared: 'Blatchington late purchased of Edward Gage of Bentlye and Edward Gage of Wormsley in Herefordshire by indenture.'

In that first court, various landholders, their holdings and rents were listed. One was John Willett, described as 'free', and he 'held a tenement and 9 acres called Hockin's 9s'. In other words, John Willett was paying nine shillings a year for the rent of a cottage and nine acres of land. He also 'held a tenement and 24 acres, rent 24s'. He owed his lord 'one heriot for both tenements', because this was the agreement that he had from a previous lord of the manor, Lord de la Warr - and custom prevailed.

Another landholder mentioned in John Gilbert's first court at Blatchington was William Cole, clerk. He was the copy-holder of 27 acres for a rent of 27 shillings. An additional note in the court book reads, 'the same, by charter, a small croft, 4d.' This may have meant a small plot of arable land or paddock adjacent to a cottage. But only two years later William Cole, who was the rector, died and beside this information the court book notes, 'heriot a gelding', which means that service was owing to the lord.

In the court of 1606, one of the villagers sued his own son. 'Coortes sues Coell his son and heir.' This is odd, as Coortesse Colvill, born in 1587, and given an unusual anglicized version of a Spanish name in the midst of the Spanish invasion scare, would in 1606 have been nineteen. As a minor, he would not have been able to sue anyone. Coell could not have been Coortesse's son and heir; if he had one, the son would have been only an infant and unable to do anything to justify being sued. The meaning could be 'Coortes sues Coell's son and heir', but the puzzle does not end there. Unusual though the forename is, *another* Coortesse appears in the parish register. He is Coortesse Coell, who appears as the father of William Coell, baptized in 1600. Given that both 'Coortesse' and 'Coell' are mentioned, the entry in the court book may refer to Coortesse and William, but it is still unclear why a man would sue his six-year-old son.

The situation becomes more puzzling still when Coortesse Coell is mentioned again in the court book for 1614, where we read of a 'surrender by Cortesius Cole, gent, to the use of Robt Goffe, clerk'. This tells us that Coortesse was regarded as a gentleman and he handed property over to a priest. The priest in question was none other than the rector (from 1605 until 1631). Robert Goffe's predecessor as rector was – William Coell. So there were two William Coells living at Blatchington in 1600, the newly born son of Coortesse Coell and the rector, a man of mature years who would die in 1605. Perhaps the meaning of the 1606 entry is that Coortesse sued the son and heir of the late rector, William Coell.

Robert Goffe was installed as rector on 13 March 1605, presented by John Gilbert just a year after John Gilbert's first court, so the village had a new squire and a new rector in rapid succession. Robert had been born in Lewes in 1564, and graduated at St John's College, Cambridge in 1588. He was ordained priest by Thomas Bickley, Bishop of Chichester, in February 1590. He first married Martha Barber of Camberwell at St Mary Woolnoth in 1618, then nine years later he married Joan Burton at Friston. He held two benefices: Bletchington and Ripe.

We can be sure that fear of a Spanish invasion was real and ever-present in the months running up to the Armada. The Armada passed along the Channel ten miles offshore on the morning of 5 August (in the New Style calendar), and Blatchington was a worryingly attractive landing-place. The 1587 Armada Survey map shows 'Bletchington hille a mete place to plante ordnance.' The report did not think much of Newhaven's defences, with its guns 'unmounted and littell worthe'. It stated that 'a bullwarke of earthe were needfully to be raised there for the planting one demi-culverin and two sacres.' For the defence of Blatchington there was also a recommendation. 'At Bletchington Hille, where an entrie was made by the French, two rampiers of earth, to plant one demi-culverin and one sacre in each; they have there one sacre, mounted and furnished.'

Blatchington Down was a place to be sure to defend. The French had, after all, landed on Blatchington's short coastline in 1545. The alarm, 'Haste, haste, post haste, for thy lyffe haste,' was sent from Seaford to the Justices of Kent. The French had landed 1,500 men on what is now Marine Parade between the southern ends of Claremont and Edinburgh Roads and made some progress inland over Blatchington Down in the direction of the village. They reached the village, where they set fire to five or six cottages. Sir Nicholas Pelham raised the men of the neighbourhood and successfully 'drove them [the French] back to their ships with the loss of a hundred men killed or drowned.'

The threat of invasion by the French or the Spanish was very real at Blatchington. Yet the ordinary everyday concerns of the village still continued, preoccupying the villagers in the midst of the Armada crisis. A *Liber Detectorum* from 1586-7 deals with the need to repair the chancel of St Peter's church. This was first reported in November 1586, when 'the church is not whitelimed', though this had been put right two months later. On 16 January 1587, the

Archdeaconry Court held in Lewes ordered that the question of repairs should be postponed until Pentecost (Whitsun); the church was to remain open 'whiletimes' (in the meantime) so it looks as if the chancel roof was not in danger of falling in. The court said that the rector would have to bear the cost of repairing the church, not the parishioners. Apparently the churchwardens had made a point of alerting the Court to the need to spare the village the expense. Many other churches were in a state of disrepair at this time. It was reported that at Brede church 'The chancel is not well.'

In the court book for 1614 we read that 'John Willett has alienated to Robert Goffe 11 acres.' Two years later, 'Edward Mabb, clerk, a tenant, *in extremis* on 8 August last, surrendered 16 acres in Willingdon to John Foster and John Giles to sell.' The mortally ill cleric, Edward Mabb, may have been Robert Goffe's curate.

1628 was the year of the first court of Nicholas Gilbert. It was also the year in which the new lord of the manor married his first wife, Ann Parker. In 1661 he was one of the signatories at the induction of the Revd John Saxby as rector. Four years later, Nicholas Gilbert and his son, also called Nicholas, signed to the reading in of the Revd John Cooke. Nicholas Gilbert Senior's wife Ann died in 1652. He remarried, and his second wife was Elizabeth Westbourne. Nicholas Gilbert Senior died in 1678.

Misbehaviour and untimely ends

In the reign of Henry VIII, pigs were causing problems in Blatchington, apparently by running about, getting in the way and being destructive. This is implicit in a ruling in the court book for 1532. 'Any tenant from this time to the feast of St Edward in October, not having ringed his pigs yearly shall incur a penalty of 20d.' The reason given was that pigs not ringed cause 'so much damage at this time of year [March and April].' The pigs of Blatchington were friskier in the spring and racketed about if not ringed and roped.

Some villagers continued to allow their pigs to run free. Six years later, in the court held on 28 September 1538, the order that pigs must be ringed was repeated, along with the threat of a fine of twelve pence for each offence.

Church services in the days of compulsory attendance were not always peaceful or harmonious. In the middle ages, there were no seats in churches for the congregation. This led to lounging, leaning against walls, wandering about, collecting in small groups and chatting. Services could become dangerously informal. In the thirteenth century there was move towards installing seats, to allow priests to exert a level of discipline over their congregations. This change meant that many of the traditional alternative uses for the church became impossible, such as feastings, ales, markets, dances and plays. No doubt rectors were pleased and congregations disappointed.

Reluctant church attenders sometimes misbehaved, even when there were pews. One such in the seventeenth century was a Blatchington villager called John Willett. His misbehaviour in St Peter's was noted in the Act Books of the Archdeaconry Court of Lewes;

11 Nov 1628 East Blatchington. John Willett, for his irreverent behaviour in the church as sitting with his hat on his head in tyme of divine service; as also for his rude and disorderly behaviour as throwing stones at others that sit in the chancell in tyme of divine service and sermon to the disturbing of the minister and the rest of the congregation; as also for fighting in the churchyard, and for a very negligent comer to the Church on the Sabboth day.'

A multiple offender. I cannot help feeling a certain admiration for John Willett, for being his own man, for refusing to be coerced into worship. There may have been a hidden grievance behind his misbehaviour. In 1614, Willett had alienated, or transferred, 11 acres to Robert Goffe, and this may have been the Robert Goffe who was the current rector's predecessor. The circumstances of the land transaction are not recorded, but perhaps Willett felt he had sold his land too cheaply or in some other way been unfairly treated by the Revd Robert Goffe.

It was not only members of the congregation who stood to be reprimanded. Sometimes it was the rector himself. Just six years after the John Willett incident, on 4 November 1634, 'Nicholas Pope, cleric, the rector' was admonished 'for not walking the perambulations.' This routine duty entailed walking, checking and asserting the parish boundaries. In the same year, he had given ten shillings towards the repair of the medieval St Paul's Cathedral, which was by then in a very poor state. That donation was recorded in *The Contrebution of the Clergy for Repairing St Paul's*, where Pope is described as 'Nicholas Pope, parson of Blatchington and vicar of Ffokington'.

Nicholas Pope was in difficulties again in 1645, when the Committee for Plundered Ministers decided to take action against him. This committee had been set up by the Long Parliament after the start of the Civil War in 1643. Its purpose was to replace and silence clergymen who were loyal to Charles I. The committee operated from London, but delegated most of the work to county sub-committees. If an allegation of loyalty to the King or of high Anglicanism (which was regarded as the same thing) could be proved, the offending rector was replaced. His property was also sequestered or confiscated, and the only way a sequestered rector could regain his property was by buying it back. Why a charge was brought against Nicholas Pope is not known, but often discontented parishioners used the committee as a means of getting rid of a rector they disliked.

On 11 March 1645 the Committee appointed 'the cause against Nicholas Pope for 10th April', whatever that cause was. Then the case against Mr Pope was adjourned until 22 May. He was uncertain what he was being charged with, and asked for an indication of the nature of the evidence being brought. On 3 May the Committee noted that 'The peticon [petition] of Nicholas Pope Minister of Bletchingdon was read thereby desiring a copy of the exaicons agt [exactions against] him,' continuing in some obscure seventeenth century legal terminology, 'but in regard he was put at ye taking ye said exaicons this coittee consisting of the same.' There were more adjournments, from 22 May to 17 June, to 10 July, to 28 August 1645. On that day in August it was ordered 'that the cause concerning Mr Pope of Bletchingdon be *sine die* for that the parties on neither side doe attend the Co[mm]ittee herein.' Neither side had turned up for the hearing, so it would be postponed indefinitely. There were further adjournments, to 21 October, then to 13 November, then the 'cause' disappears. It looks as if the proceedings against Mr Pope fell through for some reason; perhaps there was no evidence against him.

Mr Pope died in the autumn of 1661, his wife Joane having died at Blatchington two years before. Nicholas Pope's gravestone at Blatchington reads, 'Here lyeth the body of Nicholas Pope, Rector of Blatchington Sone of Ralf Pope of Hendall, in the Parish of Bucksted Esq, who died the 15 daye of October 1661 buried the 20th being 69 years old.'

Nicholas Pope had children. Anthony Pope was baptised at Blatchington on 29 May 1634, John on 4 September 1636 and Mary on 6 February 1638. In his will he refers to his daughter Frances Standford, widow of Edward Standford, who died in Ireland 'where shee still liveth'. Frances was not born at Blatchington. He also refers to his sons Ralph and Thomas and to the latter's sons Thomas and Ralph. Nicholas Pope left the residue of his estate to his son Anthony and his daughter Mary, 'they having continued with me & hindred themselves of their preferment for my sake.'

Nicholas Pope was succeeded as Rector by John Saxby in February 1662.

In a Survey of Pevensey Rape dated 1649, Blatchington parish was assessed as having about one-third of the value of Seaford parish. 'Blechington' was worth £326 compared with Seaford's £969. This is an increase in relative value compared with 1334, when the assessment for King's Tax showed East Blatchington having one-quarter of the value of Seaford; now it was worth one-third. In 1650 Bletchington Rectory was valued at £40.

In 1653, a body was found in one of the ponds at the bottom of Blatchington Hill. The East Blatchington parish register records that 'Sarah Reynolds, servant to Miles Marchant, came to an untimely ende, as is thought, May the 1st at night, for from that time shee was not seene [living], being found in the pond at the lower ende of the parish; shee was laid in the ground the 5th of June.' Her master, Miles Marchant, was born at Newick in 1608, and he was 45 at the time of Sarah's death. He died at Blatchington in 1679.

Sarah's body would have been buried not long after it was discovered, which means that it must have in the pond for several weeks before it was discovered.

This is odd because Blatchington Pond was the village pond, a major focus of village life. It was a watering place for flocks of sheep passing between downland pasture and market along the drove road; the road passing along the north side of the pond is still called Sutton Drove. It would also have been used to water horses going up and down Blatchington Hill. It was a place where villagers went to catch waterfowl and fish. Carters ran their carts into the shallows to moisten the wheels. It was a busy place. But there was a second, smaller pond on the western side of Blatchington Road, called the Water Lily Pool. This was on the site of the now-demolished Elm Court Centre. The two ponds were fed by small streams, the Lynn Brook and the Dane River, which have now disappeared. Perhaps Sarah's body was found in the Water Lily Pool or, if in the larger pond, it was hidden among reeds or bulrushes. Another possibility is that Sarah's body was not in the pond from the time when she went missing. Maybe she was somewhere else, and still alive, from 1 May until 1 June. During that time 'shee was not seene', but it is possible that she was, even so, alive.

The cryptic account in the register does not say whether Sarah drowned herself deliberately, or died by accident, or whether foul play was suspected. She may have been murdered, but the neutrality of the entry suggests that suicide was assumed. Was Sarah Reynolds the victim of the commonest kind of betrayal, a seduction by a member of her master's family leading to a pregnancy that would lose her her job and her good reputation? If so, her despair can be imagined. But there are other possible explanations, such as depression or insanity.

On 7 December 1663, Samuel Pepys tells us, there was an extraordinarily high tide affecting the south-east of England, causing enormous flood damage: 'the greatest tide that ever was remembered in England, all White Hall having been drowned'. This will very likely have caused seawater to penetrate right up the valley to the Water Lily Pool and Blatchington Pond, and kill the freshwater fish there, as it did in 1824.

It was probably this high tide that stranded a Dutch ship, the *Hope* of Flushing, on Blatchington Beach: the date is right, December 1663. The ship's master, Adrian van Hover, sold the ship's anchors, cables, masts and rigging for £33. The records say that Nicholas Pope, gent, of Blatchington and Mr William Humphrey of Newhaven bought the tackle, but Nicholas Pope had died two years earlier; probably this was a recording error and Nicholas' son Anthony was intended: Anthony would have been 29 at the time of the wreck of the *Hope*.

In a gale on 13 March 1914, two vessels were blown onto Blatchington beach, the barge *Jackin* and the brigantine *Catherine*.

The barge Jackin (extreme left) and the brigantine Catherine (right), aground in a gale in 1914. The Catherine broke up in a few hours.

The Ussuri grounded on Blatchington beach in 1936

Even steamships have grounded here, sometimes driven by gales, sometimes by navigational error. On 17 May 1936 the Soviet steamship *Ussuri* rammed the beach in a fog, its bow coming to rest against the concrete promenade. Across the centuries, scores of ships have been driven ashore on Blatchington beach.

There was a significant level of mobility in the Tudor and Stuart period, with families moving from village to village. In the 1660s, one of the farming families in East Blatchington was the Bradford family. The Bradfords lived in East Blatchington from the time of their marriage. They had a son called Richard, who was born there in 1656 or 1657 and died at the age of two. He was buried at East Blatchington. They had a daughter Ann in August 1666, who outlived her parents. There was also a daughter Elizabeth, who was born at East Blatchington in 1665. Peter Bradford died and was buried at East Blatchington in August 1666. His widow lived on for another 51 years; she was buried at East Blatchington in 1716 or 1717. Their daughter, Anne Bradford, died a year later. The Bradford parents were incomers. Peter Bradford, described as a yeoman, had been born at Pyecombe in 1618. Ann Seaman, his wife, 34 years younger, had been born at Wilmington in 1652.

In 1676 there was a Religious Census of Sussex. This revealed that there were 61 Conformists at East Blatchington, no Papists

(Roman Catholics), no Nonconformists. The congregation was about the same size as those at Alciston (64), Buncton (66), Crawley (67), Hove (57), Iford (64). There were very low numbers of Nonconformists at other Sussex parishes. So East Blatchington was a representative Sussex hamlet of its day, with an exclusively Anglican congregation. The Nonconformists, or Puritans, had long before this adopted the practice of giving their children baptismal names that were evangelizing phrases made of two words, often hyphenated. In the Blatchington parish register for 1586, we find Humphrey Rowe christening his daughter 'Syn-deny'. But there was not another Puritan name of this kind until the year 1648, and then it was a family from Seaford, not Blatchington.

The times were unusual, with new ideas of personal responsibility in the air. It is still possible to sense the shock the rector felt as he added his comment in the parish register in April 1659, on the burial of John Hollibone. *Castrat propria manu ne plures haberet liberos.* He castrates himself with his own hand, so that he may have no more children. . . Nicholas Pope wrote it in Latin, because it was too terrible for anyone else to read.

The surge of religious zeal and resulting conflict in the seventeenth century did for one of the rectors, Edward Wilson. He was born in Eastbourne in 1652, and was a scholar at Queen's College Cambridge, where he graduated in 1674. It was an age of string-pulling and in 1675 Edward wrote to his father, Sir William Wilson, to get the King's mandate for a Fellowship at his college. Sir William in turn recruited a friend to secure this and the friend wrote to Sir William at length on the best way to get the fellowship.

'I have consulted Mr Cooke, secretary to Mr Secretary Coventry; a very honest and ingenious gentleman, who tells me the King will not deny the grant to my Lord, but will refer the matter to one of his secretaries, whose answer shall be that his Majesty has promised the Vice-Chancellor, and Heads and Fellows of Colleges of both the Universities, to impose none upon them, but leave them to their own elections, unless recommended by a certificate. Now, sir, if you think your sonne's merit will obtain a certificate from popular hands, there will be no difficulty in this matter. The Duke of Monmouth is Chancellor, who, I am also informed, is the first and properest steps to climb by. I doe assure you I will serve you in what I can. . . Jo. Jeffs.'

In other words, Charles II's officials would not interfere in the appointment of fellows of Oxford and Cambridge colleges, but there was a way round this propriety. The Duke of Monmouth, Charles II's illegitimate son, turned out to be a more dangerous ally than Jo. Jeffs thought. Following Charles II's death, Monmouth tried to usurp the throne from his half-uncle, James II, and was beheaded for treason in 1685.

Meanwhile the Revd Edward Wilson had acquired a better preferment than the one he was trying to engineer in 1675. On 20 December 1680 Edward Wilson was installed as rector of East Blatchington, on presentation of John Gilbert, gent. He had been ordained priest by Guy Carleton, Bishop of Chichester, in March 1680. On 27 February 1688, Wilson married Mrs Catharine Greaves at Firle.

But in 1690, he lost his rectory. He had sworn loyalty to (Catholic) King James II and then, when the state required him to swear loyalty to (Protestant) King William III while James II still lived, he demurred. By this action dictated by conscience he became a 'non-juror' – and he was deprived of his living as a result. Robert Nowell, the Vicar of Seaford, was another who suffered in the same way.

Notes & sources

Anon 1942

Manor court books of Blatchington. (These were formerly in the possession of Robert Lambe, the last lord of the manor, and found in a cupboard, apparently in about 1940; then they were handed over by F. R. Williams to the Sussex Archaeological Society; now they are in ESRO.)

Palmere and Covert 1587 (The Armada Survey)

Renshaw 1906 (repairs to church)

Sawyer 1880 (persecution of Nicholas Pope)

Sawyer Notes & Queries No 14, *SAC* 232, 236-7.

Sawyer 1887.

Spanish Armada defences. A demi-culverin was a medium cannon with a barrel 3.4m long and a 10cm (4-inch) calibre. A sacre or saker was a slightly smaller cannon with barrel 2.9m long and an 8.25cm (3¼-inch) calibre. A rampier was a rampart.

Torr 1920.

Valuation of the Rectories and Vicarages within the Rape of Lewes 1650.

Will of Nicholas Pope 1661.

SAC 11 (Paxhill and its neighbourhood.) (Revd Edward Wilson)

Chapter 5
The eighteenth century

The lie of the land

One family moved out of Blatchington Court: a new family moved in. It had been the pattern for centuries. In 1717, Blatchington Court and the lands and rights that went with it were up for sale: 'the Manor of Blatchington and lands (153 acres), [and] the advowson of the Manor House called Blatchington'. There were nine acres of arable of which the last occupier had been a man called Rowe and the occupier before him Willett. There was also a barn, with 33 acres, and that too had been occupied by Rowe. There was a barn and close called Lambs with 27 acres of arable land that had been occupied by Goff. Part of what was being offered to the incoming squire of Blatchington was the advowson, the right of the occupier of Blatchington Court to present the living, to appoint the rector. It was an opportunity for patronage - and nepotism; in landed families there were often younger sons who went into the Church.

The land holding offered in the lease amounted to about one-fifth of the area of the parish.

Some manor houses in England stayed in one family for many generations, across centuries. Blatchington Court was not one of them. The house changed hands repeatedly. In 1600, the manor of Blatchington, together with Blatchington Court and advowson, belonged to Edward Gage the elder of Bentley in Framfield and Edward Gage the younger of Wormsley Grange in Herefordshire. In the year of Elizabeth I's death, 1603, the Gages sold the property to John Gilbert of Willingdon: the lordship of the manor of Blatchington along with the manor house and 'a piece of land', presumably the gardens. There is no evidence that John Gilbert went to live at East Blatchington and it may be that the house was let to a tenant. John Gilbert died in 1627 and was succeeded by his eldest son Nicholas who married Ann Parker in 1628. Their eldest children were baptized at Folkington, the younger ones at East Blatchington, which tells us that Nicholas and his wife Ann moved to East Blatchington, and therefore into Blatchington Court.

From 1639 on Nicholas is described as 'of Blatchington', and he probably lived at Blatchington Court continuously from then until 1677. Arms were granted to him in 1662; *Argent, on a chevron sable, three roses argent. Crest, on a wreath of the colours, a squirrel sejant erect gules, holding a nut* - a silver and black shield with a red squirrel sitting on top. The Gilberts by custom adopted the squirrel on their arms in recognition of their famour navigator-ancestor, Sir Humphrey Gilbert, whose ship was called the *Squirrel*. Nicholas Gilbert's motto was *Mallem mori quam mutare*: Death rather than change.

The Gilbert property in Wilmington may have passed to Nicholas's brother John, who was described as 'of Wilmington' when he made his will in 1696. Nicholas's wife Ann died in 1652, and her Folkington property passed to their youngest son Edward. In 1656 Nicholas Gilbert remarried; his second wife was Elizabeth Westbourne. He died in 1677 and was buried in the chancel at Blatchington. When the chancel floor was repaved in 1860, the Revd Robert Dennis found and recorded Nicholas Gilbert's grave. Inscribed on rough slabs underneath the chancel floor were two simple inscriptions, 'Anne wife of Nicholas Gilbert, gent, died 8th March 1652' and 'Nicholas Gilbert, gent, died Febry 25th 1677'.

Thomas Gilbert inherited East Blatchington from his father Nicholas in 1678 and bought extra land both there and at Eastbourne. Thomas had been managing the Blatchington estate as his father's steward for the previous 21 years.

Thomas Gilbert died in 1704 and was buried in Eastbourne. His son Nicholas inherited Blatchington manor, together with the manor house and the advowson. Nicholas had been educated at

Horsham Grammar School and trained as a lawyer like his father. He was admitted to the Middle Temple in 1692. He married Mary Eversfield in about 1695. She was an heiress, a property owner in her own right, and they may have moved into Gildredge House in Eastbourne rather than live at Blatchington Court.

By 1710 the second Nicholas Gilbert seems to have overstretched himself financially, as he mortgaged Blatchington Court to Elizabeth Jeffrey and Francis Green. A rental of the manor made in March 1710 notes that there were seven freeholders and ten copyhold tenements; the total rent amounted to £9 16s. 7d.

Three years later the second Nicholas Gilbert died, leaving a seven-year-old son as his heir and instructions for his executors to sell East Blatchington. A cache of legal papers assembled in 1717 deals with the case of Francis Green gent v. Charles Eversfield in Chancery, concerning the East Blatchington estate, reaching back right through the seventeenth century to the time when John Gilbert bought the manor and its manor house. In February 1717 Colonel John Fermor purchased Blatchington manor house and the 153-acre estate that went with it.

By 1733 the manor was owned by Sir Henry Fermor, Baronet,

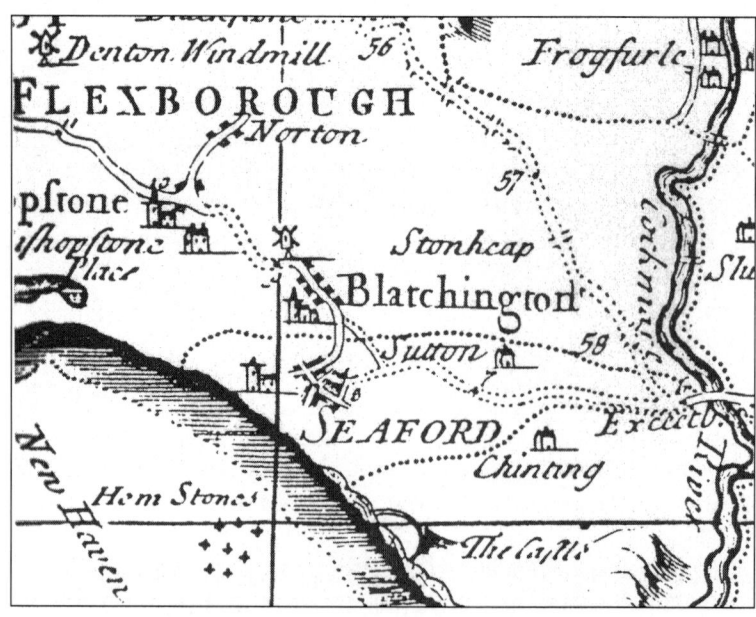

Blatchington in 1724, from the Budgen map of Sussex

who had (the third) Nicholas Gilbert serving there as his steward. So the youth who might have inherited Blatchington Court became its manager instead. This arrangement continued when the ownership of the manor passed in 1742 to John Fermor, who afterwards went into the church. John Fermor was the illegitimate son of Colonel John Fermor (1674-1722) and Ann Johnson; he was born at Sevenoaks in Kent. At birth, the baby was given his stepfather's surname, and so was baptized as John Boorder. In 1746, the Revd John Fermor (or Boorder - he had two identities) married Elizabeth Austen, also born in Sevenoaks. They had two sons, Henry, born in 1750 and John Sherley, born in 1754, both in Sevenoaks.

At Blatchington, a John Fermor (also spelt Farmer) was still in place as lord of the manor in 1789, but this was John Fermor's son, the Revd John Sherley Fermor. John Sherley Fermor was wealthy, and consequently permitted to pay court to the Earl of Conyngham's eldest daughter, whom he married in Dublin in 1785. Fermor owned the manor of Blatchington, but never lived there. It seems likely that his wealth enabled him to have Blatchington Court rebuilt at this time. He may also have bought up all the land holdings in the furlong closest to the house, on the west side of Blatchington Hill, and laid it to grass to create The Lawn, an elegant landscaped park for the new manor house.

The Lawn occupied the long slope down to the dell where the Water Lily Pool lay, creating a foreground and middle distance for the fine view from the house across to Seaford Head and the bay. The expanse of grass was given added interest with two small clumps of trees; a spinney ran down each side of The Lawn to frame the view. This was landscaping very much in the 'Capability' Brown tradition, if on a modest scale. The likely date of the Blatchington Court garden, 1785, comes shortly after Lancelot Brown's death in 1783. The Yeakell & Gardner survey (1778-83) confirms that most of the 'Lawn Furlong' was still laid out in arable strips right up to that time.

In spite of this work, the Fermors never resided at Blatchington Court. Instead there was a succession of tenants including, in chronological order, John Cooper (born in Blatchington in 1715), John Washer (born in Blatchington in 1718), John Brooks (or Brooke) and a Major Boorder, who was presumably a relative of the owner. John Brooke was in residence in 1765, as the manor court book makes a point of mentioning that the 1765 courts were held 'at the house of John Brooke'. Perhaps this was thought to be worth mentioning because the manor court was more usually held at the lord of the manor's residence, and in this case the lord was the landlord though not the occupier of Blatchington manor house. Major Boorder was evidently there from shortly after that date, perhaps from 1766, until 1789, though like John Brooke he does not appear in the parish register at either end of his life. In 1789, the Revd John Sherley Fermor was described in a document as Proprietor and Major Boorder as Occupier.

The manor court books note the death of the rector, John Robson, who was buried at St Peter's on 16 October 1765, and also the sale of a brown gelding to his widow, for £15. At the spring manor court in 1766, it was noted that the Revd John Fermor was lord of the manor, while Samuel Topping, clerk, was the rector, who 'held land called Locage, being in the garden of the rector at the west part of the barn and close to the south part of the garden'. This curious statement must have had some significance, as it was repeated elsewhere. The Minutes of Court for June 1735 note 'John Goldwright, clerk, who held Lockage resigned, Henry Lushington, clerk, then in possession'. Then again in February 1743 the Minutes tell us that 'Henry Lushington resigned, James Tattershall then in possession of Lockage'.

The statements about the possession of Lockage are strange in several ways. The rector always owned the rectory and its pair of walled gardens - that can never have been in question – so why was attention being drawn to his ownership of an integral part of the property? Another peculiarity is the fact that a special plot name, Locage or Lockage, was given to a part of the property. The description is slightly ambiguous. Lockage was close to the southern part of the garden. It was also 'at the west part' of the barn. This could mean that the land lay to the west of the barn, in which case it would have been in the southern part of the rectory's kitchen garden. Or it could mean that Lockage was the western part of the barn itself. Given that the tithe barn had been subdivided, Lockage could have referred to the western part of the building, which is now Orchard Cottage. On the other hand the wording suggests a plot rather than a building - 'land called Locage'.

Lockage is one of several mysteries surrounding the rectory. Like the manor house, it was built in the eighteenth century, and must have had several predecessors, yet (again like the manor house) nothing whatever is known of their architecture.

The 1790s brought changes. The Revd John Sherley Fermor died in Margate in the autumn of 1791, and 'the manor house and lands (200 acres)' were purchased by Mr Thomas Harben, an important and colourful figure in Seaford at a time when its public life was turbulent, and full of personal disputes and enmities.

Seaford was a classic rotten borough; attempts were made to expose it as a prime example of electoral corruption, and Harben was at the heart of this corruption. Harben's father became rich suddenly as a result of purchasing some of the quicksilver (mercury to the value of £30,000) from the wreck of the *Nympha Americana*, the captured Spanish ship that ran aground in front of the Seven Sisters in 1747.

Thomas Harben built his political career on his father's wealth. His son Thomas Henry Harben, born in 1768, was a friend of the Prince Regent and regarded as the scamp of the family. When he was 28, Thomas Henry was described in a Brighton newspaper as 'a sprightly young magistrate'. It was through his father's influence that he became a magistrate. In 1784 the *Sussex Weekly Advertiser* announced his appointment as Distributor of Stamps for East Sussex. He was sixteen years old at the time, and his appointment was a clear reflection of his father's influence with the Duke of Newcastle – and the corruption of the times. By the age of 23 he was appointed Keeper of Stamps at Somerset House.

The father, Thomas Harben, acquired Blatchington Court in 1791, but did not want to live there; he had a house already in Seaford: Corsica Hall. Thomas Harben was born in 1736, the son of a Lewes clockmaker, and was himself a watchmaker and silversmith, maltster and shopkeeper, Jurat and Bailiff of Seaford, magistrate and ironmonger, banker and bankrupt. A friend of the 3rd Duke of Newcastle, Lord Lieutenant of Sussex, he acted as Newcastle's agent and adviser, and became actively involved in manipulating borough elections. In 1791 he and another justice,

Thomas Harben

Thomas Chambers, judged that Thomas Evans - the vicar of Seaford - had sworn *six* profane oaths. Sometimes Harben worked *with* Thomas Chambers and his two brothers, James and William, sometimes *against* them. Harben took his oath as Jurat in 1790 and was elected Bailiff of Seaford in 1799. By then he had switched his loyalties from Newcastle to Pelham, who had been appointed Home Secretary in the Addington administration. Harben wrote that the Chambers brothers were mortified by his elevation to bailiff in Pelham's favour - at their expense.

At the Quarter Sessions in Lewes on 9 October 1795, Sir Godfrey Vassal Webster delivered an extraordinary denunciation from the Bench.

I understand that this is the person who was a Shopkeeper, Maltster and Banker at Lewes who was Bankrupt in the London Gazette of last November. I conceive that appointment to be not only a studied disrespect to every Magistrate, but further classing such a man as Thomas Harben with them an attempt to degrade them in the opinion of the County. . . Thomas Harben is notorious for his want of education, for his illiteracy, for his ignorance particularly of the laws of this country. . . Let Thomas Harben continue to thrive while his unpaid creditors are impoverished, let needless offices be created for him and his friends. . . but do not let Thomas Harben be a magistrate for the County of Sussex.

This was reported verbatim in the *Sussex Weekly Advertiser* and Harben offered a long and spirited defence in the same newspaper on 17 October. Experience in trade was a benefit to a magistrate, not a disgrace, he said. 'I must unfortunately admit it to be true that I have not had the advantages of Education which belong to your rank in life and which probably you have enjoyed and I shall not contest that it might be wise to confine the magistracy of the County to persons who had taken their degree in schools. That the law has not made such a qualification necessary may probably have remitted from its being thought that the demands of business and much intercourse with the world may as to the discharge of duties which belong to the office supply the advantages of a finished education. . . No effort has been spared to ruin my reputation and fortune.' Harben finished by openly threatening Sir Godfrey. 'By insulting my misfortunes you have given me the right to advert to the history of your private life. You too have known embarrassments and I shall not shrink from a comparison between us.'

People in Seaford were less concerned about Harben's lack of education, more about his absenteeism. He expected to influence public affairs in Seaford while spending 'a great deal more time at Lewes – ten times', according to one comment in the press. He was 'objected to as not being an inhabitant housekeeper [in Seaford]'.

By early 1793 Thomas Harben had serious financial problems. All three of his banks stopped payment and the following year he was declared bankrupt in the *London Gazette*. It was in the midst of this financial crisis that Harben either mortgaged Blatchington Court and the rest of his property or it was taken into receivership.

A document dated 11 May 1793 at first appears to represent the *sale* of the manor of Blatchington together with the manor house, but it is a receivership or a mortgage, because two years later it was announced that the manor and manor house were to be sold by auction – by order of Thomas Harben's trustees. Both the mortgage or receivership and the eventual sale are symptoms of Harben's acute financial difficulties.

The 1793 'mortgage' named Harben's trustees, described the manor house at Blatchington, and went on to list further properties that Thomas Harben was mortgaging to Mr Creak, Mr Simon, Mr Rickman and Mr Leach: the manor of Alfriston, the advowson of Breedon in Worcestershire, two houses in Lewes, three tenements in the Cliffe at Lewes, three tenements at Sompting, ten tenements in Seaford. The urban occupations of Creak, Simon, Rickman and Leach suggest that they were not intending to get their hands dirty doing any farming, and they were not even in Blatchington, so it must be assumed that they were intending to sub-let the land to local farmers.

On the same day, 11 May 1793, Harben's Bank ceased to exist, and its business was, by implication, taken over by Comber, Whitfield and Co.

Harben's financial difficulties were only temporary, though, because he owned enough property to cover his debts. The collection of documents deposited with the Official Receiver included deeds for the manors of Blatchington and Alfriston, as well as for properties in Seaford, Lewes, Cliffe, Ringmer, Sompting, Cranbrook, Northiam and Newenden. In 1795, Thomas Harben's trustees' tenant was William Chambers. In that year the trustees put the manor, advowson and manor house up for auction, presumably to settle Harben's debts.

January 1795. South Downs, Sussex. To be sold by auction by Verrall and Son at the White Hart Inn in Lewes on Saturday 31 January, 1795 at 3 o'clock in the afternoon, by order of the trustees of Mr Thomas Harben. The Manor and perpetual advowson of the Rectory of Bletchington, with the capital

Mansion House and estate there consisting of about 187 acres of freehold land, and 10 acres of copyhold land, together with the two copyhold cottages and 21 bullock leazes [pastures] on Bletchington Down. The Mansion House is an elegant and commodious building, with coach house and stabling adjoining, situated on the South Downs about half a mile from the sea, of which it commands a beautiful and extensive prospect. NB The 10 acres of copyhold land in Bletchington, in two tenements, is holden of the manor of Alciston by the yearly rent of 5s 4¾d. and 2d also to a fine and heriot on death and alienation.

It seems curious that ten acres and two cottages forming part of the focal manor house property in the village should not be available freehold, and it can only be assumed that this anomaly is an inheritance from the village's medieval history as a satellite of Alciston under Battle Abbey. The copyhold can only have been of long-standing, 'by custom immemorial'.

In 1795 the new owner of Blatchington Court and new lord of the manor was William Chambers, though it seems Mr Chambers did not want to live there either: he let the manor house to Edward Harvey, who was Thomas Harben's son-in-law. Edward Harvey had married the 23-year-old Elizabeth Harben in Lewes in 1794. In January 1795, Harvey was one of four candidates for election as freemen of Seaford; the Revd Thomas Evans was one of the others.

William Chambers did not move into Blatchington Court, yet both before and after that date he appears to have been residing in the parish; he married Susanna Brook at St Peter's in 1782 and they had their daughter Barbara baptized at St Peter's in April 1783. Perhaps the explanation is that he was living at Chyngton Farm, which is the address given in the parish register at the time of his burial; this would make sense, as Chyngton had no church of its own.

Another document dated 1795 is a declaration of trusts. This explains that William Chambers mortgaged his property in Seaford and East Blatchington to his brother James and that James had then died without making a will. The mortgage was to be vested in William and Thomas Chambers – for the benefit of Harry Chambers of Kingston in Surrey.

The 1798 notice of an auction of the household furniture belonging to a departing tenant provides evidence that the house had been rebuilt not long before. The auctioneer's advertisement describes the house as 'newly erected'. The house itself was on the market in December 1797;

12 December 1797. *Bletchington House. To be Lett and entered upon immediately, all that newly erected mansion called Bletchington House situated in Seaford in the County of Sussex and lately inhab. by Edward Harvey Esq with convenient attached and detached offices and 10 acres of rich pasture land adjoining if required.*

29 January 1798. *To be sold by auction by Verrall & Son on Wed & Thurs 13th & 14th Feb 1798. The elegant Household Furniture of Edward Harvey Esq of Bletchington House near Seaford in the County of Sussex, who is going into the army. Mahogany and satinwood tables of every description with chairs, sideboards, wardrobe and basin stands, sofas and paired chairs with chintz. . . dressing glasses, bedsteads with fluted mahogany pillars . . . Wilton floor and bed carpets, a suite of rich chintz drawing room furniture, lately new, elegant register stoves and appurtenances and a profusion of glass, china and stoneware, Kitchen and laundry requisites of the very best. At the place of sale, the Cliffe Lewes.*

A register stove was a closed fire fitted with a plate to narrow the chimney and reduce smoke, along the lines of a modern wood-burner.

The new tenant at the manor house, for what was left of the eighteenth century, was Thomas Flight. William Chambers was very active at this time. Not only did he acquire the manor of Blatchington in the wake of Harben's bankruptcy, and the mansion to go with it, but with Thomas Chambers he also took on the tenancy of Chyngton Farm. The lease was signed in April 1795. So, just three months after taking on the manor of Blatchington, William Chambers took on the tenancy of a very large farm nearby, but outside his manor. 'Chinting', as it appears in the lease, covered a large expanse of Downland on the western side of the Cuckmere valley, together with the reclaimed brooklands down on the valley floor. It amounted to 1014 acres in all.

On 15 January 1798 William and Thomas Chambers of Bletchington were robbed. John Towner was convicted of stealing a sack of oats from them and sentenced to seven years transportation. If this was the John Towner who was born at Blatchington in 1780, he would have been 18 at the time of the robbery.

The Yeakell and Gardner map (page 294) shows us what East Blatchington was like in 1778. From the centre of Seaford, Blatchington Road curved down and round to a road junction beside the Pond. Sutton Drove continued along the north side of the Pond up to Sutton. From the west side of the Pond, Blatchington Hill went up to the church, continuing northwards as Firle Road. From the corner of the churchyard, Belgrave Road ran down to a small fort on a low cliff where the parish met the sea. These roads were in place then as now. Conspicuously absent were Avondale Road, Homefield Road and Upper Belgrave Road, which were later additions. The western part of Sherwood Road seems to have existed as part of a footpath, a short-cut from Blatchington across the fields to Sutton. Robin Post Lane is now a dead-end, but in 1778 it continued, curving south to join Belgrave Road just to the west of Field Cottage.

There were houses all the way up the west side of Blatchington Hill. A long narrow plot ran along the north side of Blatchington Road, its eastern end marked (now) by Chichester Road. This represents Spittal Croft and Chapel Croft combined, and so commemorates the location of the Hospital of St James. A path ran diagonally across the fields from opposite the southern end of Robin Post Lane, at the western end of Blatchington Court, to join Blatchington Road at the western end of Chapel Croft; in other words it joined the headland footpath that crossed the fields from Bishopstone, the two field paths converging on the alley that still exists to the west of the Trek Club.

In the late eighteenth century, with France in the throes of a revolution that threatened to spread across the Channel, this was an increasingly militarized coast. There were two small forts in the area, one on the beach at the seaward end of the Causeway in Seaford, the second, the Blatchington Down battery, on the site of the later Blatchington fort. In 1794, the government bought twelve acres behind the Blatchington fort in order to build a permanent barracks that could accommodated 1500 men. The *Sussex Weekly Advertiser* noted in December 1794 that, 'The Barracks at Bletchington were finished last Saturday. They are . . . expected to be occupied by the Somerset Militia on Wednesday.' Later more land was acquired in order to create a hospital and chapel. Although the Barracks were several fields away, they made a major impact on the village.

The war with France and the threat of invasion brought with it all kinds of turbulence and mischief. One Bletchington villager, a labourer called William Akehurst, decided to make trouble for a man in Alciston, a cordwainer named Charles Coleman. Akehurst spread a rumour that Coleman was in league with a press gang in Newhaven, and was encouraging them to go and impress (abduct) several Alciston labourers. The workmen concerned were employees of Mr William Ridge. The rumour was designed to put Coleman in danger from the threatened workmen. Charles Coleman retaliated by bringing a prosecution against Akehurst. It was only Akehurst's public declaration of his lies, signed on 22 June 1793, that made Coleman withdraw his prosecution.

The main road through the area in the eighteenth century followed a different route from the modern A259. The milestones marked on the 1724 Budgen map show the main road passing from west to east through Denton, Bishopstone, Blatchington and Seaford, then along the present A259 route via Sutton, Exceat and Friston. Blatchington was no backwater; it was on the main road and a significant amount of through-traffic would have passed up Blatchington Hill and Firle Road on its way to Denton (and Lewes), and down Firle Road and Blatchington Hill on its way to Seaford or Eastbourne. No doubt some travellers would have by-passed Seaford by turning left at the Pond and following Sutton Drove.

This arrangement persisted throughout the eighteenth century. When the Duke of Richmond came to Seaford in late September 1789, he would have arrived by the eighteenth century main road route, by way of Firle Road and Blatchington Hill. Just before he reached Seaford, in other words in Blatchington, a number of young men dressed in white greeted the duke's carriage on the road and ran with him into town. The duke gave them five guineas for showing him this mark of respect.

Other modern lines of communication were open to those villagers who were able to read. There was a county newspaper, the *Sussex Weekly Advertiser*, which was established in Lewes in 1745 by William Lee. The newspaper cost threepence in 1785. This was also (in 1797) the cost of sending a letter a distance not exceeding 15 miles; it cost 4d to send a letter 15-30 miles, and so on, so sending a long-distance letter was very expensive. Poor people found ways of communicating by using codes. An unstamped letter might be sent to 'Mrs **W.** Mace' if the sender was well, 'Mrs **I.** Mace' if the sender was ill, 'Mrs **B.** Mace' if the sender had been ill but was now better. The receiver of the letter could glance at the envelope, recognize the handwriting, and refuse to accept or pay for it, yet still get the main news for nothing.

In 1785 Samuel Grimm drew a picture of Seaford from the shingle bank to the south. St Leonard's church is prominent in the middle of the picture, but to the left of it, just visible above the rooftops of Seaford, Blatchington can be made out. St Peter's spire peeps out behind a clump of trees, Blatchington mill can be seen

Blatchington from the south-east in 1785: detail of S. H. Grimm drawing.

a) Blatchington Hill in 1785, enlarged and traced from Grimm.

b) Southern part of Firle Road in 1785, from Grimm.

further to the left, and a straggle of cottages and barns between the two. But the village is almost on the horizon, and no detail can be made out.

Another drawing by Grimm (above) shows the view of East Blatchington from Sutton, and this tells us a little more about the village in 1785. The scene is a long sweep of open Downland with a panoramic view of the village as seen from the east-south-east. The houses can just be made out, crouching in a belt of trees maintained as a windbreak. The double gable of Blatchington House is identifiable, with a Sussex barn right beside it to the west and Field Cottage beyond that. To the north of Blatchington House there are four more houses or barns up Firle Road. Next, moving southwards from Field Cottage, comes the church, then The Gables and its outbuildings, the rectory and then a little further south what seems to be The Star Inn; behind this group of buildings is a dense clump of trees.

To the south of the central huddle of buildings and trees the roofs of four or five more cottages can be made out on the lower part of Blatchington Hill. These houses seem to lie down in the hollow lane; the lower half of Blatchington Hill is today noticeably eroded by long use into the chalk rock, and it would have been the same in the eighteenth century. In the days before roads were metalled, their surfaces were worn down by horseshoes and the iron tyres of cartwheels. Wheel-ruts acted as conduits for rainwater, which washed the powdered rock away. Sandstone and chalk especially were eroded by this kind of wear, so it was common for roads to turn into ravines. But it took a long time for this to happen. The fact that the southern part of Blatchington Hill is a hollow lane three metres deep shows that it is a very old road. A stretch of Firle Road between Alces Place and Firle Drive is also a hollow lane, though only a metre deep.

By the late nineteenth and early twentieth centuries, the Widows' Cottages and Seagull Cottage were the last houses at the southern edge of the village (map on page 220) – there were no dwellings below them – yet in the eighteenth century cottages lined the lower hill. This is borne out by a map from 1780 (page 294), which shows six houses below the church on the western side of Blatchington Hill (three below Seagull Cottage), though none below the Widows' Cottages on the eastern side apart from a cottage or farm building near the Pond.

Somewhere down on the bay between the Buckle and Newhaven, not visible on Samuel Grimm's drawing, were the Tide Mills. In 1761 three Sussex grain merchants, John and William Woods and John Challenor, built a series of grain mills, operated by the tide. They had studied the use of tidal energy for milling in France and decided that this location was ideal. It lay beside a tidal creek near the mouth of the River Ouse and close to commercial centres at Seaford and Lewes. Grain grown further up the Ouse valley could be brought down to the mill on barges.

By the final decade of the eighteenth century, the Tide Mills were a going concern, and turning into a small autonomous settlement. Occasionally there were problems with storms, but sometimes even these brought unexpected treats. In a storm in 1785, the same year that Grimm drew his picture, high waves washed a smugglers' boat with a full cargo of spirits into one of the

Tide Mills ponds. This was a great treat for the mill workers. Other wrecks provided timber for roofs and building, coal for the hearth and thousands of candles.

On the skyline of Grimm's drawing, it is possible to make out the main coast road heading towards Brighthelmstone (pronounced Bright-*Hemp*son) winding up and over Newhaven Hill. The road passes a windmill on the hilltop, just as shown on the First Edition Ordnance Survey map.

What the Grimm drawing shows above all is how the village sat in the wider landscape in 1785, exposed on the long slope of the

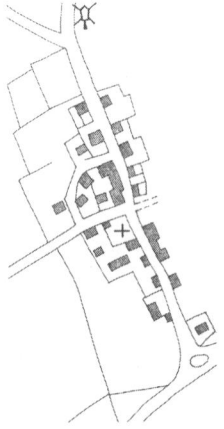

Blatchington village on the 1789 OS manuscript draft

Downland fields towards the sea. It looks windswept, hunkered down in its shelter-belt of mature trees, but it also looks more grounded in its landscape than it does today. It is a traditional English village, surrounded by the large expanse of fields on which its livelihood depends, whereas today it is stranded, fossilized, cut off from its setting by street after street of suburban houses.

The finely detailed two inches to the mile map drafted for the Ordnance Survey in 1789 gives us another view of the lie of the land at Blatchington in the late eighteenth century. This is the view from above, complementing the ground-level view shown in Grimm's drawings of the village from Seaford and Sutton. The draft map is meticulously hand-drawn in black and red ink. My version (above) is traced from the original, enlarged and retraced, then enlarged and retraced again. On the original map the village is very small, so the reader should not attach too much significance to the way buildings are rendered. The Blatchington Court stables, for example, are shown *inside* the churchyard when they were *outside*. The tithe barn is shown to the south-west of the rectory, when it stood to the south, next to the road. But all the key elements of the village are there in this remarkable map.

It shows the Pond in the middle of the Y-junction of Blatchington Road, Sutton Drove and Blatchington Hill. The village appears as a random scatter of cottages with walled gardens and paddocks and the church at the centre. The back road now called Robin Post Lane is shown continuing to Belgrave Road. What we now know as Firle Road, and was then just a continuation of Blatchington Street, is shown with its southern end rather narrow, which it was until the early twentieth century. Firle Road leads up onto the Downs, passing on its way a turning to Bishopstone to the left, and the windmill to the right.

A problem at the rectory

But the maps and landscape drawings give no clue to the everyday problems of the villagers. Even the rector had problems, with too little money coming in to maintain his buildings properly. In the Revd James Tattershall's time (1742-55), the rectory was a seriously dilapidated complex of buildings. There was a barn in the gardens, along with a stable and a brewhouse, all in disrepair. The newly appointed rector knew his income would never cover all the work that needed to be done. It was the spring of 1743 and James Tattershall could only think of one solution. If the brewhouse and stable were pulled down altogether, they would not need to be repaired. The parsonage house was large enough for him to be able to set apart one room for a brewhouse. The barn was very large. It would be possible to make part of that into a stable.

There is other evidence that there were insufficient funds to maintain the church properly. At about this time the lower half of the east window was blocked up, perhaps after the glass was broken, and the priest's door and one of the small lancet windows in the south wall of the chancel were also blocked up. It was a way of avoiding maintenance that had to be paid for by the rector, not the diocese.

The rector drafted a letter to the Bishop. He explained the situation: he was willing to pull down the brewhouse and the stable at his own expense and adapt the house. It would improve the property, not only for himself but for all the future rectors of

> *and were of Opinion that the pulling down the said Brewhouse and Stable and making a Brewhouse in the said parsonage House and a Stable in the said Barn according to the plan aforesaid laid before them will be greatly for the Benefit of the Rector of Bletchington and his Successors. We therefore said*

Bletchington. After all, even when he had set apart a room for a brewhouse, there would still be two parlours and a large kitchen on the ground floor. Because of the modest living, these facilities would be as much as any incumbent could afford to keep in good repair.

And that tithe barn designed to hold one-tenth of the wealth of the parish? Even after the stable was taken out of it, it would still be large enough to hold the tithes of the parish.

The rector drafted his letter. Then he sent it to his bishop, who gave his consent.

Mutiny

As well as being a burial ground for the villagers, St Peter's churchyard is a military cemetery, if a secretive one. All but two of the military graves are unmarked, and one of those is the grave of Elizabeth Ward, wife of Sergeant Ward of the Derby Regiment. She died in 1799 and is buried just outside the church porch. There was also a memorial to a famous officer, Colonel Coote Manningham, though that was shattered in the 1987 storm and the pieces were removed.

It is as if the village has tried to blot out a turbulent military episode, an intrusion on its rural way of life that one might have expected to be unwelcome. The barracks and fort at the seaward end of Belgrave Road formed a substantial but largely separate community, an army colony. Yet by the end of the eighteenth century this colony had doubled the population of the parish. It led its own independent life, which was determined from outside and had its own dynamic, but both soldiers and their families fell ill and died – and the parish church was where their funerals were held, and the churchyard was where they were buried.

At least 187 members of army families are known to be buried in St Peter's churchyard. And we know why they died. Even though efforts were made to improve living conditions at the barracks at the end of the eighteenth century, they were still extremely unsatisfactory and unsanitary. In the early days of the barracks, when they were no more than a tented camp, the local newspaper ran a facetious piece about the weather there one September night.

A sharp gale about the dead of night struck a number of tents belonging to the Wilts Militia at Seaford and left the astonished soldiers without any article of raiment (save their <u>buff birthday jerkins</u>) beneath the agitated cape of Heaven to bear the pelting of the pitiless storm.

The piece, published in September 1794, was no doubt expected to raise a smile, but it is easy to see how wretched and demoralized the soldiers might have become on such an exposed site.

In 1807 the *Sussex Advertiser* wrote a piece about the Blatchington barracks; 'A bowel complaint has of late been very rife here and in many instances proved fatal. Upwards of thirty children belonging to soldiers in our barracks have been carried off by it in a short space of time.' One of the few with a marked grave was Stephen Rabbit, a private in the 11th Regiment of Light Dragoons; he died in 1804, in his 25th year. His headstone in St Peter's churchyard is decorated with a pistol and a sword.

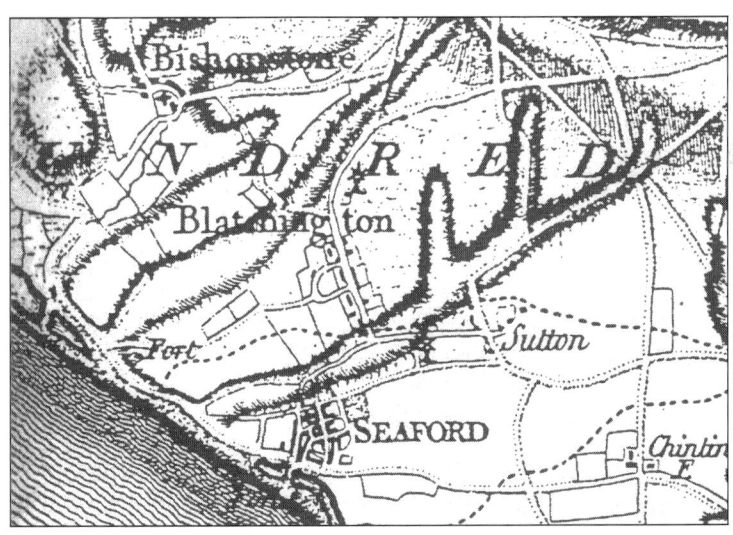

Blatchington in 1795: map by William Gardner and Thomas Gream

The biggest impact of the barracks on East Blatchington and Seaford came when the mutiny broke out in 1794. A small fort already existed but as the threat from France intensified the installation was enlarged. There was a ten-cannon battery and work had begun on the building of an extensive barracks beside it on Blatchington Down, just above the low cliff where the parish met the sea. Blatchington Down is the name given to the seaward end of the long low chalk spur which forms the spine of the parish. The fort and barracks complex filled the triangular area bounded by Claremont Road, Marine Parade and Edinburgh Road.

The militia units had to live under canvas, which was very difficult on such an exposed site. There was no cookhouse or hospital and there were no proper roads. Even what we now know as Belgrave Road was in the late eighteenth century little more than a track connecting barracks and village.

The men of the Somerset and Oxford militias arrived. They were paid sixpence a day plus fourpence for food, which they were expected to buy and cook for themselves. The Seaford shopkeepers exploited the situation by raising their prices and supplying rotting meat and stale flour. Conditions at the barracks became intolerable, as the men became ill and starved. In anger and desperation, five hundred men of the Oxford militia marched on Seaford, seized all the bread, flour and meat they could find, then sold it off cheaply to the other soldiers. Captain (Thomas Henry) Harben led the Volunteers, pleading with the mutineers to return to the barracks, even offering to buy the looted food back and sell it to them at lower prices. Some of the men were content to go back, but most of them marched on the Tide Mills and loaded wagons with 200 sacks of flour. They forced the crew of the sloop *Lucy* to take a cargo of 300 sacks of flour to Newhaven and unload it there. They began selling the flour off in Newhaven. That nightfall, most returned to the Barracks, while just sixty stayed behind to guard the warehouse.

The next morning Captain Harben took over the guns of Newhaven Fort. When two field pieces arrived with a contingent of regular troops, the mutineers put up little resistance, as many were now drunk. Twenty-five of them were marched to the House of Correction at Lewes, while the rest were sent back to Blatchington barracks. Two days later the Duke of Rutland, Lord Lieutenant of Sussex, sat in judgment.

Several of the mutineers were sent to the assizes in Horsham. Four were pardoned, one was transported to Botany Bay, six were sentenced to be given 500-1500 lashes, three were hanged and two were shot.

Living conditions at the barracks were improved in 1795, immediately after the mutiny.

The part-time volunteer forces set up during the Napoleonic Wars were the forerunners of the Home Guard of the Second World War. The volunteers went about their normal work, but had to be available when required. Uniforms were of prime importance in attracting volunteers; they provided an opportunity to dress up and swagger in front of the ladies.

At Blatchington, from 1798 until 1802, a unit of Coastal Artillery Volunteers was raised by Edward Harvey, ready to man the guns in the battery. Volunteering boomed. Nationally, there were 87,000 infantry and artillery volunteers, enough to make conscription unnecessary.

The Experimental Corps of Riflemen came into existence at Blatchington in 1800, when standing orders were created by Lt. Col William Stewart, to be under the command of Col Coote Manningham.

Oh! Colonel Coote Manningham, he was the man,
For he invented a capital plan.
He raised a corps of Riflemen
To fight for England's glory!

Coote Manningham

He dressed them all in jackets of green
And placed them where they couldn't be seen.
He sent them in front, an invisible screen,
To fight for England's glory!

Stewart and Manningham had proposed forming this special corps of highly trained riflemen and in 1800 Stewart set about organizing it. Although Manningham was the colonel and justly shares the credit for founding the corps he seems to have spent little time with it. He was an equerry to George III and therefore often at Court. Stewart did the work at the barracks.

In 1801, Stewart was ordered to take the 49th Regiment and a company of the Rifle Corps to Portsmouth to embark with the fleet commanded by Admiral Sir Hyde Parker. The Rifle Corps were moved from ship to ship. When they reached the Baltic, its members were distributed among the ships of Vice-Admiral Lord Nelson's squadron, and then they took part in the Battle of Copenhagen. Nelson wrote afterwards in his despatch, 'The Hon Col. Stewart did me the honour to be on board the *Elephant*, and himself, with every officer and soldier under his orders, shared with pleasure the toils and dangers of the day.' After Trafalgar, Stewart was to name his son Horatio.

In the autumn of 1802, the Rifle Corps returned with Stewart to Blatchington Barracks and changed its name to the 95th Regiment of Foot. The newly named regiment was back in Blatchington again for the summer of 1803. Later, in 1806, it would change its name again to Rifle Brigade; eventually in 1958 it became the Green Jackets.

In November 1804 the 10th Prince of Wales' Own were reviewed by the Dukes of York and Cumberland on the North Downs near Guildford. Then the Prince of Wales' Own marched to Blatchington to take up coast duty. This was part of the build-up of forces to repel the French in the event of an invasion.

In 1809 Manningham went off to Spain and after the Battle of Corunna he returned home, to die in Maidstone at forty-four of exhaustion. A monument erected to him in Westminster Abbey bears a long inscription including the line, 'Yet, reader, regard not his fate as premature, since his cup of glory was full.' A second monument to Manningham was put up in St Peter's churchyard, to commemorate his connection with Blatchington and the creation of the Rifle Corps there. So on Blatchington Hill a monument was raised, in effect marking the end of the long tradition of the thin red line of the British Army.

In the year of Coote Manningham's death, a regiment stationed at Blatchington barracks, the 81ˢᵗ Foot, helped rescue the crews of seven ships wrecked *in one night* in Seaford Bay. Thirty-three sailors lost their lives that night, four from the *Weymouth*, fifteen from the *February*, twelve from a Prussian ship, two from the *Harlequin*.

East Blatchington's turbulent connection with the army came to an end for the time being, when the barracks were demolished in 1818. Now there is very little evidence of the episode. Not a trace of the barracks remains. Col Manningham's memorial in St Peter's churchyard was shattered in the 1987 storm and has not been restored. Except for two, the graves of 187 other military personnel buried there (129 soldiers and their wives and children) are unmarked.

One of the soldiers who visited Blatchington barracks in the wake of the Mutiny was Thomas Skeel. He was an unusual soldier for his time, in that he wrote a two-volume autobiography, covering the years 1803-15. Only the first volume has survived, taking his story to 1807. Thomas Skeel was a Welshman and he had been a farm servant at Tickenham near Bristol; from there he 'went a soldier', enlisting in July 1803 in the 2ⁿᵈ Somerset Militia. Skeel was intelligent and observant. He was a tolerant, kind and loyal young man, always glad to see his family and his former employer, and glad to help his comrades. He took a simple approach to soldiering. In his own words, 'I done according to orders'.

When he was on leave Skeel sometimes walked very long distances, up to forty miles a day, day after day, to go west to see his brothers and sisters in Bristol or his parents in South Wales.

July the 2ⁿᵈ [1806], marched [from Hailsham] to Blatchington Barracks 14 miles. The 12th of July 1806, William Gay and I went to Lewes on a little business 10 miles, and from Lewes went to Brighton 8 miles. We went on the coach from Lewes to Brighton, for it we paid one shilling and sixpence. We remained in Brighton that night and in the morning returned to Blatchington Barracks 17 miles. The 11th of August, the 2nd Somerset Militia and the 88th Regiment of Foot and the Northumberlandshire Militia and the East Devonshire Militia and the 17th Light Dragoons was reviewed by the Duke of York and the Prince of Wales at Beachy Head.

Blatchington Barracks is built close on the sea beach, half a mile from a small town called Seaford. It is a no-market town, but a Cinque Ports town. There is no market town nigher to it than Lewes and that is 10 miles. On October the 10th furloughs began to be given out in the Regiment. All the men cast lots to see which would go first, but the men that was on forlough the last year was not to go. So I was one of that number, but there was a man by the name of William Hurle one of the same Company which drawed the 3rd number, which was to go on the 10 of December, and he offered to sell his chance to any man that would give him 10s and 6d, which I give it to him, immediately, and share of a pot of beer in the Bargain, as I had a great inclination to go to Wales to see my father and mother, as I had not been in my own country for 4 years and 8 months. All the way was very far, about 300 miles, and only 1 months [leave], to go and to return in.

'On the 12 of December 1806, I and one Isack Ledbury, one of Frome in Somersetshire, which was my comrade at the time. . .'

After a long difficult journey, Skeel reached Laugharne.

' . . . I had been absent from home 4 years and 8 months. In going down the town I accidentally met with my father. I knew him, but he did not know me at first, until I spoke to him, which brought tears from the old man's eyes. I found all my friends as well as I left them. I shan't trouble the reader with the particulars during the time I remained in Laugharne, but I spent a Merry Christmas.'

He managed to get his leave renewed by a JP, and then, mid-January, set off again for Blatchington.

'I travelled to Lewes. . . Billeted at the White Swan, it being cold weather all the way as there was a good deal of snow on the ground. The 12th, I march to a village called Newhaven 7 miles. I lodge at the White Hart, a very civil house, the next day being the 13 of February 1807 joined the Regiment at Blatchington Barracks 3 miles. They were in the same place where I left them. I had been absent 2 months.

I gave in my furlough and my voucher to the Command Office, everything was well, I being on duty for some time after having my liberty so long. I thought it hard to be compelled at the time but it wore off by degrees. The 7th of April I went with a detachment to Crockmare Barracks, 3 miles, to do duty there over smugglers. Remained there 1 month, then returned to Blatchington.

On the 23rd of June I went with an escort to Brighton with one deserter. Was quartered at the Grey-Hound, and returned the next day to Blatchington, 14 miles.'

Thomas Skeel has little to say about Blatchington, and nothing at all about the mutiny there twelve years earlier. The turbulence of the time and the swift comings and goings of successive regiments had erased the memory.

Notes & sources

Ellman 2004 (Using codes to avoid paying postage)

Gentleman's Magazine Vol 70, 1791.

Hudson 1984 (Volunteers)

Jones undated (Thomas Skeel)

Lease of Chinting Farm. Lord Pelham to William Chambers and Thomas Chambers. SAS/ A549, 7 April 1795.

Mortgage of Blatchington Manor and Manor House. Thomas Harben to William Creak and others. AMS 958-959. May 1793

Skeel 1815 (In this text the spellings have been modernized)

Sussex Weekly Advertiser (Contemporary issues)

Thorne 1986

Thomas Harben died of dysentery in January 1803 at Isleworth.

Chapter 6
The early nineteenth century

John King's emergence as squire

At the start of the nineteenth century, Blatchington Court was owned by William Chambers, the Seaford property tycoon who lived at Chyngton Farm. He owned large areas of Blatchington parish freehold, and held about two-thirds of the East Laines (then still divided up into medieval strips) copyhold of the manor of Alciston. The eighteenth century pattern of occupancy continued, with Blatchington's manor house home to a series of tenants. In 1800, a tenant left and the house was once again available. An advertisement appeared on 28 July in the *Sussex Weekly Advertiser*:

> *To be let for five years by auction by Verrall & Sons at the Star Inn in Lewes on 3 August 1800 at 7 o'clock in the evening if not disposed of in the meantime or by private contract. The Manor House of Bletchington with stables, coach house, garden and about 10 acres of land lying contiguous thereto . . . Mr Wilson of Bletchington will show the premises.*

The new tenant was John Bean. The owner of the house, William Chambers, Jurat of Seaford, had held a position of responsibility in the Port of London before retiring to Seaford to make a living out of farming. He died on 7 May 1808 at the age of 57. An inscription in the chancel of St Peter's reads, 'He was a sincere friend and an honest man. His Widow erected this monument as a tribute to her affection.' He was one of the three Chambers brothers who were sometimes friends and sometimes political rivals of Thomas Harben. William Chambers left a daughter, Barbara. She was his only child, and she inherited the manor of Blatchington.

William Chambers left his farms and tenements in Seaford and Blatchington, freehold and copyhold, to be managed by three trustees and executors until his daughter Barbara was of age; then the property was to be conveyed to her. The three executors were his brother Thomas, the Revd Edward Robert Raynes of Lewes and James Brooke of Blatchington. Five years after her father's death, in 1818, she married Stephen Hasler Challen. At the end of that year Barbara gave birth to Caroline, who was baptized at St Peter's in December. The Challens were described as 'of Blatchington House', implying residence at Blatchington Court.

St Peter's church from the south-east in 1802. Watercolour by Henry Petrie. Note the openness of the churchyard before the Dennises' landscaping, the farm gate which was there before the lych-gate, and the entrance pillar to Blatchington Court's drive on the left.

On 13 October 1818, Thomas Chambers, the brother of William Chambers, acted on Stephen Challen's behalf to sell a major property in Blatchington to John King of Wilmington for £1,980. The property sold was 'all that messuage & tenement and 17 acres of land thereto with the barn and stable, garden, yard and appurtenances.' It had in recent times been John Bean's and before that it had been Baker's. It is not explicitly stated that this was Blatchington Court. It included a toft (homestead) with 6 acres and 2 roods of land, which had also been held by John Bean, and this too was handed on to John King. If the modern Blatchington House was intended, the toft may have been Lambe's Cottage, on the other side of Firle Road.

On the other hand, we know that John King was residing in Blatchington *Court* in the 1840s, so it is more likely that that is what he purchased in October 1818. On the Tithe Map of 1843, Mr King appears as the owner of 665 acres of farmland which he let to a relative, William King Sampson, but in addition he had 16 acres and 2 roods of land to himself: Blatchington Court and its outbuildings and gardens. The two figures, 17 acres and 16 acres 2 roods, are so close that it seems likely Blatchington Court was intended in the 1818 conveyance.

The John Bean mentioned as the earlier occupier of Blatchington Court as tenant was one of several men of that name who have lived in Blatchington and Seaford. This particular John Bean was born in Blatchington in 1749, the son of Robert and Ann Bean. He was a prosperous farmer, to judge from the fine low table tomb in the churchyard that bears his and his wife's well-carved names. John Bean married Mary Hyde at St Peter's in June 1788, when John was 39; they had no children. He described himself as 'yeoman' and died at the age of 65 in March 1813. In his will he instructed that, after his wife's death, everything was to go to his nephew William Towner of Seaford. His wife Mary died, also at the age of 65, in November 1816.

In 1827 a Declaration of Trust was drawn up, in effect concluding the business of William Chambers' estate. Blatchington Court and its estate, and all the other properties left by William Chambers, had been sold by the three trustees, Thomas Chambers, James Brook and the Revd William Raynes, and the proceeds invested on Barbara and Stephen Challen's behalf. The Declaration along with a stock receipt was sent to the Challens at their home in Devon; they received £9,660 of New 4% Bank Annuities. This estate eventually went to Barbara's two surviving daughters when she died in 1854.

Meanwhile, by the autumn of 1818 John King had legally established himself as the owner of Blatchington Court and much of the land in Blatchington parish. But Lord Gage, lord of the manor of Alciston, wanted to establish *his* holdings in Blatchington parish. On 4 December 1818, a Deed of Covenant was signed and sealed by him and John King. The Deed preserves the remembrance of the details of the tenements that had been held of Alciston Manor, perhaps preparing the way to consolidating the many separate strip holdings. A fine map surveyed by William Figg shows the component strips in Blatchington's North and East Laines, where Lord Gage owned two-thirds of the land, much of which had been held by William Chambers. The Deed also established that Bullock Down, the open pasture on the chalk hillside immediately north of the village, constituted the tenantry down. Its acreage was noted. Mr King owned the freehold of this land. Its 189 acres of pasturage were divided up into 52 leazes – the tenants' only right of pasturage on the Downs. Today Bullock Down is the golf course, but it still has its Bullock Barn.

John King worked to acquire more land as it became available. An example of this was the aftermath of the death of Henry Mace, who was buried in St Peter's churchyard on 4 March 1827. He had occupied as a tenant a cottage and a fairly small plot of land, larger than a garden but smaller than a field – a rood of land. He had paid a peppercorn rent, two pence a year, to the lord of Alciston manor. Henry had been born and baptized in Blatchington in 1749, and he had four sons by his wife, Elizabeth: George, Henry, William and John, George being the eldest and John the youngest.

The owner of Henry Mace's cottage and land was the lord of the manor of Alciston, who at the manor court shortly after Henry Mace's death formally invited Henry Mace's heirs to claim them. What remains unclear is what happened to Henry Mace's widow, Elizabeth, who lived on in the village for another 8 years. Whether she was still living in the cottage the documents do not say, but the formality of property transfer had to be gone through, then as now. At a court later in the year, on 31 October 1827, an heir at last stepped forward. It was Henry Mace's youngest son, John, who came to the Alciston manor court to be admitted to the property as the new tenant. John had a mother and three elder brothers, but the ancient custom of both Blatchington and Alciston manors was that the youngest son had the right of inheritance, and here he was, at the age of thirty, to claim it, to have and to hold the property in perpetuity and leave it to his heirs. The fine or fee for having this claim recognized was £4 10s.

Mr King had evidently already discussed the situation with John and they had come to an agreement beforehand. Either John Mace did not really want the property, or he had been reluctant to claim it ahead of his mother and brothers - but Mr King did want it, and he was there to take part in the next transaction, which followed 'immediately afterwards', as the Alciston court book tells us. John Mace sold all his rights in the property to John King for £80. Normally a heriot would have been required of John Mace for this, but the court humanely recognized that John could not pay it, so 'for a Heriot nothing because John Mace has no living beast.' A heriot was a common fee for this kind of transaction, but it was for many ordinary people a crippling one, and had been for centuries. A heriot was a tenant's best animal. Sometimes it was difficult for a tenant to continue without his best beast, perhaps his only beast. Sometimes a tenant pleaded to be let off surrendering the animal until it had helped with the next major agricultural task, but even when this was allowed there was a cash penalty for the delay. It was generous of Lord Gage to let John off paying altogether.

We can only speculate about the views his elder brothers may have had about John Mace collecting £75 10s net in this way. Was there an expectation that they would share it?

John King was in court with his lawyer, Robert Picknell, to ask to be admitted to the property. The property John King acquired that day in the autumn of 1827, albeit formally as a tenant on a peppercorn rent, is neither named nor described, so it is hard to be sure where it was. The plots which came closest in size lay along the eastern side of the southern end of Firle Road. The Tithe Map (see below) was made less than 20 years later, by which time the village would not have altered much. On this, any of the plots numbered 41, 42, 43 or 44 could have been Henry Mace's, and then John King's; William Figg's 1818 map shows that of these plots only 41, where Lamb's Cottage now stands, belonged to the manor of Alciston.

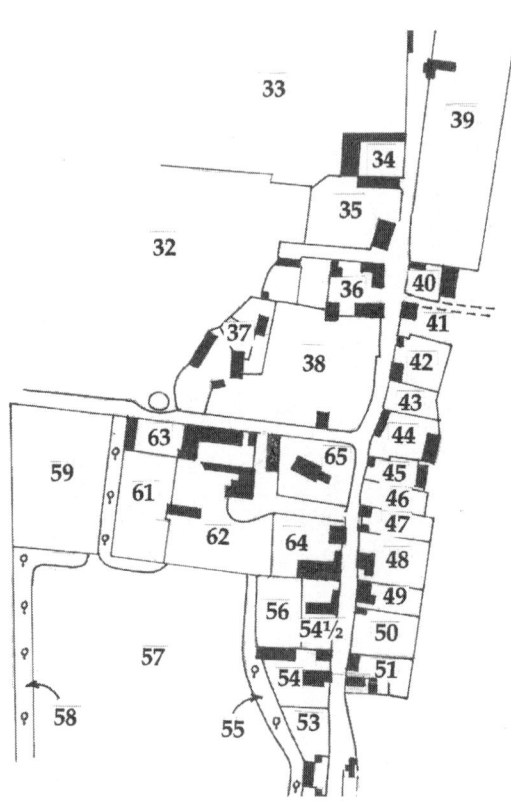

The village as shown on the Tithe Map of 1843, with the original plot numbers. Blatchington Court is 62, St Peter's 65, the rectory 64, Alces Place 34, Blatchington House 36, The Star Inn 51. 55 & 58 are the spinneys flanking The Lawn (57).

For John King it was another piece in the jig-saw of land ownership, or virtual ownership, and the degree of consolidation he achieved can be seen in the Tithe Map. An oddity of the transaction is that John King, lord of the manor of Blatchington, was going to *rent* this property from the lord of the manor at Alciston, Henry Hall, 4th Viscount Gage. He was required to pay only a peppercorn rent, but the wording of the Admittance is clear: 'and he [John King] is admitted *Tenant* thereof'. The hold of Alciston over Blatchington continued, as Horsfield commented in 1835, 'About 72 acres [of the parish of Blatchington] are copyhold, holden of the manor of Alciston; the rest is freehold, and in the manor of Blatchington, belonging to Mr King.'

This continued in the paperwork through the rest of the nineteenth century. At the time of John King's death in 1853, it was noted that he was 'well entitled to the advowson and Manor [of Blatchington] and to such pieces of land and hereditaments as were of freehold tenure and well entitled to the customary inheritance of such of the hereditaments as were of copyhold tenure according to the custom of the *Manor of Alciston of which the same were holden*.' At a court held for the Manor of Alciston on 5 July 1885, 'F. H. Gell was duly admitted to such of the hereditaments as were then of copyhold tenure, to hold the same according the custom of the said Manor [of Alciston]'.

In 1829, not long after John King's acquisition of Henry Mace's cottage, there was a sudden death at Blatchington Court. Mrs Mary Ann Rose was living in Mr King's household, perhaps as a house-keeper or house-guest. By this time, Mr King had lost his two infant sons and his wife. The newspaper reported what happened.

The deceased was a widow lady of amiable disposition and accomplished manners and had been living for a considerable time past at the residence of John King Esq. On Thursday last she was called from the parlour by one of the domestics and on her way to the store room she fell in a fit into the servant's arms and instantly expired. Medical aid was promptly resorted to unhappily without effect.

The inquest was carried out in the usual way for those days, in the village where the sudden death occurred, and with the body of Mary Ann Rose on view. The verdict was that she died of a visitation of God.

The 1831 census listed men's (though not women's) occupations. It showed two farmers employing labourers and one farmer not employing labourers, three men involved in retail or crafts, one capitalist or professional - and twenty-eight agricultural labourers. The emphasis on agricultural labour was even greater than the census suggested, though, because many village boys between the ages of 9 and 19 were farm labourers too. Their labours produced good results. It was a matter of comment in the local newspaper (9 May 1831) that 'last week green peas were gathered in the garden of J. King Esq of Bletchington. They were produced in an open border [ie not under glass] and were full and fine grown.'

Shortly after this time, Blatchington was 'by-passed'. All through the eighteenth century, the main route east to Exceat from Newhaven ran through Denton, Bishoptone and Blatchington. In 1833 a map was prepared for a Newhaven-Eastbourne turnpike road, showing a significant diversion of traffic – away from Blatchington. The new route hugged the eastern side of the Ouse floodplain, then passed along the coast in front of the Buckle Inn and the site of the former barracks, and reached Seaford along Marine Drive. This must, to an extent, have pushed Blatchington village off the beaten track.

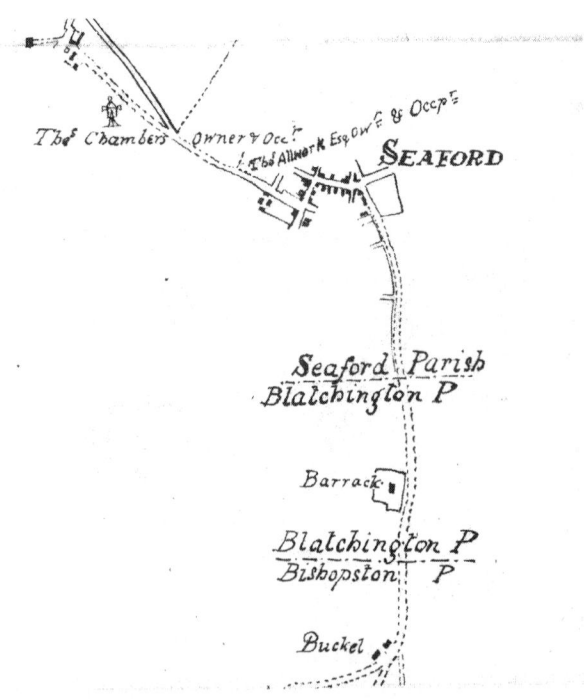

Rusticated battalions: parties at the barracks

Following the Mutiny, successive regiments were stationed at the barracks, though rarely for very long. Perhaps the intention was to keep the soldiers on the move and preoccupied, as a way of forestalling mutiny. But individual soldiers were even so dissatisfied, and they expressed their dissatisfaction by running away. On 11 November 1799, the press reported that two Kentish men had deserted from the East Kent Regiment. They were musicians and went off in their distinctive band uniforms: white coats faced with blue-grey, with blue-grey tassels. They must have been very conspicuous runaways.

There was a press report on 28 January 1799 about the way one regiment settled in;

The 2nd Battalion of the Derby Militia are quite rusticated at the little barracks at Bletchington which though their situation is somewhat exposed are better fitted up and more comfortably accommodated than any we have visited in the neighbourhood. The officers, a few evenings since, gave a ball and supper at their mess room for the ladies of Seaford and the neighbourhood, which turned out so agreeable that the company did not break up till 6 o'clock the next morning.'

In this way the soldiers made themselves very popular with the villagers. When the newspaper reported in March 1808 on a regiment's departure, it commented on the sense of regret that the villagers of Blatchington felt;

The gentlemanly demeanour of the officers and peaceful conduct of the men of the Royal Berkshire Militia who lately quitted the barracks in Bletchington rendered their departure greatly regretted by all the inhabitants of both Bletchington and Seaford.'

The regiments laid on parties the like of which the village had never seen. This was one they gave in November 1808:

'On Wednesday evening last Bletchington Barracks, a most splendid entertainment was given by Lt- Col MacDowall of the Renfrew Militia to all the beauty and fashion of Seaford and its adjacents [ie Blatchington], dancing commenced between 9 and 10 to the most lively Scottish tunes performed by the band of the regiment, and was kept up with unusual spirit till nearly 3, when the company sat down to a very elegant supper, after which the cheerful dance

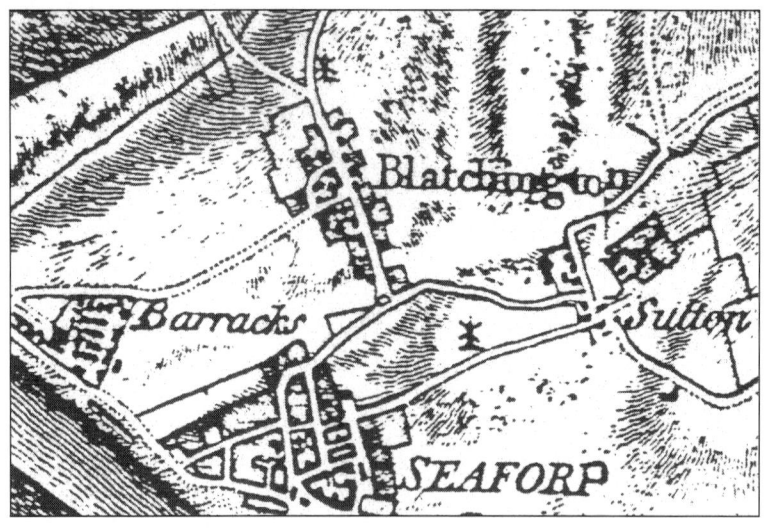

*Blatchington in 1813. The road system is shown
very clearly and accurately for the first time.*

*was renewed, and continued till the dawning light announce the approach of
returning day. The company then departed, highly gratified. . .'*

In October 1809, a similar treat was laid on by the
Nottinghamshire Militia to celebrate the fiftieth year of King
George III's reign. There were fireworks, wine, roast beef and
Yorkshire pudding, and as much ale as you could drink - and all at
the expense of the officers. Twenty empty ale casks were rolled out
of the barracks the next day.

No doubt one of the intentions was to attract into the barracks
as many impressionable young women as possible, and turn their
heads, but there was a political motive as well. These enter-
tainments made the regiments extremely popular in Blatchington
and Seaford. As the end of the Napoleonic wars drew near, there
were fewer soldiers, and the barracks were often empty. In April
1812, the newspaper commented, 'The 2nd Battalion of the 36th and
45th Regiments of infantry at Horsham, we understand, are under
marching orders for the barracks at Bletchington, which have been
a long time unoccupied, to the great regret of the inhabitants of
Seaford, who always appear dull without the society of military
gentlemen.'

Having the regiments stationed at the barracks added colour and excitement. The newspaper reported on 11 March 1799 that a duel had been fought 'on the beach near Bletchington Barracks between Captain D---n and Lieut L---n. The captain was shot in the abdomen and not expected to recover.' But he was still alive a week later, with good hopes of recovery. The duel was fought over 'a matrimonial connection'. A year later another duel was averted, this time between Lieut T. and Mr J. O-E, 'touching the priority of claim to a certain young lady in the neighbourhood'. An order went out to take the two men into custody. One hid in a bathing machine all night and so was able to appear on Blatchington beach at the appointed time and place for the duel, but his opponent did not turn up: he had already been taken into custody.

No doubt to the locals these incidents added to the interest and excitement of having soldiers at the barracks. The young women of Blatchington must have savoured the glamour and romance of being fought over. It more than made up for the rise in petty crime. In 1797, John Steward of the Royal Artillery was committed to prison by Thomas Harben and another magistrate for burglariously entering Mrs Washer's house and stealing ten women's shifts, ten pairs of cotton stockings, six pocket handkerchiefs and three bottles of brandy. Two weeks later, John Steward was sentenced to seven years' transportation - from Seaford Bay to Botany Bay.

A good deal of the crime was home-grown, in any case. In March 1793 the house of Mr Hurdis of Seaford was broken into and '7 or 8 fine grown fowls' were stolen. The newspaper report added a prejudicial footnote: ''Tis supposed the stolen fowls are gone into the Weald.' The assumption was that Blatchington Hill and the Greenway over the Downs were the natural route for stolen goods.

Other social problems were home-grown too. The Pauls were a well-established Blatchington family. James and Susannah Paul had five daughters, Anne, Susannah, Mercy, Mary and Betty, and two of them behaved in a way that was disapproved of by, at least, the parish clerk, who noted illegitimate births in the parish register. In September 1784, Ann Paul was baptized, and it was noted that Mercy Paul was the mother but the father was not known. Mercy was 19 at the time. Four years later, on 23 March 1788, either the rector or the clerk noted the baptism of a second illegitimate child, 'Noah, baseborn son of that notorious whore, Mercy Paul, pauper.' This is all the more startling for being virtually the only personal comment made in the Blatchington parish registers.

In spite of these lapses, Mercy found a husband: John Cowstick came and married her at St Peter's on 22 June 1792. Then it was Mercy's sister Mary's turn to take on the role of scarlet woman. On 14 April 1795, 'James Paul, baseborn son of Mary Paul,' was baptized at St Peter's. In 1802 Mary gave birth to a baseborn daughter, Sarah, who died two months later. She gave birth to a *third* illegitimate child in April 1804, and it too died a few weeks later. The burial is recorded: 'William, baseborn son of Mary Paul'. Curiously there is no rebuke in the parish register: for some reason Mary is *not* referred to as a notorious whore.

It is possible that some of these illegitimate children were the result of one-night stands with soldiers from the barracks, but there is no particular reason to think so, other than the free availability of soldiers.

The military presence in Blatchington was stepped down after Napoleon's exile to St Helena. In June 1818 the barracks stores were auctioned off. In the autumn that year another auction disposed of the fabric of the barracks: the tiles, rafters, roofs, floorboards, weatherboarding, doors and glazed sashes. The battery continued in use, remaining effective during the 1850s, but it was severely damaged during storms early in 1880.

Another relic from the Napoleonic Wars was Rear Admiral James Walker, who was living at Blatchington at the time of his death in 1831. For some reason he is buried and memorialized at St Leonard's Church in Seaford, not St Peter's in Blatchington, which he perhaps saw as not grand enough. His naval career was a phenomenal series of adventures. When he was 16 he nearly drowned when a captured French privateer suddenly and un-expectedly sank underneath him while he was trying to pump her dry. At 19 he nearly lost his life again when the coach in which he was travelling across Germany was attacked by ten highwaymen. Characteristically, he was the only passenger to put up a fight and he was cut down with a sabre and left for dead in a ditch.

He attained the rank of Rear Admiral in 1821 and it was strange that he received no further honour. The Duke of Clarence proposed a knighthood for him, but Walker declined it, hoping that if he did he might instead be made a Knight Commander of the Order of the Bath. But he was disappointed.

His memorial tablet explains that he was 'a most brave and distinguished Officer, who served, fought and conquered with Rodney, Howe, Duncan, St Vincent, and the Immortal Nelson! . . . and after serving his King and Country for Fifty-nine years with conspicuous valour, zeal, skill, and fidelity, he departed this Life at

Blatchington, July 13ᵗʰ, 1831 in the 67ᵗʰ year of his age.' The Dictionary of National Biography gives us little further detail, other than the fact that he died 'after a few days' illness'. Where in Blatchington he died is not recorded; he may have been a house-guest of John King's, and it is hard to think of another house in the village at that time that would have been suitable to accommodate someone of Walker's social status. He would have made a good house-guest, kind, cheerful, and liking nothing better than to make those around him happy.

William Catt

John King established himself as a central figure in the neighbourhood by becoming Blatchington's squire. He acquired friends among the other notables in the neighbourhood. He was regarded as a friend by William Harison of Folkington. When Mr Harison died in 1837, he left nearly everything to various relatives. But he left to his nephew John Harison and 'unto my friend John King of Bletchington House' the sum of £50 each immediately on his death. He also left them all his property to manage, for the benefit of the six daughters 'of my brother Charles Harison'. John King was evidently regarded as a man of probity, a man to trust.

Mr King enjoyed shooting and the other people in the area who set themselves up as gentlemen can be identified in the annual list of certificates for killing game. If you wanted to be considered a gentleman, a huntin' an' shootin' man, you needed a licence. A spring issue of the *Sussex Weekly Advertiser* gives us the following, from the list of licences granted in 1809:

John King (Wisborough Green [not yet in Blatchington])
John Farncomb (Bishopstone)
George Farncomb (Bishopstone)
Thomas Chambers (Seaford)
Thomas Harben (Seaford)
Thomas Henry Harben (Seaford)
Charles Harrison (Seaford)
William Hodson (Bletchington)
Thomas Ker (Bletchington)
Edmund Catt (Bletchington)

William Catt did not figure in this list of local grandees, yet he was to become a very important figure in the economic life of the area in the early nineteenth century. He ran the Tide Mills, but his presence was felt in neighbouring settlements like Blatchington too.

Under Catt's management, the Tide Mills grew in commercial power and also grew as a community. By the middle of the nineteenth century there was a thriving settlement at Tide Mills with offices, a forge, carpenters' workshops, houses and communal washing and laundry facilities for about a hundred people. It was a new village of about the same size as the old village of East Blatchington.

William Catt was a fierce but fair boss. Many of his family's servants and employees stayed with him happily enough through all their working lives. But he was an uncompromising master. He imposed a curfew; at 10.10 pm the Tide Mills village gates were locked. Villagers who stayed out too late had to climb over the gates and risk punishment from their employer if they were caught. Catt was hard on himself too. It is said that the morning after his marriage at the age of nineteen he was out in the woods at the crack of dawn hauling hop-poles with his father's team of horses. When he took over Tide Mills, he and his wife rose every morning at three o'clock to begin their working day.

When William Catt died in 1853 he was given a massive table tomb in a prominent position close to the entrance to Bishopstone churchyard, and a memorial tablet inside the church. It said, among other things, that 'his transactions were characterized by a strict adherence to justice, great firmness, energy of mind and sound judgment.'

Catt was a man of property, and he rented eight properties in Blatchington village. The 1843 Tithe Map shows him and his brother Edward Catt as the 'occupiers' of a piece of land running down the western side of Blatchington Hill, and including all the roadside properties south of the Rectory. The squire, John King, owned Blatchington Court, The Lawn stretching from the mansion right down to Blatchington Road and the Water Lily Pool, the two flanking spinneys and the walled peach garden where Four Walls now stands. Mr King also owned most of the fields round the village, amounting to 665 acres, all of which were let for farming to Mr William King Sampson: the parish as a whole, fields, village, beach and waste land, amounted to 755 acres. Of those, 21 acres were the barracks, owned and used by the government. John King held back just 16 acres for his own use. So the Tithe Map gives us the following picture of Blatchington;

Owner	Occupier	Area
William Alce, Jr	William Alce, Junior	1 acre 1 rood
Government	Government	21 acres 1 rood
John King	John King	16 acres 2 roods
John King	Wm King Sampson	665 acres
John King	Wm & Edward Catt	5 acres 1 rood
John King	Cottagers	2 acres
Revd Robt Dennis	Revd Robert Dennis	0 acres 1 rood
Revd Robt Dennis	Church, churchyard	0 acres 1 rood
Common	Beach, roads, waste	43 acres 3 roods

The Catt family also rented all the roadside properties on the eastern side of Blatchington Hill, from and including The Gables down to the Star Inn and the Widows' Cottages, but excluding William Alce's property, now The Cottage.

What use would the Catts have had for these properties? The Catts did not live in them. Although described as 'occupiers' they did not literally occupy them, so they must have sub-let them.

As was the custom in the nineteenth century, William Catt socialized with those he regarded as his social equals. These included the squire of Blatchington, John King, and the rector of Blatchington, from 1846 the Revd Robert Dennis. The three men were keen on shooting; they shared an interest in wild birds which would have provided a common currency for their conversation. It is fair to assume that Mr Catt sometimes dined at Mr King's house, Blatchington Court. William Catt might have had occasion to visit Blatchington for supper, but this does not explain why he rented some cottages there from Mr King. The answer may lie in his paternalistic attitude towards his work force. Perhaps there was not sufficient accommodation at the Tide Mills, and he acquired the Blatchington cottages in order to provide additional housing for his mill workers.

The growth of the Tide Mills settlement, in effect a 'new village' in Bishopstone parish, to some extent compensated for the loss of the barracks. In 1811, when the barracks existed, Blatchington had a population of 362. In the 1840s, after the closure of the barracks, the population fell back to 163.

Catt may have been a fair employer, but there were other employers in rural areas who were well hated by their workers. In 1831 there was an eruption of violence among farm workers

Henry Hall, Lord Gage

because the introduction of threshing machines threatened their livelihoods.

At Firle, Lord Gage cannily averted trouble by meeting his workers and agreeing an increase in wages - in spite of his strongly reactionary political views. Lord Gage was an unusual reactionary. When out walking he habitually dressed in a smock and a battered hat, and was sometimes mistaken for a labourer. On at least one occasion when making a social call he was turned away at the front door and scornfully told to go round the back, which he did; it amused him. During the Captain Swing unrest, he kept fire-watch over his tenants' barns, and narrowly avoided being caught and injured as a suspicious loiterer by one of his own tenants. In the Cuckmere valley, barns were burnt at two farms and one man was hanged at Horsham for the Cuckmere burnings. Whether there was any unrest at Blatchington is not recorded, but if so it must have been minor. No wage riots were recorded in the relatively acquiescent Eastern Downs. The rioting was concentrated to the north of the Downs; it was the Weald that was the major focus of unrest - and the Weald was another place altogether. And yet - in 1835 a huge barn on the Earl of Chichester's farm at Chyngton was burnt, with everything inside it, and that was a case of arson. No-one was ever caught.

The flood of 1824

On 23 November 1824, the whole of the lower part of Seaford was flooded by the sea, including the ancient valleys on each side of Blatchington Down. The valley to the south-east of the ridge was flooded as far inland as Blatchington Pond. Thomas Horsfield described it;

'At Blatchington, the waves flowed into a large pond, more than half a mile from the sea, and destroyed all the carp and tench, whose ancestors had dwelt there in safety for many generations.'

The 'large pond' was Blatchington Pond. A week later 'A letter from Alfriston' in the *Sussex Weekly Advertiser* described the pond as 'the fishpond of J. King'. The fort was badly damaged under the sea's onslaught; much of the structure was destroyed in the storm. Subsequent sea-wall building and housing development has obliterated every remaining trace of this important installation. The main road from Seaford to Newhaven was also broken up by the sea in the 1824 storm and for many years afterwards it was necessary to make a long inland detour, through Blatchington, until a new cut was made across the foot of Hawth Hill in the 1880s.

Another change was the building of the railway, which arrived in the centre of Seaford on an embankment. When there was another flood in 1875, the railway embankment acted as a flood barrier, preventing water from surging up the valley towards Blatchington Pond.

John Lewis

This chapter opened with the death of William Chambers, whose wife erected a stone memorial to him, or rather to her affection for him, in the chancel of St Peter's. There are three such memorials in the chancel. The second in time sequence is that of the Revd John Lewis.

It reads, *'To the memory of The Rev. JOHN LEWIS, upwards of 36 years Rector of this parish, who died on the 8th day of December, 1843, in the 76th year of his age. Also of ELIZABETH, his Widow who died on the 2nd day of October, 1853, in the 77th year of her age.'*

The third memorial in the chancel of St Peter's is a severe and stately classical black marble monument that seems to belong to the eighteenth rather than the nineteenth century. The inscription on its top half was evidently carved by the hand of one mason, the inscription below by another, the style perceptibly different. This is the monument of John King and his family. Their story is really the subject of the next chapter. When the inscriptions were recorded in the nineteenth century, only the upper half was transcribed. It tells a sad story of a squire bereaved;

'To the memory of MRS MARY KING, Wife of John King, Esqre., (and second daughter of Thomas Rogers, Esqre., of Kingston, near Lewes) who departed this life May 13th, 1822 in the 35th year of her age. Also of their two sons HENRY and JOHN KING. The former died Novr. 22nd, 1818 aged 3 months; and the latter July 30th, 1821 aged 4 years and 10 months. Also of MARY, wife of Lieutenant GEORGE WATSON, R. N., and eldest daughter of John and Mary King, of this parish, who died at Stonehouse, Devon, the 12th of January, 1836, aged 25 years. Also of JOHN KING, Esqre., of this parish, who died July 5th, 1853, aged 78 years.'

What happened next, and how the tablet was completed much against John King's wishes, we shall see in the next chapter.

Ordinary lives

It was an ordinary village. Thomas Horsfield described it in 1835 as 'consisting of a single street of indifferent looking houses. The parish is small containing not more than 170 inhabitants. . . As the greater part of the parish lies on the downs, the surface is considerably undulated, and the soil light, producing excellent crops of barley.' Most of the men living in Blatchington in the early nineteenth century were farm labourers. From this it might appear that the prospects for their children were bleak. But there was a well-established tradition of apprenticeship. At the age of 14 or 15, boys were formally indentured as apprentices in neighbouring towns: Brighthelmstone (Brighton), Southover, Lewes and even Hastings. Most of the boys went to Brighton, and by far the commonest apprenticeship was in shoemaking.

A typical indenture dating from 1822 shows William Stace, aged 14, the son of Thomas Stace of Bletchington, labourer, becoming indentured to John Bearman of Brighthelmstone, cordwainer. Two years later another fourteen-year-old boy, John Towner, was indentured to John Bearman. The fourteen-year-old Charles Stace, son of James Stace, a Blatchington labourer, was indentured in 1835 to George Barton of Brighthelmstone, cordwainer (shoemaker). This took them away from home, so it was an experience equivalent to going to college, living under someone else's roof while acquiring skills that would be the basis of a livelihood. Other Blatchington boys who took apprenticeships in the 1820s and 30s were Edward Coates, William Hoad, William

Ade, Daniel and Stephen Horscroft, John Shalton (or Shelton), William Button and George Mace. The apprenticeships were often for four years, sometimes five.

So there was a way out of the village for the boys who wanted it. And for the village girls there was always 'service'. In the 1890s, Jacob and Anne Squibb's teenaged daughter Rebecca, who grew up in Blatchington, was working as a servant in Beckenham.

Notes & sources

Abstract of Title, Arlington House (King holding land of Alciston Manor)

Anon 1832 (Rear Admiral Walker)

Copy of entry in the Alciston Manor Court Book (31 Oct 1827).

Corner 1853 (Borough English custom)

Ellman 2004 (Lord Gage)

Horsfield 1835, Vol 1, 278 (land in Blatchington parish holden of Alciston manor)

Langton and Morris 1986, 187. (Captain Swing riots)

Robinson 1822 (Borough English)

Tithe Commutation Map (1843)

'Visitation of God' was a common verdict on a sudden unexplained death.

Will of John Bean, dated 1812, proved 1813.

Chapter 7
The Revd Robert Dennis

The new rector

1844 was a landmark year for Blatchington. A new rector arrived, the twenty-nine-year-old Robert Dennis, not long since graduated from Clare College, Cambridge, and given the living by John King, the squire who both owned and lived in the mansion house. The rectory next door was in effect a tied cottage, though it was not always occupied by the rector. In 1802, for instance, it had been empty and available to rent.

> *To be let. Ready furnished for six months certain or longer – Blatchington parsonage – house fit for the immediate reception of a small genteel family and pleasantly situated half a mile up from the sea and the same distance from Seaford. For further particulars enquire of Mr Lambe, upholsterer, Lewes or Mr John Wilson, Bletchington, who will show the house.*

John Wilson had been born in Blatchington, and would die there soon, in 1810, at the age of 40. From 1802 to 1804 the old rector, Samuel Topping, was ill, languishing in a Dorset vicarage, and he let Blatchington rectory to tenants. But the burials - of soldiers and Blatchington villagers alike - continued, and clergymen from neighbouring parishes had to cover Mr Topping's duties. The *Gentleman's Magazine* for 1804 announced that Mr Topping had died on 21 April - 'At the parsonage-house at Boscombe, aged 83, the Revd Samuel Topping, rector of Blatchington, Sussex.'

Robert Dennis was a conscientious rector, but he had an interest quite outside the Church. He was fascinated by birds. There was nothing he liked better than walking out, especially with his dog and a gun, in the hope of seeing and shooting some new specimen. On a cold sunny December day in 1846 Robert went on one of his favourite walks, down Blatchington Street and over the fields to Sutton and Chinting, down the slope to Cuckmere and the sea. There, in the estuary, he saw a great variety of birds: divers, redwings, larks, lots of small birds busy on the shingle, and geese, grebe, rail and waders on the marshes.

Blatchington was a fine place for bird-watching. The village was close to high chalk cliffs that were breeding places for ravens, peregrines and the last of the Sussex choughs. Not far from home

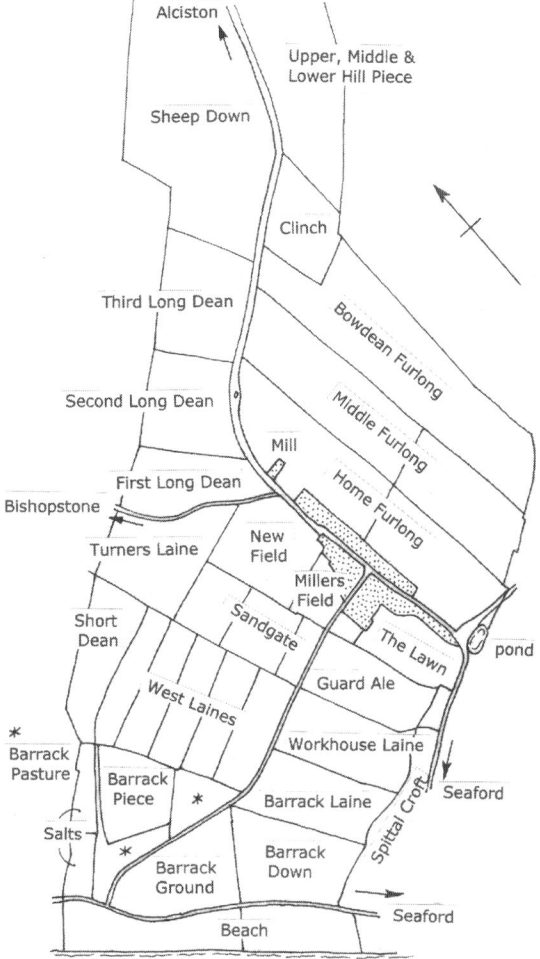

Field names in the 1840s (from the Tithe Map)

was the beach and its long shingle bank with the lagoons of the old estuary of the Ouse behind it. Another favourite walk took him down the long farm track from the church past Blatchington Court and across the fields towards the Barracks. To his left were John King's fields, let to tenant farmer William King Sampson: Way Field, Guard Ale, Workhouse Laine, which took its name from the Poorhouse at its lower edge, and Barrack Laine. To his right were more fields worked by Mr Sampson: Millers Field, Sandgate, West Laines and Barrack Pasture. Passing the Barrack Ground, Robert stepped out onto the long shingle bank that swept across the bay towards Newhaven. He watched flights of chaffinches on the shingle bank, and gulls tumbling in the air. From there he went on to the Tide Mill ponds.

Robert owned only a handful of ornithology books to help him identify birds; one was Bewick's *History of British Birds* and he had come to rely on it.

A ten-foot flint wall separated Robert's kitchen garden from the grander gardens belonging to Mr King. The birds moved with enviable freedom from his garden into Mr King's, and back, singing, hawking and building with equal disrespect on both properties. Mr King was friendly and sociable enough; he too was interested in birds. Recently he had told Robert that he had seen a saddleback crow pounce on a reed-sparrow and swallow it whole. But he was a good deal less sympathetic regarding Robert's interest in his daughter Elizabeth.

Mr King was a man of substance, a landowner, and he was not going to allow his daughter to marry so far beneath herself. He made it clear that Robert's courtship was to go no further. But Elizabeth was neither so young nor so biddable as to take this as absolute. In an age when women were expected to marry young, she was close to being left single for ever. She was three years older than the rector, thirty-two now, and may have seen him as her last chance. It seems she secretly encouraged Robert, and they took to talking to each other over the high flint wall separating their two gardens. But the wall was twice as tall as she was, so they piled up stones on each side of the wall. Then they could stand on the stones and talk to each other. As the weeks passed, the heaps of stones grew higher, until they could see one another, and - it is said - high enough for them at last to kiss. In the course of these forbidden conversations, screened by the spinney trees from the disapproving eyes of Mr King, Elizabeth finally accepted Robert's invitation - to come over the wall for good. Elizabeth's father was unbending. He doggedly refused to allow her to marry Robert. They would have to wait until Mr King's death before they could marry - and wait they did. It was a long engagement.

Will Reed was Robert Dennis's neighbour and contemporary; they shared an interest in birds. Social station was the key difference between them; Will was a labourer, and he became Robert's gardener. Will and his sons, especially his son William (who would later live at Rookery Cottage), went on bringing Robert Dennis specimens and reports of birds for many years.

On May Morning, sweeps turned up at the front door of the

rectory with shovels and bells; they were fantastically dressed up with gilt paper caps and ribbons, and they danced at Robert's door.

Mr King continued to be friendly, and he let Robert shoot birds in his garden. The two men were on good enough terms to go out together. Mr King drove Robert over to Firle, where they walked round Lord Gage's park together.

Robert took home injured birds, nursing them back to health in the rectory bakehouse, which he treated as an aviary. Later, in the 1860s and 70s, he kept injured birds in cages on the south-facing rectory verandah, where they would catch the sun. But the caged birds did not always survive, and Robert seems to have been surprised by this. Robert Dennis's attitude to his birds was ambivalent. If he could, he would shoot a bird dead, send it to Swaysland's the bird-stuffer in Brighton to be turned into a display specimen. But if he winged it he would take it home, and try to nurse it back to health. He was a great slayer of birds – like his neighbours he must have killed hundreds of them – yet sometimes he regretted it. He wrote, 'I really think that no creature can exceed the tern in lightness, grace and beauty. I felt sorry to fire.' But fire he did.

Robert Dennis suffered from headaches and attacks of biliousness, perhaps migraine symptoms. If he was suffering from stress-related migraines, it is not hard to guess the source of the stress. It seems he was sometimes not able to take services, leading to a strange incident. The vicar of Bishopstone, John Harison, lived at Sutton. One Sunday morning he travelled over to Bishopstone, no doubt travelling up Blatchington Hill and passing St Peter's church on his way, only to find when he reached Bishopstone church that a strange clergyman was already at the reading-desk and had started the service. Mr Harison was puzzled, but found a place in a pew and let the stranger carry on. When the service was over, he went over to the strange clergyman and discovered that he believed he was in Blatchington church, which is where he had been sent. Meanwhile the Blatchington congregation had waited a long time, wondering whether anyone was coming to take their service. Eventually Mr Catt, the churchwarden, stood up and took the prayers. This irregularity was reported to the Bishop, Ashurst Gilbert, who wrote Mr Catt a letter of gentle rebuke, asking him 'not to do the like again'.

It was the Revd Edward Ellman, rector of Berwick, who recorded this episode. Ellman was also secretary to the Rural Decanal Chapter and in this capacity in 1861 he proposed undertaking a survey to find out how many churches had chanting of psalms, and which hymn books they were using. He found that of the seventeen churches, nine had chanting, nine used the (old) Tate and Brady psalms and hymns, five used *Hymns Ancient and Modern* and one a local hymn book. At Arlington and Robert's church at Blatchington there was 'no singing of either Psalms or Canticles'.

As Robert grew older, he became more infirm, and went out on shooting sprees less often; he relied on people 'bringing up' specimens for him. Neighbours, landowners, coast-guardsmen, farm labourers and children brought him birds, dead or living.

Mid-nineteenth century Blatchington

The 1851 census tells us about the state of the village in the middle of the nineteenth century. Two-thirds of villagers had been born in Blatchington. A further one-quarter had been born not far afield, and still in Sussex. Two percent came from Kent. This much is unsurprising, and as in any community there were a couple of people with far-flung origins. The rector had been born at Cape of Good Hope and the coastguard, Lieutenant Killop, had been born in France which, given the widespread suspicion of the French, cannot have made life easy for him.

There were 138 people living in Blatchington, of whom 43 were men (fourteen and older), 36 were women, 22 were boys, 37 girls. It is not known why there were so many more girls than boys. Of the children under the age of four, four were boys, eleven were girls. Some people were living to a great age – one pauper woman was 82 but only six people in the village were 70 or older (unusually, four men and two women).

Most of the men, 37 of them, and five of the boys were agricultural workers. One of the boys, John Reed, was only ten and his brother Will was only eight years old. They lived with their parents, William and Elizabeth Reed, along with their five siblings, in Glebe Cottage. Some of the agricultural workers took pride in their specialized occupational skills, describing themselves as cart-ers, cattlemen or oxmen. Jesse Wood was a wheelwright. The miller, William Seymour, lived in the cottage up Firle Road beside the mill with his wife Mary and their family of eight. Thomas Young, a 24-year-old journeyman miller, is described in the census as a visitor.

The postman was George Mace. At the seaward edge of the parish there was the coastguard, Henry Killop. He was married, but his wife was not at the coastguard station; instead he was attended there by an 18-year-old servant called Sarah Simmonds.

Then came the village's upper class, the rector, Robert Dennis, the squire, John King, who described himself as 'landed proprietor', and William Lambe, who described himself as 'farmer', adding '720 acres, 25 employees'. He was a tenant or yeoman farmer.

The odd man out was William Alce, who owned his property, the site of The Cottage on Blatchington Hill. There were but three property owners (according to the Tithe Map) in Blatchington village: the rector, the squire and William Alce. Even William and Edward Catt were tenants at Blatchington, not owners. Somehow, in spite of John King's careful acquisition of estate, William Alce had managed to retain ownership of his cottage and rood of land.

While most of the men in the village were engaged in agricultural work, most of the women were keeping house. Twenty were housewives, three were housemaids, housekeepers or servants. There were six other house servants, such as the rectory cook, 57-year-old Ann Bodle. There were also two paupers, one described as a milkwoman, the other a needlewoman. As these were the only two female paupers in the parish and both were widows, it is possible that they were living in the pair of Widows' Cottages.

The southern edge of the village in perhaps 1880 or 1890, with Widows' Cottages on the right (the single-storey building at right angles to the road). This was the place where Blatchington Hill (foreground) became Blatchington Street (middle distance).

Only half of the the 28 children under the age of fourteen are described as scholars: only half of them were going to school. There is one four-year-old, Kitty Alce, described as a scholar and one fourteen-year-old, the miller's son, William H. Seymour. Eight children from eight to twelve years of age, all boys, are described as agricultural labourers or shepherds; over one-fifth of the village's agricultural work force was child labour.

The 1851 census gave each household a number, but unfortunately not its location. It is, even so, possible to reconstruct some of the addresses. Lieutenant Killop was based at the Coastguard Station, which lay close to the sea just east of the barracks. Robert Dennis lived at the rectory, John King at Blatchington Court and William Lambe at Blatchington House, having moved there just a few months before. William Seymour lived in the cottage beside the windmill. Carter, the shepherd, probably lived in the cottage to the north of the Mill, while William Reed and his family lived at Glebe Cottage. William Alce lived in one of the cottages immediately north of Glebe Cottage. The two pauper widows probably lived in the Widows' Cottages. John Shelton and his family may have lived at The Gables, as an 1892 conveyance mentions that Mary Shelton had once occupied the house.

The census shows that no-one in the village was acting as a carrier, which means that for public transport the villagers must have relied on the Seaford carriers. There were four of these to choose from, two going to Lewes, two to Brighton. George Lower took a waggon to Lewes every Wednesday and Saturday, while Mrs Ann Earl (in 1855) or Mr William Earl (in 1865) ran the same service on a Tuesday and Friday. Edgar Hilder's omnibus went to Brighton on a Tuesday and Friday. William Wood's omnibus went to Brighton on Monday, Thursday and Saturday.

In his diaries, Robert Dennis mentions travelling on Hilder's van on 17 November 1848: 'Went to Brighton and back by Hilder.' Then, more graphically, ten days later, 'Jolted to Lewes in Hilder's van'.

In the 1890s, when the recently widowed Mrs Dennis was giving properties to create a glebe for the church, she handed over three acres of meadow round the Water Lily Pool. At that time, the meadow was in use by Mr Hilder, who may have been grazing his horses there. It would have been a good location, midway between Blatchington, Sutton and Seaford and within easy reach of all of them. In 1899, the directory shows Hilders' still in action as butchers (Hilder & Son), but no longer as a carrier service. The

Seaford carriers then were John William Lower & Son, Collingham Bros and William Cosstick.

The brink of change

In October 1853, just when Robert's life was being transformed, members of the Sussex Archaeological Society arranged to hold a meeting in Seaford. They visited Bishopstone Church and East Blatchington Church on their way to Seaford, where they met with the 'greatest hospitality'. Doubtless Robert gave them a guided tour of St Peter's. At the meeting, the local historian Mark Antony Lower read a paper on the History and Antiquities of Seaford.

In 1853, everything changed for Robert Dennis. On 5 July that year Mr King died at the of seventy. Mr King had forbidden Robert to marry his daughter; doubtless he saw the rector as too far beneath his daughter's social status for such a union to be thinkable, and perhaps he also suspected that young Dennis might be a fortune-hunter. And perhaps Mr King was just too emotionally attached to Elizabeth to let Robert take her from him. John and Mary King had had two sons and two daughters, but only Elizabeth lived beyond the age of thirty. The two boys had died in infancy, Henry dying aged 12 weeks in 1818 and John junior in 1821 at the age of four. Then Mary herself died in May 1822, at the age of only thirty-four. Their daughter Mary survived into adulthood, but died

Blatchington Street in the 1850s (painting by Rodney Castleden)

in her twenties in 1836. Elizabeth, the only survivor of his family, was too precious to lose.

Robert and Elizabeth were condemned to what must have seemed like an endless engagement. But now that Mr King was dead there was nothing to stop them from marrying. After a few months, on 26 September 1853, they did marry, and in St Peter's church. He was thirty-seven; she was forty. Elizabeth had not only become free to marry, she had inherited half of the Blatchington Court estate, become its beneficial owner, and the newly-married couple moved into the mansion, while Robert's father took over the rectory as his son's curate. It was like the happy ending to a novel by Trollope.

The terms of John King's will show his ambivalence towards Robert. He had not wanted his daughter to marry Robert, but he trusted him enough to leave to him the responsibility of looking after Elizabeth's financial interests, appointing him one of three executors and trustees; the other two were F. H. Gell of Lewes and Lt-Col George Watson of Surbiton. Watson features on the King family memorial as 'Lieutenant George Watson RN', but now he seems to be in the army. He was John King's son-in-law, the widower of his daughter Mary. The trustees were to see that Elizabeth and her (curiously anticipated) children received half of the rents and profits of the estate. The other half were to provide an annual income of £100 for Mr King's son-in-law Lt-Col Watson and to be held in trust for his grandchildren, Robert and John Watson.

John King died on 5 July 1853 without altering this will, which was proved at Canterbury in August by F. H. Gell and Robert Dennis. The trustees of Mr King's will, including Robert Dennis, were to hold in trust the mansion house, the manor of Blatchington, the advowson of the rectory and all the freehold properties.

Robert's interest in birds continued unabated and now, at Blatchington Court, he had a larger and more varied garden in which to watch them. Will Reed was still his gardener and helped by reporting what he and his twelve children saw. Will's son John, now a twenty-one-year-old ploughman, saw two buzzards every morning on the Downs immediately above the village when he went to plough, and described the buzzards as 'quartering the rape like dogs'.

Not long before, Robert had been unable to purchase the lavishly illustrated books on birds that he wanted. Up till now he had been forced to lean on Gilbert White's *Natural History of*

Selborne and Thomas Bewick's *History of British Birds* as his only reference books. In 1847 he wrote, 'I am sadly at a loss for books of reference, good ones with plates are so expensive.' He managed to purchase Hewitson's *British Ornithology* in 1848. He badly needed Yarrell's *British Birds*, but for a time the price was beyond him. Because of the lack of reference books, he could not identify many of the birds. Now it looked as if he could afford them.

He might also restore the church, on which he started work in 1857. But all was not as it seems. It was not his wife's money that paid for the restoration; a large sum was raised by subscription. The fact that in 1861 Elizabeth needed to *borrow* a large sum suggests that there was some difficulty in gaining access to her half of the rents from her father's estate. Meanwhile, the restoration work went ahead. The Manx architect Ewan Christian (1814-95) took out and replaced the old pews, added the vestry on the north side and built a new porch on the south side. The floor of the tower was dug up in order to re-pave it, which is where our story began, a link right back to the very beginnings of the village.

The result of the restoration was a tidy, sturdy structure that was well set to last for another century or more.

The one negative aspect of the Dennises' restoration was the loss of some traces of medieval wall paintings. When a survey was undertaken of murals in Sussex churches in the late 1890s, there were no visible traces of any in East Blatchington church, but the Revd Arthur Richardson believed that some murals had been discovered 'at the restoration of 1860'. It is not known what the origin of Richardson's belief was. Did Robert Dennis mention it during the hand-over? Or did Richardson hear it from the men who had worked on the restoration? And was it true? Certainly Bishopstone had its walls painted, with garish zig-zags.

The parish of East Blatchington was neither exceptionally rich nor exceptionally poor by the standards of the area. In 1867, the yearly value of the Blatchington rectory was £200, which was significantly higher than Alfriston's £135 and a little higher than Newhaven's £186, but lower than Seaford-cum-Sutton, which was worth £240.

After the work on the fabric of the church, in 1859-60, Robert and Elizabeth set about landscaping the churchyard, an open and neglected plot. They planted it up with trees and shrubs. Then they turned their attention to the rectory. Robert's father died in 1860, so the two-storey Georgian building then stood empty. It seems likely that it was Robert and Elizabeth's money that paid for the lavish memorial east window dedicated to Robert's father, although on the window the mother, Ann, is named as donor. It was also in 1860, in February, that Robert Dennis made his will - one that would not be superseded by any later will - leaving everything he had to his wife.

In 1861, Elizabeth Dennis reached the age of 45. This triggered a new legal agreement. She had passed the age at which she might be expected to produce children. She was also entitled, according to the terms of her father's will, to raise a mortgage to the extent of one-third of the estate, and for this sum to be paid over to her for her sole use. The estate, both freehold and copyhold, was valued at £42,260 (£1,823,950 in today's money). The significant sum of £6,000 had had to be raised by the trustees on her behalf, though it is not clear from the documents what she needed this money for. It represents around £260,000 in today's money. The trustees agreed to pay interest on this at 4.5%.

Elizabeth Dennis was entitled to the proceeds from half of the estate (the half that was freehold), and one-third of that half was £7,043 6s 8d. The trustees had earlier paid Elizabeth £1,043 out of the trust money. She was entitled to claim the further sum of £6,000 from the trust, which would enable her to repay the £6,000 which she had been voluntarily lent through the trustees by Thomas Lambe. This Thomas Lambe was Robert Lambe's Uncle Tom (1812-1900).

The rectory, enlarged by the Dennises, view facing Blatchington Hill

Richard Lambe's Abstract of Title for Arlington House is worded very precisely. The trustees 'applied to and requested Thomas Lambe to lend the said £6,000'. Richard, who was Robert Lambe's solicitor son, was careful to point out that it was the trustees' idea to borrow money from Thomas Lambe; the initiative had not come from Thomas Lambe. If the loan had been offered by Lambe, it could be construed that members of the Lambe family were trying to put Elizabeth Dennis under an obligation to them, which they might later use as a lever to acquire her estate.

Immediately afterwards, in March 1861, F. H. Gell, the trustee who had been admitted to the copyhold (ie Alciston-owned) half of the estate in 1855, covenanted with Thomas Lambe to surrender his half into the hands of the lord of the Manor of Alciston to the use of Thomas Lambe. There was a proviso: that the trustees of John King's estate had until 18 August to pay Thomas Lambe the £6,000 owed to him. Whether the sum was paid is not known, but Thomas Lambe was not admitted following the surrender. F. H. Gell died in October 1864, leaving everything to his son Inigo Gell, who was accordingly admitted to the copyhold property held of Alciston Manor in May 1867.

Following the death of Robert Dennis's father, the Dennises decided to move back into the now-empty rectory, perhaps finding Blatchington Court too large for their needs. The rectory, on the other hand, was too small. The Dennises ambitiously had the rectory roof removed, and an extra storey added. From the evidence of the diaries, we know that this happened in 1862. Robert noted in March that long-eared and pipistrelle bats were found 'when unroofing the rectory'. Apart from this cryptic diary entry, Robert typically tells us nothing about his major project, the remodelling of the house, only about the bats, which were 'rather torpid until aroused by the warmth of the hand, or the fire'.

Another change probably made at this time was the blocking-up of the front door on Blatchington Street and its replacement with a front door opening onto the south garden, beneath an elegant new wrought-iron balcony. This was a reorientation of the building through ninety degrees, and the Dennises may have been consciously copying the layout at The Gables (opposite) and Blatchington House (William Lambe's house just up the road), both of which presented their sides to the street.

Once the Dennises moved into the rectory, which they probably did in the summer, they were able to let Blatchington Court. The advertisement for the let, dated 7 October 1862, ran as follows;

Blatchington House Nr Seaford. To be let. Very desirable and commodious residence. 3 sitting rooms, 6 bedrooms, 2 dressing rooms, laundry & man-servants room, kitchen, housekeepers room, back kitchen, bakehouse, store room, larder, dairy, 4 dark attics, water closet, also 2 cow houses, shed, cattle yard, 4 stall stable, loose box, coach house, harness room and granary, walled kitchen garden, orchards. 10 acres grass land adjoining. Very pleasing situation. ¾ mile from sea. Gell &Sons, Lewes.

Attics often had dormer windows and were used for servants' bedrooms, and the phrase 'dark attics' signalled to prospective tenants that at Blatchington Court the attics were not usable for staff accommodation. Blatchington Court was sometimes called Blatchington House, as in this advertisement; at those times the building we today know as Blatchington *House* was described as Blatchington *Farm*. There can be little doubt from the description of the lavish accommodation and its date that it was the mansion, Blatchington *Court*, that was being offered, not the farmhouse. The 'ten acres of grass land adjoining' is identifiable as The Lawn. The Dennises' tenant in 1867 was Dr William Tyler Smith, a London doctor and magistrate, and he was probably their tenant from the beginning.

In June 1865, Will Reed told Robert that he had been listening to the call of the golden oriole at intervals all day and had seen a pair, specially noting the bright yellow breast of the male. Robert was excited because he had not met with the golden oriole for some years. He too heard the male singing in the clump of trees

On the 12ᵗʰ of July 1864, the Great Eastern steamship passed across the bay near shore, the wind being fresh from the east. She was on her way from Liverpool to the Thames to take on the Atlantic cable.

above John Shelton's garden (The Gables), and while the men were gone to dinner Robert and Elizabeth together listened to the male and female answering each other. The female seemed to be in among the trees on the coach-road (presumably further up Firle Road).

The January of 1868 was another hard winter with snow. Joe Banks the bricklayer shot a red-legged chough in good plumage and condition on Seaford Head. Banks took the bird to Robert Dennis, who examined it and understood that he was looking at a rare bird. Robert wrote to William Borrer about it and Borrer replied that within his experience no Sussex specimen had been seen. Robert looked in his reference books and found in Knox's *Birds of Sussex* that the red-legged chough was believed to be extinct in Sussex. Perhaps now it was. The specimen ought to go to Swaysland to be stuffed. Robert's most important contribution to Borrer's list of Sussex birds was to be the rose-coloured pastor, which he recorded at East Blatchington, but no notes about this rare bird survive.

In his later years, ill health set in and Robert Dennis became withdrawn and reclusive, enjoying only the company of his friends and intimates. He would still be seen walking about the village, and he was now a big stout man with a white beard. Increasingly, his bird-world shrank to the walled enclosure of his rectory garden, but even there he was able to see, on the ground, in the trees, on the walls and in the sky above, a fair proportion of the 162 bird species he had observed in and round Blatchington.

The 1871 census shows a sixty-three-year-old Robert running a frugal household in his spacious rectory with his wife Elizabeth, then sixty-seven. They had two live-in servants, Sarah Coppill, the housemaid, and Frances Coom, the cook. Frugal though their household may have appeared, the Dennises were people of property, by Blatchington standards.

There was a flurry of activity towards the end of 1877. In November there was an agreement between Thomas Lambe, George Watson and Robert Dennis that all the interest due on the £6,000 loan had been paid up to date and the capital sum too had been repaid. The half-share in the Blatchington Estate was duly returned to Watson and Dennis. At the same time Thomas Lambe formally cancelled the conditional surrender of copyhold lands to Alciston Manor made in 1861. It was also noted that the two Watson boys, Robert and John, had passed the age of 24 in 1857 and 1859. Under the terms of John King's will, with the written consent of Elizabeth Dennis and Robert and John Watson, the way was now clear to *sell* Blatchington Court and its estate.

Robert Dennis

On 20 December 1877, they agreed to sell Blatchington Court and its estate to Robert Lambe, the son of William Lambe of Blatchington House. The sale price agreed was £34,500, a sum that was 9% lower in 'real money' terms than the valuation of the property 16 years before. Robert Lambe wanted the copyhold properties to be enfranchised, ie changed to freehold. E. T. Gage and Viscount Gort, the lords of the Manor of Alciston, agreed to this, on Robert Lambe's payment of £1,505 11s 9d. Inigo Gell was recognized as the (outgoing) holder of these copyhold lands and it was agreed that he would convey the enfranchised lands to Robert Lambe. This way, Robert Lambe would own the entire estate freehold, which is what he wanted. The Gages established that although Henry Hall, the Viscount Gage who died in January 1877, had left his estate to the use of his grandson H. Charles Gage and his heirs, it was lawful for any freehold or copyhold properties to be enfranchised, so long as the current tenant for life agreed to it in writing. The enfranchisement of the Alciston lands in Blatchington parish could go ahead. The centuries-old obligation to Alciston was coming to an end.

Robert Lambe at this point acquired the freehold of East Blatchington Farm (now Blatchington House), in which he was then living with his parents. Also included were 'the Windmill Cottages barns stables stalls waggon lodges buildings yards closes and several pieces of land arable meadow pasture and down to the said Manor and farm belonging or appertaining all which said premises were known by the general name of the Blatchington Estate'. Excluded were the lands conveyed to the railway company in 1864.

Robert and Elizabeth Dennis bought three small properties out of the estate back from Lambe. They acquired The Gables, and a single cottage in two tenements, the cottages now known as Glebe Cottage and Rectory Cottage, and also three acres of land at the bottom of the Lawn of Blatchington Court, the piece of meadow that contained the Water Lily Pool. What their intention was in buying these small properties is not known, but immediately after Robert died in 1892 Elizabeth negotiated with the Bishop of Chichester, the ninety-year-old Richard Durnford, to transfer them to church ownership to generate income for the current rector, Arthur Richardson, and his successors.

Robert and Elizabeth had reached a decision to leave Blatchington, when lightning struck the church. They put up a commemorative brass plaque on the west wall of the nave, just behind the organ, headed 'From lightning and tempest, Good Lord, deliver us'. It reads, 'On 30th Dec 1879 this Church was struck by lightning at the spot where this tablet is now placed to mark the very place where the lightning struck.' On it they offered thanks to 'the mercy of God in sparing the fabric from destruction.'

The plaque was not entirely accurate regarding 'the very place'. *The Times* described the lightning striking the west side of the spire, tracking down to the north-east to hit the nave roof-ridge. It was guided by the iron stove flue, which then ran to the roof-ridge, to the vestry chimney and down into the vestry floor. A branch of lightning travelled along the guttering on the north side of the church, descending each of the drainpipes. The shingles were completely wrecked on three sides of the spire and a large hole was left in the north side of the nave roof next to the tower.

Whether the Dennises saw the lightning strike as an omen cannot now be known, but by then they must already have made their decision to leave Blatchington.

Robert resigned as rector and he and his wife retired to Paignton in 1880, but the connection with Blatchington Hill was not forgotten. After Robert's death, Elizabeth generously erected a sturdy lych-gate to his memory, on the eastern corner of St Peter's churchyard, right on Blatchington Hill. It replaces a traditional farm-gate (see page 89). The weighty central roof-beam of the lych-gate is inscribed: 'In memory of Robert Nathaniel Dennis, B.A., for thirty-five years Rector of this Parish, and of his pious care of the churchyard this lych-gate was erected by his widow, AD 1892.' The lych-gate was dedicated by Robert's successor, Arthur Richardson, in a ceremony on Sunday 6 November 1892. Elizabeth came to stay in Blatchington for the event.

Later that month, while she was still in Blatchington, Elizabeth attended to another piece of business, again to commemorate her husband's ministry. She gave a trinity of properties - three cottages and three acres of meadow land - to the Church glebe; this included the triangular flint-wall-bounded hollow down at the foot of Blatchington Hill where the Water Lily Pool lay and the grassy slope above it where Glebe Drive and its flanking row of houses now runs.

The vellum conveyance, covering the three cottages and the meadow, was signed by Elizabeth Dennis, the rector, Arthur Richardson, and the nonagenarian bishop. Elizabeth lived on until 1908, when she died in Paignton at the age of ninety-four.

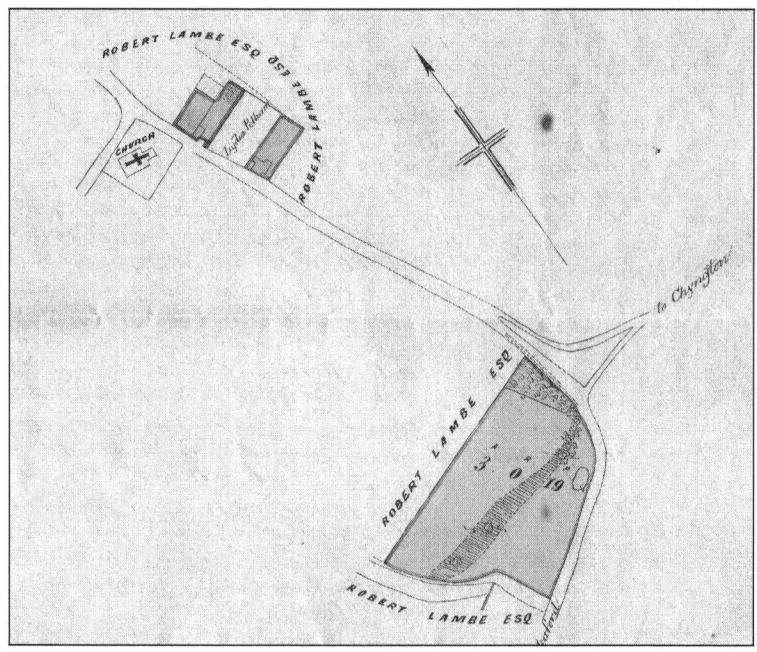

The new Glebe lands

Now at last the monument to John King and his family could be completed. The upper part of the inscription in the chancel had ended half a century before with the death of John King in 1853, the John King who had stopped his rector from marrying his daughter. To this could now be added the significant tailpiece –

Also of the Revd Robert Nathaniel Dennis, Rector of this Parish, who died the 17th of February 1892. Also of Elizabeth, his wife, daughter of the above-named John King, who died at Paignton, Devon, the 12th of February 1908, aged 94 years.

The names of John King, Elizabeth Dennis and Robert Dennis, the forbidden husband, all huddle together on the King family monument, and are together now for ever.

Robert Dennis left £300 stock to the rector and church-wardens of St Peter's. The yearly dividends were to go towards maintaining the paths and graves in the churchyard, in particular the grave of his father. He also expressed the wish that Will Reed and his family would always be employed by the rector and churchwardens of St Peter's.

Robert Dennis's gardener, long-term general helper and friend, Will Reed, died in 1904. Will's wife Elizabeth died aged 84 in October 1903, and Will, 'husband of the above and Sexton of this Church', followed her three months later at the age of 86. It was a measure of their standing in the village that they were given the privilege of being buried in the closed churchyard.

Notes & sources

André 1900 (Murals in the church)

Castleden 2011 (Robert Dennis)

Census 1851 (village in 1851)

Dennis 1861a (Memorials in St Peter's)

Ellman 2004 (St Peter's congregation left in the lurch)

Franks, B. (transcribed) 2006 *Bequest by the Revd Robert Dennis*. Seaford
  Museum.

Sussex County Directory (1855)

Simpson's Lewes Directory (1865)

The Times, 1 January 1880 (lightning strike)

Abstract of Title for Arlington House (terms of John King's will)

Chapter 8
Blatchington Court
in the late nineteenth century

Dr Tyler Smith

Once the Dennises had moved into the enlarged rectory, they were able to let Blatchington Court. Their first tenant was William Tyler Smith Esq, MD, JP, a doctor, a magistrate, a pillar of the community, a man of substance, and an eminently suitable tenant for the Dennises' mansion. Dr Smith was fifty when he moved into the house, and at the peak of his career. He was co-founder of the Obstetric Society of London and had been its president from 1860. He was also a businessman, co-founder of the New Equitable Life Assurance Society.

Dr William Tyler Smith was also to prove surprisingly active in Seaford, where he had the idea of developing the town into a health spa. Once Tyler Smith ruled the roost at Blatchington Court, things were set to change. There would be Development. There would be Progress. He launched a concerted campaign for commercial expansion.

As with later developers in Seaford, soon after settling at Blatchington Tyler Smith became a Seaford Jurat. His ascendancy in Seaford is marked by the years in which he was Bailiff – the 1860s. But Tyler Smith remains something of an enigma. No personal papers have survived and even his professional dealings are recorded only in a number of official documents, so his motives remain obscure. Was he trying to help the local community or was he trying to make a lot of money? Was his interest philanthropic or commercial?

He bought a considerable amount of land in and next to Seaford, setting up the Seaford Improvement Society; one of the improvements was the building of a long and lofty row of terraced houses in Pelham Road. He helped to found the Convalescent Hospital. Given his responsibilities in London, Smith was startlingly active in Seaford.

While Tyler Smith was active, another Seaford developer, Thomas Cook, founded a Seaford Gas Company with an unsightly gasworks on the Blatchington-Seaford parish boundary, on the site of the leper colony. Then the disruption of gas pipe-laying began all round the town. At the same time, Tyler Smith built the Terminus

Dr William Tyler Smith. The background is a painted studio backcloth, not the interior of Blatchington Court.

Hotel in Dane Road in 1863, in anticipation of the increased numbers of visitors the Newhaven-Seaford railway line would bring when it opened the following year. It was Tyler Smith, through his Seaford Improvement Committee, who persuaded the Brighton and South Coast Railway Company to extend the line from Newhaven to Seaford. At a public dinner at the New Inn, Bailiff J. S. Turner hailed the arrival of the railway as 'the means for the regeneration of Seaford'. Tyler Smith made a speech in which he speculated ambitiously about continuing the railway line east to make a direct link to Eastbourne and Pevensey. That did not come to pass. Nor did Turner's vision of a fifty-fold growth in the size of Seaford.

The main focus of Tyler Smith's development ambitions was the Beame-lands, the low-lying marsh marking the former estuary.

Smith's plans were not universally popular in Seaford. In 1859 he took a 299-year lease from the Corporation on 29 acres of Salt and Beame-lands. Local people criticized this move as it alienated the traditional common rights from the town's inhabitants. The plans divided the corporation in two. The lease was renewed and revised in 1866, and Smith started building houses at the top of Pelham Road and in Marine Parade. Another firm independently applied for consent to build a pier and landing place. In 1869 Smith turned the old baths into Assembly Rooms and started work on the Bay Hotel in Pelham Road.

This may seem to have no bearing on Blatchington, but Tyler Smith's ambitious schemes for Seaford were to have a profound influence on Blatchington's future, as we shall see in Chapter 10.

The historian Mark Antony Lower mentioned Tyler Smith when he described a walk from Seaford in 1868.

'A short and agreeable walk is that to Blatchington and Bishopston, two neighbouring villages. Leaving the town by Broad Street, the pedestrian soon reaches an abrupt turn in the road near Cinque-Port Place, and the gas works in a deep dell on the left. Near this spot stood the old hospital of St James. Further on, near a pond, the road takes another sharp turn northward, and the village of Blatchington is soon reached. It is picturesquely situated among trees, and commands a beautiful view over Seaford and the Channel. The churchyard is remarkable for its neat and elegant arrangement arrangements, a perfect garden, the graves being planted with flowers of every hue. This attention is due to the care and taste of the rector, the Rev R. N. Dennis, and his wife. Blatchington Court is the residence of Dr Tyler Smith, and stands in agreeable grounds on the left. Passing the church, a road turns at a right angle westward.'

Then Tyler Smith died suddenly. It happened in June 1873 at Richmond, when he was fifty-eight, and he was brought back to be buried in a double-width grave on the north side of St Peter's Church. The ambitious plans to expand and develop Seaford came to an abrupt halt. There was uncertainty about his executors' interests and intentions. Then came a major storm in 1875 which caused flooding and serious damage to the Assembly Rooms; the billiard table was swept out to sea and found, several days later, floating in Cuckmere Haven. It marked the symbolic end of William Tyler Smith's dreams.

Pevsner later described Seaford as 'the least gay of the chain of south coast seaside places.' A uniqueness worth conserving, perhaps; why try to make all seaside settlements the same?

Tyler Smith's widow, Tryphena, remained in Seaford. She was still there five years after his death. She was invited to attend the Honourable Artillery Company's Camp Fete, held at The Millberg in Seaford on 5 August 1878. The Honourable Artillery Company visited Seaford with a flourish, taking the salute as they passed Blatchington Battery. Once in town, the artillery retired to the New Inn 'to mess'; the pub was their HQ in Seaford.

The Fishers and the Bloomsbury Group

Smith was succeeded as tenant of Blatchington Court by Herbert William Fisher. He had the house from 1872 or 1873 onwards, moving from Onslow Square in Kensington with his wife Mary and their two sons and three daughters. He was forty-five when they moved in, with none of Tyler Smith's aspirations to put Seaford on the map. Throughout that alarming episode, Blatchington had remained unscathed. There were only a hundred or so people living in East Blatchington village in 1801, and that remained the same until the final quarter of the nineteenth century. Fisher was not interested in commercial or any sort of growth in Seaford or Blatchington, quietly pursuing his career as a barrister and historian. He was married to Mary Jackson. They had a son, John Francis Fisher, who was born in 1866 and who would later be killed at thirty-five in the Boer War in 1901. A daughter called Emmaline was born in 1869. Edward was born in 1872 and Henry in 1874.

When ownership of Blatchington Court changed in 1877, the property deeds note that the house was occupied by Herbert Fisher, who had a tenancy agreement that expired 'at Ladyday 1878'. Robert Lambe became the Fishers' new landlord.

Herbert and Mary Fisher's son Charles Dennis Fisher was born at Blatchington Court on 19 June 1877 and baptized at St Peter's on 4 August. He was educated at Westminster School and Christ Church, Oxford, played cricket for Oxford University, and was a first-class cricketer from 1898 to 1903. Wisden described him as 'a safe and steady batsman'. He graduated in 1900 and was elected Tutor at Christ Church in 1903.

Charles went into the Royal Navy and was a Lieutenant aboard *HMS Invincible*, a battlecruiser, the first of its kind in the world. At the Battle of Jutland, *Invincible* was flagship of the Third Battlecruiser Squadron, which acted as a heavy scouting force. With other ships, *Invincible* engaged the *Lutzow* and the *Derfflinger*. During this duel a twelve-inch shell hit *Invincible* amidships. The exploding magazines blew *Invincible* in half, causing huge loss of life. 1026 officers and men were killed, including Rear-Admiral Hood - and Lieutenant Charles Fisher. Only six survivors were picked up.

Charles's sister Cordelia was born in 1880. She lived on to 1970, when she died at the age of ninety. She hated war, to which she had lost three of her beloved brothers, and did her best to instil a loathing of it in others. A younger brother, Edwin, was born in 1883. He went into the Army, rose to the rank of Captain, and in 1936 became Chairman of Barclays Bank.

William Wordsworth Fisher, one of Charles's elder brothers, was also born at Blatchington Court, on 26 March 1875, and baptized at St Peter's on 2 May 1875. He too headed for a naval career. He was educated on board *HMS Britannia*, entering the Royal Navy as a Cadet in July 1894. He captained *HMS St Vincent* at the Battle of Jutland which, unlike his younger brother, he survived. In 1922 he was made Rear-Admiral; in 1929 he was knighted; in 1932 he was made full Admiral and Commander-in-chief of the Mediterranean fleet.

Admiral Sir William Fisher was an impressive and formidable figure. He respected honesty from his subordinates and they either idolized him or saw him as dogmatic and uninspiring. When one of the Mediterranean flotillas returned to Portsmouth in 1936, the crew were touched to see 'the towering figure of Admiral Sir William Fisher', standing on the quay, waiting in heavy rain to give them a welcome home.

The two sailor brothers' father was Herbert William Fisher, who wrote a book on the origins of the American Civil War. He was also tutor to Edward VII and became the Prince of Wales's Private Secretary.

The household's eldest son was Herbert Albert Laurens Fisher (1865-1940), better remembered as the writer H. A. L. Fisher. He was an historian like his father, and he became another great public figure. He spent some of his boyhood at Blatchington Court, graduated in 1888 and later went into politics. He was President of the Board of Education in Lloyd George's 1916-22 government. As part of the reconstruction legislation promised by Lloyd George during the war, Fisher was given the task of working on a new Education Act (1918) which made school attendance compulsory up to the age of fourteen.

On 15 October 1918, Virginia Woolf had tea with Herbert. He said, 'We've won the war today. The Germans have made up their minds they can't fight a retreat. There is now a prospect of a complete defeat of the German army.' She reflected, 'I tried to think it extraordinary but I found it difficult - extraordinary, I mean, to be in touch with one who was in the very centre of the very centre, sitting in a little room in Downing Street. . . The fate of armies does more or less hang upon what two or three elderly gentlemen decide.'

Herbert became Warden of New College, Oxford, in 1926 and continued as Warden until his death. During that time he wrote a three-volume *History of Europe*. He became a Privy Councillor and was eventually awarded the Order of Merit. He died in 1940 at the age of seventy-five, somewhat anticlimactically, when he was knocked down by a bus. Yet in a way his career was not quite over. He was posthumously involved in a bizarre hoax.

In Operation Mincemeat, the body of a Welsh tramp was disguised as that of an aristocratic officer. The tramp was furnished with an officer's uniform, a bank account and even a girlfriend called Pam. The aristocratic underwear he was supplied belonged to the late H. A. L. Fisher. This detail was passed on to Harry Judge (at Brasenose College) by Hugh Trevor-Roper in 1978; Judge thought at the time that the story was unlikely to be true, but it was corroborated by Fisher's daughter, who was then Principal of St Hilda's.

Operation Mincemeat (1943) was a plan to mislead the Germans into believing that the Allies were planning landings on Sardinia, when in fact they planned to land in Sicily. False documents were to

H. A. L. Fisher

be planted on a dead body, which would then be allowed to fall into enemy hands. A suitable corpse was found, the body of a Welsh vagrant named Glyndwr Michael. After the body had been in the Med for a while it would be difficult to establish cause of death, and hypothermia or drowning would be assumed, though Michael had taken rat poison.

He became 'Major William Martin'. Suitably dressed and salted with documents, Major Martin was taken by submarine to the Mediterranean and released off the Spanish coast, where he was picked up within a few hours by a local fisherman. The authorities examined the papers, and their contents were reported back to Hitler, who responded by sending extra troops to Sardinia. After the war was over, Montagu wrote a book, *The Man Who Never Was*, which was an immediate best-seller and then was made into a successful film two years later. The Man Who Never Was wore the underpants of a one-time Blatchington resident on his final – indeed only – mission.

But long before that, in the summer of 1880, on the lawn sloping down in front of Blatchington Court, we might have witnessed an unhistoric scene of upper middle class domesticity. Two brothers playing, the three-year-old Lieutenant Charles Fisher, who would one day die at the Battle of Jutland, and the five-year-old Admiral Sir William Fisher, who would survive Jutland and climb the ranks. Watching, perhaps, was the fifteen-year-old future historian and President of the Board of Education, H. A. L. Fisher. Also looking on was another sibling, Adeline, the ten-year-old wife-to-be of the composer Ralph Vaughan Williams, wondering if anyone would play tennis with her.

The cool and elegant Adeline (1870-1951) married Vaughan Williams in 1897. It was a mis-match, a marriage Vaughan Williams must have regretted almost at once.

When RVW went up to Cambridge in 1892, he used to visit the Fishers at their term-time home, the Lodge at Downing College. RVW's father had known Herbert Fisher at Christchurch, and it was through this family connection that RVW came to know the eleven Fisher children. In the summer holidays, the Fishers had taken houses not far from RVW's home near Dorking. The Fisher cousins were not popular with Virginia and Vanessa Stephens (later to become Virginia Woolf and Vanessa Bell). Virginia and her sister thought the Fishers a rather bloodless lot. The family's matriarch, Mary Fisher, was described as a saint by her son Herbert, but Virginia and Vanessa regarded Aunt Mary as a washed-out ghost. Virginia took a positive dislike to Adeline, referring to her as 'ice-cold Adeline'. They came close to a separating quarrel.

Virginia finally disgraced herself in the eyes of the Fishers by her involvement in the 1910 *Dreadnought* hoax instigated by Horace de Vere Cole. Cole, Virginia, her brother Adrian, Guy Ridley, Anthony Buxton and Duncan Grant dressed up in costumes and pretended to be an Abyssinian prince and his entourage. They were welcomed on board the *Dreadnought* as it lay at anchor at Portland, and Admiral Sir William May gave them a guided tour of the ship. They repeatedly cried 'Bunga! Bunga!' to express amazement. Adrian Stephen, as their interpreter, was unsure how to address his foreign friends, so he spouted chunks of Vergil and Homer, which the admiral did not recognize. Although Admiral Sir William May met the hoaxers, William Fisher was the *Dreadnought's* flag commander, and he was furious when he found that his cousin Virginia had been involved.

The Bloomsbury aesthetes were pacifist by tendency, and the hoax could be seen as a pacifist gesture against the Navy. But it was more personal than that. The prank's real target was the Stephens' priggish cousin, Commander Fisher. When they had all been younger, there had been bitter rivalry, doubtless some of it acted out at Blatchington Court, between the earnest, dull, conformist Fishers and the clever, sarcastic Stephens.

How the Fishers were regarded in East Blatchington is not known: aloof, probably. No doubt when they lived at Blatchington Court they kept themselves to themselves. Virginia Woolf observed

The Dreadnought hoaxers: Virginia Woolf is on the left

uncharitably that 'the Fishers would have made Eden uninhabitable.'

Ralph Vaughan Williams was too folksy to be accepted by the Bloomsbury group and too warm, restless and romantic a figure to find the Fisher family culture congenial for long. Yet he proposed to ice-cold Adeline in 1895, and they were married in Hove in 1897. (The Fisher family moved from Blatchington Court to Hove in 1881.) The marriage was a disaster from the start, with Adeline always putting her family before RVW. He loyally remained with Adeline until her death, in spite of being in love with someone else.

Did Vaughan Williams visit East Blatchington when he and Adeline were young? It would be pleasant to think of a youthful RVW walking up Firle Road from Blatchington Court with Adeline on his arm, she picking a flower, he a folksong sung by a labourer at a cottage door along the way. RVW did collect folk songs in Sussex villages, though not quite this early. When he was an undergraduate at Trinity College, Cambridge, Vaughan Williams frequently visited the Fisher family: they were living (in term-time) in the Lodge at Downing College. The courting seems to have happened there, after the Fishers had left Blatchington Court.

There is nothing to connect Vaughan Williams to Blatchington, except perhaps indirectly. RVW collected Sussex folk song, as did his younger protégé and friend, George Butterworth, and they enjoyed walking the Sussex countryside together. Butterworth was at Oxford from 1904 until 1908. While there he became involved in the English folk song revival, and a collaboration and friendship with RVW began. Butterworth started collecting folk songs, mostly in Sussex in the summers of 1908-10. It was then that he wrote a piano piece called *Firle Beacon*: this is the name of the nearest high hill to Blatchington, just four miles away.

Vaughan Williams loved Butterworth's piece, but the manuscript vanished without trace: it was neither published nor even performed in public. Butterworth may have seen Firle Beacon while he was on one of his song-collecting expeditions, and walked up onto it. Did he perhaps visit Firle Beacon with Vaughan Williams?

Pass on, weak heart, and leave me where I lie

Fifty years before, in 1856, the novelist George Meredith visited Seaford, just about the time when William Tyler Smith arrived there. There were aspects of Seaford that Meredith liked very much, though he and his friends poked fun at its sleepiness. He described it as 'an ill-conditioned sort of place with a straggling row of villas facing a muddy beach.' And he referred to 'DULNESS' – not specifically the dullness of the place, just to dullness, and in truth he was carrying an intense melancholy within him that he was perhaps projecting onto the place. He commented that he was able to write there, 'though, engaged as I am, the DULNESS is something frightful, and hangs on my shoulders like Sinbad's Old Man of the Sea'. Meredith was experiencing what we would now call depression. That was due to the failure of his marriage, not Seaford.

He loved the wildness of the seafront.

'Today it has been blust'rous, as they say here. The water within a foot of our little room and surf raging up wrathful-white all along the shingle and breaking in feathery masses on the sulphur gray curtain of cloud. . . Blatchington beach is battered to bits.'

He liked the simple pleasures of the place.

'Here is fishing, bathing, rowing, sailing, lounging, running, pic-nicing, and a cook who builds a basis of strength to make us equal to all these superhuman efforts.'

He stayed for several months that year at No 3 Marine Terrace, which was kept as a lodging house by Richard Ockenden, the village carpenter and wheelwright, and his wife, who was the famous cook.

Meredith used this experience for his description of the fictional Crikswich in *The House on the Beach*. Meredith even included the wonderful Ockendens in his novel, as the Crickledons, and they took in paying guests, who were Meredith and his friends, thinly disguised. He started writing *The House on the Beach* in 1856, but did not get round to publishing it until 1877. He heard about the Great Flood in Seaford in 1875, and that gave him the ending he needed for his piece.

But Meredith's visit to Seaford was not a conventional seaside holiday. He was 28 and still a young, unknown writer; he felt that he had failed to make his mark as a poet. His poems had been published and favourably reviewed; some critics commented on his kinship with Keats, though he did not have Keats's high abilities. He was turning to prose in the hope that he might make his way as a novelist instead. While at Seaford he wrote part of *The Ordeal of Richard Feverel*, which would be his first full-length novel. He had brought his wife, Mary Ellen Nicolls, and their three-year-old son Arthur to live for a few months in Seaford because he had found lodgings on the seafront where they could live very cheaply. He was having difficulty in supporting his family and his marriage was in a state of collapse. One of his friends was seducing her and trying to persuade her to go off with him instead. She was on the point of leaving Meredith, and he was in despair over it.

George had recently been the model for the Pre-Raphaelite painter Henry Wallis's painting *The Death of Chatterton*. George posed for the dramatic picture in the very room where Chatterton had taken poison and killed himself in 1770. In 1856, the year of George's Seaford visit, the picture was exhibited at the Royal Academy and it was an immediate and enormous success; it was universally praised and is still regarded as one of the landmark paintings of the Victorian era. There was a peculiar aptness about Meredith being the model for Chatterton, the young poet in utter despair at ever being taken seriously, and ending it all with a phial of poison. Meredith was intelligent enough and self-aware enough to have seen this aptness. He saw himself at that time as a neglected genius, as Chatterton did, and he had a tendency to morbid melancholia. But there was a further twist of the knife: it was the artist *Henry Wallis* who was his wife's lover. It was that same Wallis who had painted Meredith with such painstaking care as the pale stricken corpse of Chatterton; the lover had in effect already murdered the husband in lurid oil paint. Wallis came down to Seaford to be with Mary Ellen. She was in difficulties, in debt and in distress; he consoled her while Meredith went out walking.

Meredith was lean, energetic and physically very fit. He loved the Downs, which were an immense attraction for him. He had loved hill-walking ever since his schooldays in the Rhine Gorge. Doubtless he wanted to escape the tension in the house on the beach by walking inland and up into the hill country he loved. We can imagine him striding feverishly up Blatchington Hill, away from his wife and Wallis, towards Bullock Down, the open sheep pastures and Firle Beacon, where he could listen to the larks as they rose skywards from the grass – the larks ascending. And no doubt as he strode up the hill he looked as wild and pale as the suicidal Chatterton in Wallis's picture.

He hung on at Seaford through the winter of 1856-57, writing and walking, though in despair. He had started work on *Richard Feverel*, which opens with a man being left to bring up his son single-handed when his wife runs off with another man. The autobiographical element is clear enough.

By the summer of 1857, Mary Ellen was openly consorting with Henry Wallis in public. She announced that she was going to leave George for Wallis. Meredith tried desperately to persuade her not to go, but she went, with Wallis, to Capri in 1858. There she became pregnant and produced a baby girl, and Wallis promptly left her. She wanted to come back to George now, but he would not have her, or her daughter, even though she named George as the baby's father on the birth certificate. Not only would George not have her back, he would not let her see Arthur again.

Meredith

This disastrous episode did not stop George Meredith coming back to Seaford in 1863. Again he brought his son, and a group of friends. They made a lot of noise, talking and laughing, and sat on the beach throwing stones into the sea. His friends thought Seaford comically quiet, calling it 'the Village of the Dead'.

Within three years of her Capri escapade, Mary Ellen was dead. She asked for some verse to be inscribed on her headstone.

Come not, when I am dead;
To drop thy foolish tears upon my grave,
To trample round my fallen head,
And vex the unhappy dust thou wouldst not save. . .
Pass on, weak heart, and leave me where I lie;
Go by, go by.

The lines were too despairing, too hysterical, too terrible, to put on anyone's grave, so Mary Ellen had no epitaph. George Meredith became hugely successful as a novelist and poet, and he grew a white beard to go with this new image of the great literary figure. But towards the end of his life he wrote a poem that seems to have its roots in the experience of the younger, Chatterton-like Meredith of that terrible summer of 1856, when he had walked up Blatchington Hill onto the Downs and listened to the birdsong.

The poem he composed was an extraordinary rhapsody of recollected ecstasy, a poem with phrases that seemed on first reading to be trying to describe the larksong, but then it dawns on the reader that, somehow, they *are* larksong.

> *He rises and begins to round,*
> *He drops the silver chain of sound*
> *Of many links without a break. . .*

The poem is ecstatic, leaving the troubled earth behind as bird and music fly up into the sky. It is *The Lark Ascending*. And just a decade after he wrote it Ralph Vaughan Williams wrote his masterpiece, inspired by the poem - not by the birdsong - *The Lark Ascending*. The two halves of the young George Meredith, despair and ecstasy, are vividly preserved for ever in the Wallis painting and the music by Vaughan Williams. Meredith wrote about both, in his remarkable poem cycle *Modern Love* and in *The Lark Ascending* - but how curious it is that the art *by* Meredith is eclipsed by the art *about* him.

Notes & sources

Cline 1970 Vol 1 25-6 (Meredith letter dated 4 June 1857 should be 1856)
Cooper 1998 (Meredith)
Ellis 1920 (Meredith and his friends)
Lower 1868 (Meredith and Seaford)
Lowerson 1975 (Seaford's development)

Chapter 9
At Monk's Orchard

How beautiful! How bright!

On Robert Dennis's departure from Blatchington in 1880, the village was still a place distinct and apart from Seaford. Where now Broad Street crosses Sutton Road to curve down to join Blatchington Road, there was a clear view across open country towards Blatchington. Everyday life at Blatchington was nevertheless inextricably tied into what was happening in Seaford, and influenced by events in the world outside. The 1881 census revealed that only one quarter of the inhabitants had been born in Blatchington; half had been born elsewhere in Sussex and the remaining quarter had moved to Blatchington from outside the county. Significant changes were under way; as time passed there would be more incomers, fewer native-born Blatchingtonians.

After part of the coast road was washed away in the major floods of 1875 and 1877, all the road traffic came in past the Buckle, then up Belgrave Road to Blatchington Church, down Blatchington Street and Blatchington Road, past the gas works and up the hill into Broad Street. Just as in the early eighteenth century, Blatchington Hill once more carried the main through-traffic. This inconvenient diversion led directly to the building of Claremont Road, with the permission of the landowner, Robert Lambe. For a time it was known as the New Road: it was a Blatchington by-pass.

The Revd Arthur Richardson was Robert Dennis's successor. In 1881 he was 36. He had been born at Highgate, like his wife, another Elizabeth, who was 31. They had a three-year-old daughter Frances Elizabeth, born at Glynde, and a one-year-old son Arthur, born at High Leigh in Cheshire. These addresses show the spoor of the Richardson family. Also living with them at the rectory was David Gregory Smith. He was eighteen and a student, and he was the Richardsons' lodger. He had been born at High Leigh, and moved from there with the Richardsons to Blatchington.

Arthur Richardson was intrigued by the history of the Church, the history of *his* church in particular, and of his house and the village too. Richardson had succeeded Robert Dennis as rector and inherited his rectory. St Peter's was an interesting building with an interesting history. The Revd Arthur John Richardson MA was a Cambridge man, a graduate of Magdalene College and academic by inclination. He gave a series of lectures on church history, illustrated with lantern slides. The lectures dealt mainly with the larger picture, the development of the Church in England, but on 15 March 1897 he gave a lecture on his own parish church. 'We have come tonight to the church in Blatchington, as it were to one of the little rivulets that help to form the broad-flowing stream of the Church in this country. . .'

One of the things he discovered was that there had once been 'a Tithe Barn just below my house'. This had functioned as a warehouse for agricultural produce in the days when the Tithe was paid in kind, instead of money, before the Commutation in 1836. The Tithe Map of 1843 shows the tithe barn as a substantial building running at right angles to Blatchington Hill, 27m long and 7m wide, though to judge from eighteenth century documents it is surprising that it was still standing in the 1840s. As we saw in Chapter 5, one of the eighteenth century rectors, James Tattershall, obtained formal permission from the bishop to demolish two other outbuildings because he could not afford to maintain them. After the mid-nineteenth century the barn was unroofed and the walls stood as a shell. There is still a walled courtyard on the spot, with Orchard Cottage built into the western end of the ruined structure.

In February 1892 Arthur Richardson's predecessor, Robert Dennis, died. Eight months later, Robert's widow Elizabeth was back in Blatchington to sort out Robert's affairs. Their shared wealth had in reality been hers: she had inherited it. Once they were married the wealth was theirs jointly, but now that Robert was dead she could legitimately make decisions about its disposal. She liked the idea of commemorating her husband's ministry at Blatchington by permanently endowing the rectory. She signed a conveyance that transferred The Gables, Glebe Cottage, Rectory Cottage and three acres of meadow to Arthur Richardson and his successor rectors. The income from these properties would supplement the rector's income.

Only six years later, in December 1898, when Elizabeth Dennis was still living, in an act that looks insensitive, the diocese began to sell on these generous gifts. There is a memorandum about the sale of The Gables in Richardson's handwriting attached to the conveyance and noting, 'The Cottage, Gardens, Outbuildings & Appurtenances here mentioned as "formerly in the said occupations of the said Robert Nathaniel Dennis and Mary Shelton. . . . together with the walls on the North-East & West sides thereof, were sold for £600 to the Misses E. M. & E. A. de St

Croix, December 1898, with the consent of the Rector (Rev. A. J. Richardson), Patron (B\(^P\) of Chichester) & Ecclesiast: Comm\(^s\). A. J. Richardson December 26, '98.' Who had the £600 – Richardson, the bishop, the diocese? And was this Elizabeth Dennis's intention?

Also not immediately obvious is that Ethel and Emma de St Croix were Richardson's sisters-in-law. His wife was their sister.

Arthur Richardson was interested in history but also aware of the needs of the present day. The Kodak had not yet become a craze among the inhabitants of Blatchington, indeed the electric light had only just arrived, in the form of a single incandescent street lamp at the church corner. That was a memorable event, not least because it had taken him and his parishioners four years of petitioning to move a slow-moving local authority into action. But now there was the wonder of the lamp itself, illuminating (some of) his walk up Blatchington Hill. It prompted poetry.

For lo! One evening as perchance I stray'd,
Of ugly flints and pitfalls half afraid,
I saw a gleam – 'Oh! Twinkle little star,'
I said – 'Oh! I wonder what you are!'

Nearer I drew – foreshadow'd like a ghost,
I saw a lamp – and, then, I saw a post!
Five yards' circumference made the pathway bright –
At six 'twas plunging into blackest night!

'O lamp,' I cried, 'How beautiful! How bright!
Art thou, indeed, an incandescent light?'

The Parson's tale was a serious exploration of the village and its past, but he relished its lighter side as well, with all the colourful texture of English village life. He shared with his audience the story of the village stocks. An Act was passed in 1405 which required every town and village in England to set up a pair of stocks. Being put in the stocks was a standard punishment for drunkenness, but also for other offences, such as resisting the Constable, tippling during the hours of Divine Service and stealing firewood; wood thieves were known as 'hedgestealers'. The stocks were still in use until the middle of the nineteenth century. Someone told the rector about a soldier who was put into the stocks halfway down Blatchington Hill. A man came by and said, 'Why, they can't put you in these stocks!' 'But they have,' said the soldier. 'But they can't!' said the other man. 'But they have,' said the soldier. And so

The Gables on the right, the entrance to Blatchington Court on the left, and Arthur Richardson's lamp-post standing at the junction of Blatchington Street and Belgrave Road. The picture was taken in about 1912, when Richardson was rector and Robert Lambe was living at Blatchington Court.

on. I suspect this was a time-honoured Blatchington saying. Today it has been replaced by the wise-acre Hillite stock advice addressed to someone puffing up the hill: 'It's much easier going down.'

Richardson found that maintaining the sanctity of the Divine Service had in the past been a major issue. According to the parish register, someone had to be paid an annual retainer, charged on the Church Rate, for keeping order in church; 'Whipping disorderly boys and dogs during Divine Service, 10 shillings per annum'. Richardson had not come across anything like it before. Presumably the whipping was done after Divine Service rather than during, or at least outside the church rather than inside.

Richardson was giving his lantern-slide lecture four years before the nineteenth century gave way to the twentieth. The beginning of the twentieth century was marked by a census and the death of Queen Victoria. At this moment Arthur Richardson and his wife Elizabeth were both 51 years old. They had a son and a daughter living with them, both single. The daughter was 23 years old, without occupation. The son was 21 and an assistant schoolmaster. They had a general servant, a fourteen-year-old called Eliza Harriott, who came from Westdean.

Arthur Richardson suffered in his later years from a throat infection, which was believed to have been caused by swimming in polluted seawater. Richardson resigned as rector and died in 1915; his successor was Henry Lancelot Martley. By this time the rectory was in a poor state of repair – so poor that the diocese decided to sell it off into lay ownership and use any available house that came onto the market in Kedale Road or Blatchington Street.

Miss Helen Whelon, who came from Kent, bought the rectory on 6 March 1916, for £625, and renamed it Monk's Orchard. The building was never associated with monks, and was never attached to a monastery, so it was an odd choice of name; the present name, The Old Rectory, is more apt. The house changed hands fairly frequently. By 1925 Monk's Orchard was occupied by the Revd J. E. Germon, in 1929 by R. A. Howden.

In the 1930s it became the home of Captain Basil Lubbock, the adventurer, sailor, yachtsman and marine author. He wrote books on the history of sailing ships. His first book, *Round the Horn Before the Mast*, published in 1902, was extremely popular with adventure-loving boys and adult readers alike.

Round the Horn

Alfred Basil Lubbock's father was the seventh son of Sir John Lubbock, baronet, and the brother of the 1st Lord Avebury, so Basil was born on the fringes of the upper classes. He was educated at Eton and his family doubtless expected him to go on to King's College, Cambridge. Instead he set off along the Chilcoot Trail to the Klondike, joining the 1896-7 Gold Rush for several months. Perhaps sensing that he was not going to make his fortune in the Gold Rush, Basil turned south to San Francisco, where in July 1899 he signed on the four-masted barque *Ross-shire* as an apprentice at £2 a month. It was a way of getting home, but it was also an adventure he would hugely enjoy. He sailed round the Horn, crossed the South Atlantic and North Atlantic and eventually reached Queenstown. There he joined the full-rigged ship *Commonwealth*, signing on as 'a sort of second mate'.

In one of several nearly-fatal incidents in his life, he fell fifty feet from the mizzen mast of the *Commonwealth* onto the poop rail, breaking a belaying pin with his thigh. He fought in the Boer War with the Royal Field Artillery and Menne's Scouts; in 1901 he was mentioned in despatches for rescuing a native scout under heavy

At Port Said, on the way out to India, Basil took this photograph of HMS Hampshire. The Hampshire had a special guest on board, the captain of the German cruiser Emden, whuch had been sunk a few days earlier. The Hampshire would become even better known a few months later, when she herself hit a mine and sank off Orkney – with Lord Kitchener on board.

enemy fire. Basil had risked his life to save a black comrade. Lord Kitchener wrote on 8 August:

'Lieutenant A. B. Lubbock; at Jonberfs Nek, July 15, assisted Sergeant Cima to save a native scout whose horse had been killed, Boers at time being within 150 yards and firing heavily.'

At the end of the Boer War, in 1902, he wrote *Round the Horn Before the Mast.* In 1903, still aged only twenty-six, he returned to Canada, sailing from Liverpool to New York on board the *Germanic.* Once settled in Canada he continued writing; *Jack Derringer, a Tale of Deep Water* (1906), *Deep Sea Warrior* (1910) and *The China Clippers* (1914).

In 1912 Basil married Dorothy Warner, the widow of Commander Thynne. She had no children by either marriage. When the First World War broke out in 1914, Basil took a posting to India with the Royal Field Artillery. He took Dot with him, sailing from Tilbury on board the P & O steamer *Caledonia.*

Once they arrived in India, Dot and Basil took every opportunity they could to travel and see the sights. Sometimes Basil headed off on his own to explore the more remote frontier regions. This was an idyllic time, and they recorded it in an album which has only recently come to light, after nearly a century, in rural Canada. The album contains autographs of the people they met in India, photographs and Basil's sketches and watercolour paintings of the landscapes.

Dot and Basil Lubbock, 4 October 1914: Hamble

The photographs of Basil Lubbock at this time, at the age of thirty-eight, show him lean, wiry, youthful, moustached, and good-looking too in a severe and military way. His gaze is direct, intelligent and penetrating.

In 1915 the Lubbocks returned to the mayhem of Europe. Basil served with the Royal Field Artillery in France, where he fought with characteristic dash, winning the Military Cross. A surprising survivor of the First World War, Lubbock returned to civilian life in April 1919. He returned at once to writing books that looked backwards, books about his experiences when single aboard the old sailing ships, such as *The Colonial Clippers* (1921), *The Western Ocean Packets* (1925) and *The Last of the Windjammers* (1927).

Basil was now *Captain* Lubbock: this was his army rank, nothing to do with seafaring. He was no longer a soldier, and no longer a seafarer either. But in the 1920s he did a great deal of recreational sailing, based on the River Hamble.

He was the founder of the Hamble Sailing Club in 1919, and its first Commodore, a position he only relinquished when he and Dot moved to Blatchington in 1932. In 1922, he approached Alfred Westmacott with a request to design a new class of racing yacht. What he asked for was 'an improved Mermaid'. The result, which Westmacott produced in November 1922, was the Hamble One Design Class, known as the 'Y Class', because all the boat names were to end with the letter 'y'. The class quickly became the Solent Sunbeam. Lubbock had the first one built, 26 feet long, and named it *Dainty*. It was Sail Number 1, and it was built in 1923.

Basil took his friend Wilfred Dowman racing in *Dainty*. Dowman was another square-rigger sailor. He was a man of means, who had at one time owned the *Cutty Sark*. He liked *Dainty* and ordered a Solent Sunbeam for himself, to race at Falmouth. There, the Falmouth Sunbeams became established by the 1930s, when there were eight or more of them racing. The thirteen original Solent Sunbeam owners in 1926 tried to make the class exclusive by limiting the number of boats in the class to twenty-four, but in this they failed. The Solent Sunbeams were adopted by Bembridge and then, in 1932, by Itchenor Sailing Club; they are recognized now as a classic racing keelboat. The latest one, *Milly*, was built in 1999. The wonder of the design is that the first built, *Dainty*, is still as fast as the last built. Her present owners regularly take *Dainty* to sail in the Mediterranean; she is still as beautiful as when she was launched - and treated as a celebrity.

When the Lubbocks moved into Monk's Orchard, Basil was still at the peak of his powers as a writer. The books kept coming out at the same steady rate, roughly one a year; *The Nitrate Clippers* (1932), *Sail – the Romance of the Clipper Ships* (1932), *The Opium Clippers* (1933), *Barlow's Journal of His Life at Sea* (1934), *The Last of the Windjammers (Volume 2)* (1935), *The Coolie Ships and Oil Sailers* (1935), *The Arctic Whalers* (1937), *Scourge of the Slavers: Adventures of the Famous Brig Waterwich* (1938). *Romance of the Clipper Ships* was a fine three-volume production with paintings by Jack Spurling.

Basil died at Monk's Orchard early in September 1944. Dot died just two months later. John Masefield wrote an appreciation of

Lubbock: 'He is honoured throughout the seven seas as one who wrote the history of the sailing ship as she was in the generations of her greatest splendour just before she ceased to be.'

The Times published Basil's obituary; 'Mr Alfred Basil Lubbock died at Monk's Orchard, Blatchington, Sussex, Sep 4 1944. . . During the Boer War Mr Lubbock saw what was probably the largest fleet of sailing ships ever gathered together in modern days. This was in Table Bay. In addition to the vessels in the docks, he counted over 150 ships waiting their turn at anchor.'

No more a-roving

Fourteen years later, the thirty-six-year-old Robert Back and his new wife Denise moved into the cottage at Monk's Orchard. Robert's career, like Basil Lubbock's, had a strongly nautical flavour.

Robert was brought up in the Australian outback, outside Adelaide. There were no toys, so his father dammed a creek to make a pond and Robert made models of square-rigged sailing ships to sail on it. In 1931 his father inherited an estate in Norfolk and drove his family the 1,300 miles to Sydney, to board a ship to England.

In 1933, when Basil Lubbock had been settled at Monk's Orchard for just a year, Robert won a place at St George's Chapel, Windsor. The family sailing holidays on the Norfolk Broads seemed to come straight out of Arthur Ransome's stories. Then at public school Robert won prizes for art, and from the beginning he was drawing and painting ships.

When the Second World War broke out, Robert served in the Royal Navy, and when it ended he joined the Merchant Navy. Without any real experience he found himself helming a 29,000-ton ship to South Africa, the *Edinburgh Castle*. This was the sort of life that suited him, but when he got married he went back to marine art. He made a living by teaching art and painting marine scenes.

He and Denise settled in Seaford, moving first into the cottage in the garden of Monk's Orchard, Orchard Cottage. The paintings that he created there soon gained recognition - and value - in London and New York. He became known as one of the foremost marine artists of his time. He was remembered on Blatchington Hill as a likeable, jolly, eccentric character. A friend described him as 'a Rolls Royce with no petrol'. When the children, two girls, started to grow up the cottage became too small for the Backs, so they moved to a larger house in Seaford. Robert died in Seaford in 2004.

Robert Trenaman Back

Basil Lubbock's adventuring days came to an end when he married Dot, and he settled down to *write* about the great days of sail. Robert Back's adventuring days similarly ended when he married Denise and he settled down to *paint* the great days of sail. Two parallel lives passing through Monk's Orchard, the lives of restless men whose creativity was fuelled partly by the frustration that they could go no more a-roving.

Notes & sources

Conveyance 1916 (Sale of rectory by diocese to Helen Whelon)
Pettitt 1949 (road system in 1870s)
Williams (undated) (Monk's Orchard).

Chapter 10
The last squire

The young Robert Lambe

The last squire of Blatchington was Robert Lambe. His late nine-teenth century term as Blatchington's major landowner saw enormous changes, many of them precipitated by the ambitious scale of his financial dealings. It was in the fall-out from his huge debts that land in and round Blatchington was sold off for building, and the character of the village was changed for ever.

Robert Lambe was baptized at Hamsey in 1842. His earliest years were spent at Wilmington, where several generations of Lambes had farmed. His mother was Elizabeth Bodle, who was born in Brighton, but his father, William Lambe, was born (in 1804) and bred at Wilmington. His grandfather, also William Lambe, was born at Wilmington in 1768; his great-grandfather, Richard Lambe, was born at Wilmington in 1735; his great-great-grandfather, another William Lambe, was born at Wilmington in 1700. Five generations of Lambes had lived and worked the land beneath the Long Man.

Robert Lambe makes his appearance at Blatchington in the 1861 census as William Lambe's 18-year-old son. William was 64 in 1861, and an important tenant farmer employing 19 men and 8 boys; Robert's mother was 54. Robert was the only son, with two sisters, Elizabeth and Ann. Revd Robert Dennis, and his wife Elizabeth owned Blatchington Court and were currently living in it. The Lambes lived at what was then known as Blatchington Farm, now Blatchington House, and they had moved there from Wilmington in 1850. William and Elizabeth Lambe ran a small household with two servants, Mary Burstow and Mary Goldsmith.

Among the papers left after his death is an outline of *Incidents of my Life*, written in Robert's fluent, confident hand. It amounts to a skeletal autobiography, which is intriguing for what it does not reveal. Its opening briefly covers his childhood and education.

Incidents of my Life

1850 *My Father came to Blatchington Farm. I went to Peters [?] School January. Cliffe blown down 19 Sept, 27000 lbs of Gunpowder used.*

1853 Threatened abolition [of] old Cinque Ports.

1856 Left school June. Peace proclaimed June. My sister Elizabeth married February 4th [at the age of twenty]. 10th December 1st enquiry Pub Health Act 48 Population: Town 900, Outside 97. Houses: Town 207, Outside 25.

[1857 -]

1858 National School began May 27. Fitzgerald Charity Formed 14 Aug, Advertized 15 Oct.

1859 School opened 2 March. Honorable Artillery came August. Gales 25 October & - Road washed away at Battery. Groyne removed after this.

1860 Joined Volunteer Artillery. Very wet year. Began cut Corn Sept 1st . 5 wrecks in Bay June 5. Railway to Seaford proposed 16 Oct 1860. Blatchington church restoration: £600 collected. – to Seaford Volunteers 23rd

1861 February [St Peter's Church?] reopened. Seaford census 505 Males, 578 Females; including 86 Little Sutton. To Tyler Smith 7650 [?].

1862 Honorable Artillery here in August.

1863 Engaged April 13th. Catts changed their name to Willett.

1864 Went into Partnership with Father [at the age of 22]. Carnegie died. Tyler Smith took Beamlands April 64. Buck appointed March 7. 1st Regatta July.

The account culminates in Robert's emergence as an adult, a fully-fledged farmer in the long-established Lambe family tradition. The early childhood years at Wilmington, with his sisters Elizabeth (born in 1836) and Ann (born in 1839), are not mentioned at all. It is as if life only began when he left Wilmington. He remembered the family's move to Blatchington as a landmark event, and it comes as no surprise that the spectacular blowing up of Seaford Head made a deep impression. Any eight-year-old boy would be impressed. He was also excited by the summer visits of the Honourable Artillery to Seaford. The regiment made regular appearances in August for manoeuvres, including artillery target practice along the seafront, a great event for the whole community.

Robert left school at fourteen, which in a way marks him out as a farmer rather than a gentleman. He was a relatively poorly educated man by comparison with some of the local landed gentry. But against that he appears to have been interested in public affairs from early on, noting Seaford's population in 1856, the passing of the Public Health Act, the foundation of a school and a charity, events that took place when he was fifteen or sixteen. These would be the public-spirited concerns of his adult life.

Such further education as Robert was to have would be supplied by joining the Volunteer Artillery, which he did at eighteen. The Volunteer Force had been created the previous year in response to mounting international tension; the British government appealed to the citizens of coastal towns to set up Artillery Corps as a safeguard against possible invasion. The Volunteer Artillery was a kind of Home Guard, an early 'Dad's Army'. It was a straightforward revival of the volunteer forces that had been so successfully set up during the Napoleonic Wars. Then, as in Robert's time, the artillery volunteers were to man the guns in the coastal batteries.

Robert was still living at home, at Blatchington Farm (or House), and working on the land with his father; this 'carrying on as normal' was standard practice among volunteers. He mentions a wet year in which the harvest was delayed until September. The

Blatchington House or Blatchington Farm.

public concerns continue. He was not only aware of the Revd Dennis's restoration of St Peter's church, but how much had been collected to pay for it and when St Peter's had re-opened.

He was more significantly taking note of the activities of Dr Tyler Smith. From early on, Robert was interested in money, in how much projects cost, in property speculation. The cryptic remark '. . . Little Sutton. To Tyler Smith 7650' is explained in the local newspaper, where we read that in April 1861 Tyler Smith bought Little Sutton Farm for £7,650. Tyler Smith was evidently putting into Robert's head the idea of buying farmland with a view to profitable property development later.

Robert Lambe the farmer

We return to Robert's self-account where he begins working on the farm in partnership with his father, is engaged to be married and establishes himself as an adult member of the community. This brings his early adult life to the point where he takes the momentous and misguided step of buying Blatchington Court.

1865 Railway to Seaford opened. Married Oct 19th [to Elizabeth Sarah Shoosmith, born 1845]. Extraordinary storm January 14th & Nov 22nd.

1866 Storm February.

1867 William [Robert's first son] born April 1st. Drainage committee appointed Nov.

1868 Drainage tender accepted February, completed Oct.

1869 Tom [Robert's second son] born September 21st. Dr Noakes killed by accident February.

1870 -

1871 Census Blatchington: 167; Seaford: Males 604, Females 717. First School Board: Dempster, [Revd R. N.] Dennis, J. S. Turner, T. S. [Tyler Smith] Chair, R. L. [Robert Lambe] Vice [Chairman], W. Chapman (Clerk).

1873 Dr Tyler Smith died June 3rd.

1874 Uncle John Ellis died (aged 71).

1875 Mother died 23rd Oct (aged 69). Mr Hollands property sold July. Troughton Brewery £4500, Devonshire [?] Field £500, Church & Vicarage [?] £500.
Rd Frederic [Robert's third son Richard] born 12 June. Flood Nov 14th; collected 1185£ 1908½d 1206 [= £1185 + £1206 + £19.0.8½d?] [Flood Relief?] Committee: Mr W. Turner (Bailiff), Clangy, Crook, Cullingford, Lambe, Simmons, A. D. Smith, Tuck, J. S. Turner.

1876 [Seaford?] Vicarage built February: Morling £1894. Creed's scheme Sea Wall Dr Tyler Smith lease abolished. B. J. Tuck married Oct.

1877 Bought Blatchington Estate.
Bazaar for West Dean Church Aug £150 [raised].

These notes show Robert quickly establishing himself as a major figure in the Blatchington-Seaford community. Dr Tyler Smith was the leading figure, but it is clear from the composition of the School Board of 1871 that Robert was then second only to Tyler Smith, although he was only twenty-nine.

Blatchington Court

In 1875 and 1877 Robert Lambe purchased properties in East Blatchington, Seaford and Alfriston. What is not clear is how he was able to purchase land on any scale at all. His father was still alive - he died in 1879 - so there was as yet no paternal legacy to explain it. There were no business transactions or commercial successes to explain it. Perhaps a legacy or gift from his mother lay behind it; she died in 1875. Her daughters were safely married and taken care of by Mr Marchant and Mr Downs, her sons-in-law - and Robert was her only son.

On 14 February 1877 a memorandum of agreement was signed between Robert Lambe (purchaser), Robert and Elizabeth Dennis (vendors) and Inigo Gell, the Lewes solicitor representing the devisees in trust of John King. George, John and Robert Watson were additional signatories to the agreement under the terms of the trust set up under John King's will.

The agreement allowed Robert Lambe six months in which he might decide to make a number of related purchases from the Dennises. These included the advowson, the right to appoint a rector to the parish, the manor court rents, heriots, fines, services and profits, 'and also all the capital Mansion Manor house messuage or tenement and premises called Blatchington house [Blatchington Court] with the Stable Coachhouse and other buildings thereto belonging and also the garden orchard cowhouses shed and cattle yard used and occupied therewith And also the messuage or tenement and farm known as East Blatchington Farm [now Blatchington House] now in the occupation of the said Robert Lambe and the Windmill Cottages barns stables stalls wagon lodges buildings yards closes and several pieces of land arable meadow pasture and down to the said Manor and farm belonging or appertaining All which said premises are known by the general name of the Blatchington estate'. The agreement in effect gives Robert Lambe an option to purchase, and six months in which to make a firm decision and explore ways of raising the cash with which to do it. And the sum he had to raise was £34,500. Once Rober Lambe gave notice that he wished to purchase, he had four months in which to complete. After that, interest at 5% per annum would become payable.

The provisional agreement specified that the vendors would prepare an abstract of title which was to begin with the will of John King, written in 1851, two years before his death. The purchaser was to assume that John King had at that time been the legal owner of all the property. The agreement also explained that some of the estate was freehold but some was copyhold. The copyhold property was copyhold tenure 'according to the custom of the Manor of Alciston whereof the same are holden.' John King's formal agreement with Lord Gage clarified which lands still belonged to Alciston manor. John King might be lord of the manor of Blatchington, but eight years after the 1818 agreement, when John King was trying to purchase a cottage in Blatchington village, in the heart of his own manor, he had to ask Lord Gage, the lord of the manor at Alciston, for admittance, and he was recognized as the new tenant of the cottage. The Gages were still regarded as lords of the manor in respect of some property at Blatchington - as in earlier times. But, at Robert Lambe's instigation in the 1870s, a start was made on the enfranchisement of the Alciston lands (see Chapter 7).

A small strip of the estate had been purchased by the London Brighton and South Coast Railway Company in March 1864 (for the railway line).

Robert Lambe went ahead and made his bewilderingly ambitious purchase, the purchase of Blatchington Court, and was in debt ever after.

1877 — Bought Blatchington Estate. Bazaar for West Dean church Aug 15th

The complicated legal transfer (among seven parties) was transacted on 20 December 1877, a property deal that had consequences that could not have been foreseen by Robert, or probably by his father, who then had but a year and a half to live. The elaborate conveyance represents the sale of the Blatchington Court estate by the Dennises to Robert Lambe, who was now thirty-four. He paid £34,500 or £1,667,000 in today's money. This was a large sum, but nevertheless 9% lower than the valuation of the estate sixteen years earlier. Had the estate deteriorated, or was Robert getting it at a bargain price, perhaps as a gesture recognizing Uncle Tom Lambe's £6,000 loan to Elizabeth Dennis?

On the very same day as the purchase of the estate, plans were drawn up showing four large fields that Robert intended to offer for sale for building: Guard Ale, Workhouse Laine, Barrack Laine and Barrack Down. The next day, 21 December 1877, Robert arranged a mortgage with Richard Lambe of Lewes, his uncle.

Robert did not have the money with which to buy the Blatchington Court Estate: he had to borrow in order to do it. The entire estate was mortgaged to Uncle Richard for £27,000; Robert agreed to pay 3.5% a year interest if he could pay off the mortgage within the year.

This is the first of a long stream of complicated and sometimes incomprehensible Blatchington property deals that Robert carried out across the next four decades. It led, ultimately, to the selling-off of the entire Blatchington Court estate and the end of the Blatchington squires. This act of over-reaching was Robert Lambe's undoing.

Robert Lambe the developer

In 1879 Robert Lambe offered land for a new road to be built across the south-west of his estate as a highway for public use - Claremont Road. An East Blatchington vestry meeting on 18 December 1879 agreed to accept the offer. This road was a significant help to Seaford, as it allowed people to travel into Seaford from Lewes and Newhaven without having to pass along the ancient coast road, which was very exposed to the sea, and more frequently flooded and impassable as the sea nudged closer. It also enabled people to reach Seaford without the detour through Blatchington. Robert's notes about his life show that he was particularly interested in road improvements at this time. He was also interested in the passing of friends, associates and relatives.

In 1880 Robert tried again to sell land in order to reduce his debt. This time two fields were offered for development, Barrack Laine and Workhouse Laine. The land was advertized enticingly as 'Blatchington Park' with a plan showing a tree-lined perimeter.

In the same year, arrangements were made for a well pumping station and reservoir to be built on land belonging to Robert on open downland to the north of the village, together with a pipe leading from it to a point about 5 chains north of East Blatchington churchyard. Significantly, 5 chains (100m) north of the churchyard is the location of Blatchington House, Robert's home: a roomy and comfortable farmhouse, evidently extended since 1843, with paddocks and yards next to it now tidied up and laid to gardens. A barn was removed from the front garden to improve the prospect to the south. By 1881 Robert and Elizabeth were well set up, with ample space for their children, Richard (5), Bessie (8), Thomas (11) and William (14). A governess, Letitia Waddell, looked after the three younger children; William went away to school. They had a live-in cook and a housemaid too.

Although he owned the Blatchington Court estate, Robert did not move into Blatchington Court until 1900. Blatchington Court was let first to the Fishers, then as a school. A newspaper ad dating from about 1890 reads:

Blatchington Court near Seaford, Sussex. Mr Warwick Wyatt Crouch, MA and Mr Cecil Sturges Hand, BA prepare boys for the public schools. Large covered gymnasium, carpenter's workshop, play ground, tennis lawn, cricket and football fields. DETACHED SANATORIUM.

Robert Lambe was not only a churchgoer but a churchwarden, like John King. He mentions in his notes that in March 1880 there was a presentation to Robert Dennis, to mark his retirement, and in June Arthur Richardson was inducted as the new rector. Other things were happening in the parish too. In January Sergeant Parry and his wife died. But the preoccupation with property transactions was never far away: 'J. Slee buys Tyler Smith's lease.' He notes the birth of each of his sons, but neither the birth nor the early death of his daughter Bessie, which took place in August 1914, when the account stops. He does nevertheless mention her marriage.

To acquire the Blatchington Estate, Robert Lambe had needed a £27,000 mortgage, which he got from his Uncle Richard. Uncle Richard died in December 1882, leaving a will (made in October 1879) that bequeathed most of his money, personal estate and effects to Robert, but all the real estate vested in him as mortgagee or trustee jointly to Robert and Stephen Marchant, his nephew-in-law. Robert may have been disappointed with these terms as they did not wipe out his mortgage debt. This meant that in March 1883 there had to be an agreement between Robert Lambe and his brother-in-law Stephen Marchant. The interest on Robert's 1877 mortgage had been paid up to date, but the capital sum was still owing. The money left jointly to Robert and Stephen consisted of £4,333 in 3% annuities; £5,000 was invested in 3½% India stock for Mary Lambe as stipulated in Richard Lambe's will. Robert asked for the property that remained subject to the mortgage released to him, 'discharged from all principal moneys and interest'. He wanted reconveyance of the Blatchington Estate to himself, without repaying any of the capital borrowed - and Stephen Marchant, remarkably, agreed to this.

In March 1883, a document was accordingly drawn up, conveying to Robert Lambe 'the Manor mansion house, lands tenements hereditaments and premises [as listed in the 21 Dec 1877 mortgage]'.

Then we find Robert borrowing money again. On 17 March 1883, he borrowed £8,000 from John Page of Lewes at 4% per annum interest. For this sum, he conveyed to John Page East Blatchington Farm, the land and the buildings. This was the property that Robert was living in at the time, so he was mortgaging his own home. John Page died in July 1884, leaving as executors his son John Page of Ringmer, John Jenner of Hastings and Luther Martin of Ripe, all farmers. Luther Martin died in 1889. In July 1894, Robert Lambe made a new agreement with John Page and John Jenner, noting that he owed them £3,200 but asking them to lend him a further £1,600, raising the debt to £4,800 with interest. In October he was back again, asking for more. He wanted another £1,400, raising the debt to £6,200. There is nothing on paper to explain why Mr Page and Mr Jenner agreed to these requests for money, but (like Stephen Marchant) they did agree.

In 1886 the Seaford Bay Estate Company Ltd was incorporated. Robert Lambe was one of the prime movers in the creation of the company along with Davies Gilbert, W. R. Gade, an Alfriston landowner, A. E. Carey, a Newhaven civil engineer, and P. S. Lee, a London surveyor. The company's aim was to develop all the land between the old town and the esplanade, but this was an unsuccessful project in that only the Esplanade Hotel and some houses in the Esplanade, College Road and Pelham Road were completed. Davies Gilbert, who had been the company's dominant figure holding 2915 shares by 1896, applied for voluntary liquidation in 1898, and the company finally ceased to exist in 1913.

Incidents of My Life resumes in summary form the bald events of Robert's activities following the acquisition of Blatchington Court until the end of the nineteenth century.

1881 *Census Blatchington 213; Seaford Males 744, Females 812. Enfranchised the Wilmington copyholds. J. S. Lee agrees to build Sea Wall.*

1882 *Sold land to Water Co. Bought Vidals Cottages, Wilmington. Uncle Richard died December 21ˢᵗ. Mrs H Simmons died June 5. J. S. Turner died August 7ᵗʰ.*

1883 *Aunts moved to Wilmington from Sutton, Uncle Tom to 61 Springfield Road. I retired from Seaford School Board. Order issued by Govt for Local Board opposed by E. J. Gorringe. For election: Tuck (212), G--- (200), Cullingford (189), Ade (179), Lambe (168), C--- (150), Bravery (145), G--*

- (137), Under--- (84). Unsuccessful: Banks, Martin, Brand, Tredgold, Jackson, Hanke. H. Simmons married Miss Naddell 27/ 9/ 83. R. Lambe elected Bailiff.

__1885__ Richd Lambe [of] Lewes died Oct 10th. Bishopstone Church opened 14/ 12/ 85. Earl of Chichester died Mar 1886.

__1886__ Last meeting of Corporation 22/ 3/ 86. B. J. Tuck died Nov.

__1887__ Jubilee Subscriptions £119 – 2d. Lawn Tennis Club formed May. Capt C---y died Nov. First Drainage Enquiry; I agreed to pay one-third up to £900.

__1888__ Dr Morgan married Sept. [Dr Morgan's sister Harriet was to marry Robert's son William.]

__1889__ Elected on County Council when formed. Surrey Home built £10,215. Bazaar for Seaford Church.

__1890__ William [married] 16th Oct to Harriet Gaynor Morgan. Bazaar for Tarring Neville Church.

Robert Lambe as Bailiff in 1883: the established public figure

1891 Dearsley case: he resigned.

1892 Elizth Marchant [Robert's sister] died 16 February (aged 56). Sept Road finished, obliged to take action agst District [?]. Took Wilmington Farm into own hands. Aunt Ann died 24 December (74).

1893 Aunt Kitty died 22 April (76).

1894 Sold Churchill Land. Bought Chambers Land on Front £1250. 1st Urban Council December: Gorringe (241), Brand (220), Jack (203), Lambe (179), Newman (167), Hooper (164), Farncombe (117), C---y (114), Martin (111).

1895 Seaford Relief Committee formed. Sold Flock.

1896 Thomas married Roseanna Marian Kimber Sept 16th.

1897 –

1898 Bessie married David Gregory Smith February 3rd. Mr H. Buck died March 14th.

1899 Simmons Institute opened 27th May.

1900 Moved to Blatchington Court. Uncle Tom died January 5th (aged 88). Richard Frederic married Florence Eva Hartung 17 Feb.

The Revd W. Dearsley, as vicar of Wilmington, was of interest to Robert. Dearsley's servant took him to court, accusing him of being the father of her child. The patrimony case went against him and he was forced to resign; he fled to Bosham. It was a major local scandal, and there was no further discussion at the Archaeological Society of Dearsley's scheme for outlining the Long Man in chalk.

Robert refers briefly to J. S. Lee agreeing in 1881 to build the sea-wall. J. Swanwick Lee was an architect and civil engineer who lived in London but became interested in buying land in Seaford in 1880, thinking that a judicious outlay of capital would be enough to turn the town into a resort. He bought land on the seafront from Tyler Smith's executors and went ahead with great energy, building the wall very quickly. He was a speculator in the same spirit as Tyler Smith and Robert Lambe. He died at the beginning of 1883, after being unwell for some time.

A Lambe family wedding in February 1898 – Bessie Lambe and David Gregory Smith. Left to right, front: Thomas Lambe, William Lambe, Edith, Richard Frederic Lambe, Elizabeth Lambe, Lucy Tuck, Revd Richardson. Left to right, doorway: E. L. Gregory Smith, (Mr and Mrs Andrews behind) David Gregory Smith, Conny Andrews, Robert Lambe.

Robert Lambe does not mention his good work in giving land for the building of an Infectious Hospital or sanatorium at Cradle Hill in 1888. By this time he had been Bailiff of Seaford, and public gestures like this were expected. In 1889 he announced that he would repair the road from Blatchington to Firle Beacon, and make it easier for people to visit that picturesque spot. The press reported that 'the thanks of all will be heartily accorded to Mr Lambe for kindly undertaking this much-needed improvement'.

In September 1900, Robert Lambe finally paid off the mortgage (£5,809) on Blatchington House, the money he owed to John Page and John Jenner.

The 1901 census shows Robert Lambe's household. Robert himself was the head of the household, married, aged 58; he was described as a farmer and an employer. His wife was Elizabeth S. Lambe, who was 59. They had a married son living with them aged 33, William Lambe, with the same occupation as his father. There was also a 27-year-old niece called Edith Monnington living with them. They had a visitor staying with them at the time of the census, a cousin of Elizabeth's, Hope Elizabeth Horne, who was 59. Robert and Elizabeth had three live-in servants, Mary Sherlock (cook), Lucy Card (housemaid) and Kate Brooks (kitchenmaid). The entry in Kelly's Directory for the following year, 1902, shows Robert Lambe living at Blatchington Court but, in spite of owning the estate, he had only been living in the mansion for two years.

Dogged by debt

Robert appeared to be an established local public figure. In 1911-12, for example, he was Chairman of Seaford Urban District Council. But he was by no means out of the financial wood. His debts were considerable. He was also entangled in several projects involving seafront development. In 1901 he noted a guaranteed subscription to Sea Defence and the building of a 'road & parade'. He sold some unspecified land 'to Taylor', apparently for £80,000. In 1901 he set up a limited company which gave him a certain amount of anonymity, the Seaford West Company Ltd. This had capital of £24,000 divided into £1 shares, increased in June 1905 to £30,000.

In 1905 Robert Lambe sold the two pieces of land he had bought in 1875 and 1877 to the Seaford West Company in exchange for 6,000 shares. Seaford West was a housing development company, and it committed itself to building houses of high value in certain specified locations, such as along Belgrave Road. There would also be house-building along the old field path from Seaford to Bishopstone, which was to be named Carlton Road. The idea was simple: to make money by building houses on farmland.

Robert also sold off his sheep. In the following year, 1906, he gave up farming altogether, selling off the remaining stock in a sale on 12 October.

The debts, some of them now of long standing, could no longer be ignored. Barclays Bank made it clear that a start had to be made on repaying them, or Blatchington Court would be forfeit. Robert noted simply in his list of *Incidents* 'Barclays threatened'. Straight after that, in March 1912, he noted 'Seaford West shares transferred', though it is not clear where they were transferred to or what he hoped to gain (or evade) by doing so. Robert Lambe was indebted for the sum of £7,253. 8. 5d. (or £414,000 in today's money).

An agreement dated 1 August 1912 clarified the nature of the Seaford West Company. It stated, in effect, that all the shares were held by Robert Lambe and his three sons, William Lambe, Thomas Lambe of The Lodge, Hornchurch, who was a surgeon, and Richard Frederic Lambe, a Seaford solicitor. Robert Lambe held practically all the share capital. The agreement was between them and Barclays Bank, acknowledging that they were overdrawn with the bank to the extent of £32,926 (£1.88 million in today's money), which they would repay, with interest, on 1 December.

To deal with this colossal debt, Robert had to mortgage much of his property. Barclays outlined detailed arrangements for the repayment of the debt. The bank demanded repayment of the amount owing to it by Robert Lambe and the Seaford Company. There was an agreement that the Seaford Company should secure its substantial overdraft by a mortgage before the following December and that Robert Lambe and his three sons should pay back further debts to the bank with 5% per annum interest; there would be quarterly payments to the bank.

The document amounts to both an action plan and a warning of foreclosure on Robert Lambe's estate. It mentions appointing a Receiver and taking possession. The property to be forfeited is described as 'The Capital Mansion House and other buildings and the lands occupied therewith by the said Robert Lambe known as The Blatchington Court Estate, containing in the whole upwards of 11 acres.' It was made very clear to Robert that the bank intended to take his home from him, an alarming prospect. The unsavoury details of this agreement were tactfully omitted from the (otherwise comp-rehensive) Abstract of Title for Arlington House that Richard Frederic Lambe prepared for his parents. But he went so far as to mention that 'Powers conferred on Mortgagees by Conveyancing Act 1881 and Conveyancing Act 1911 should become exercisable by Bank without notice if default made.'

A few months later, in December 1912, Mr Neal, Robert's London Wall solicitor, wrote a letter expressing both puzzlement and anxiety over Robert's financial activity.

9 December, 1912

Dear Mr Lambe,

I am in receipt of your letter this morning enclosing one from Messrs Jarram & Son. I also have one from your son Richard telling me that he has found the £50,000 and that he will be able to take the securities out of Messrs Barclay & Company's hands. . .

I take it that for the present at all events you will not wish me to interfere but leave matters in the hands of your son Richard.

I am glad, for your own sake, that you will submit every document to me for consideration before appending your signature thereto. I think this will be wise as my only interest is to safeguard, as far as I am able, your position.

With kind regards,
William P. Neal

Within days, Robert was writing to a Mr S. Halford in Chancery Lane;

With reference to my instructions to you to obtain for me a Bank loan of £55,000 in order to take over my existing loans & guarantees to Barclay's Bank I am willing to accept a loan of £60,000 from the London County & Westminster Bank on the securities comprised in the loans to Barclay's Bank together with the securities the London County & Westminster Bank now hold & on which about £5400 is at present owing. I instruct you to accept the loan from them. . . I understand from you that the London County & Westminster Bank are willing to lend up to £60,000 & that you have already received a letter dated December 13.

I undertake to accept this loan. . .

Robert accepted the terms, which included a commission payable to Mr Halford at the rate of 5% on the amount of the loan. It seems that what Robert was doing was paying off the debt to one bank by borrowing from another, and paying an additional £3,000 to arrange it. The money 'found by Richard' was in effect a new and bigger debt, and Robert had negotiated its further increase to £60,000.

In 1913, another indenture was drawn up to take account of this new arrangement. This time the agreement was between Barclays Bank, Robert Lambe (thinly disguised as the Seaford West Company) and the London County & Westminster Bank, the transferees of the loan. In effect the 1912 Lambe Mortgage was being transferred from Barclays to London County & Westminster.

Some repayments had been made, and the mortgage was now for £32,035.

The conveyances relating to the plot at the foot of Blatchington Hill, on the Sutton Drove corner, tell part of the story. In 1913 Barclays forced the Seaford West Company (Robert Lambe) to mortgage the plot to London County and Westminster Bank Ltd. In January 1914 the same plot was sold by London County and Westminster to John Pattinson Martin and Charles Joseph Bravery. The banks were moving to force Robert settle some of his debt. Meanwhile Charles Bravery was cleverly and unobtrusively buying up Robert Lambe's building land, stepping into his shoes.

Robert undertook to pay the transferees the sum owing. He seems to have taken a simple view of a very complex and serious situation; if he owed money, he would borrow some to pay the debt, and a little extra, and all would be well. He noted in 1913, the year after the bank's warning, 'Paid Barclays off', but this was only by setting up the mortgage with London County & Westminster. London County & Westminster Bank agreed to release to Robert Lambe, 'the Borrower', the hereditaments (in other words the Blatchington Court Estate) on payment of £4500.

Robert paid the agreed sum, and the estate was released to him. It was his once more. It was defined as, 'all that Capital Mansion House formerly called Blatchington House but now known as Blatchington Court with the stable and other buildings thereto belonging and also the gardens cowhouses sheds and cattle yard and also the four cottages and gardens thereon now in the occupation of F. Saunders, Thomas Stevens, Henry Bean and William Reed, and also all those several pieces of grass or meadow land with the plantations thereto adjoining. . . and coloured pink (14 acres).' The map that accompanied this indenture shows that Robert Lambe had by this stage sold off a large rectangle 200ft long from north to south fronting Blatchington Hill, for building land. He did this, presumably, to help generate the £4500 he needed to redeem Blatchington Court. The rectangle is represented today by the house plots occupied by 21-25 Blatchington Hill and the northern half of the larger plot where Sanctuary (No 19) stands.

On 2 June 1913 the East Blatchington Estate was offered for sale, freehold. The sale particulars were laid out like a bill advertizing an Edwardian music-hall. 'Particulars. . . comprising over 700 acres in this healthy Seaside Resort, forming Excellent Building Estates. . . building plots suitable for the erection of Large Residences or Scholastic Edifices, others are adapted for Small Villas, Shops and Cottages; also 4 Superior Residences, known as

Lexden House and 10 acres of land, **Dial House** and 2 ½ acres, **Upper Lodge** and 4 acres, **Eversley Boarding Hotel** and over 1 acre. . . which will be sold by Auction by Fairbrother, Ellis & Co at the White Hart Hotel, Lewes on Monday 2nd June 1913, in 118 lots.'

The sale particulars list Beach Cottages, Bullocks Barn, Cyprus Lodge (Albany Road, on the site of the Barracks), Dial House (Firle Rd), Edinburgh Cottages, Eversely Hotel (Marine Parade), Lexden House (Lexden Rd), Seaford Golf Club, Upper Lodge (Firle Rd), Sea Cottages. Not all of these were in fact sold, as they re-appear in Robert's will as still in his ownership nine years later. It is a sign of Robert's desperation that he was attempting to sell Upper Lodge, which was his son Richard's home.

Now Robert saw that he could no longer afford to live at Blatchington Court. He let it furnished, from August to October, to a Mr Martin.

In 1914, Robert Lambe was still struggling to hang on to what was left of the Blatchington Court estate, but under enormous financial pressure. He borrowed £5,000 from Margaret Elizabeth Palmer, described in the documents as 'spinster of Cricklewood', at an agreed interest rate of 6% per annum – rather a high rate for the time. If she got her capital and her interest back from Mr Lambe, Miss Palmer would be doing well. The Blatchington Court Estate itself (as opposed to the East Blatchington Estate, which covered much of the parish) was offered as collateral, but the indenture explicitly stated the cautionary reminder that 'the Borrower is indebted to the bank in a large sum of money'.

A plan shows the estate as it was at the outbreak of the First World War, a rectangle bounded by Belgrave Road, Blatchington Hill, Glebe Drive, the eastern boundary of the Kedale Rd house gardens; Kedale Road already existed by this stage. Two squares were excluded from the squire's estate, the churchyard and the rectory gardens. Robert referred blandly to what must have been a painful process as 'Plots Sale'.

In 1915, Lambe was still living at Blatchington Court, but this could not continue. In 1914, he noted that building work had begun on a house, which was presumably Arlington House.

Among his papers there is a document headed 'Priced quantities of proposed house for Robert Lambe', a long list entailing high costs. It does not identify the house and it does not bear a date or a signature, but the substantial scale of the works listed would be in line with those required for the building of Arlington House.

Saying goodbye to Blatchington Court? Robert and Elizabeth Lambe standing in the porch of the manor house.

In 1911, the site of Arlington House was still part of Home Furlong, the very large field that lay to the east of Firle Road and Blatchington Hill and ran alongside the village from the golf club nearly all the way down to Sutton Drove. In 1911, Upper Belgrave Road did not exist. By the time of Robert's death in 1922, Upper Belgrave Road been made, Arlington House been built, with its two drives, one opening westwards onto Firle Road, the other opening southwards onto Upper Belgrave Road - and Robert Lambe and his wife had moved into it. Presumably this was a means of keeping dignity, of remaining resident at the centre of Blatchington, while letting Blatchington Court itself go. He must have known by this stage that most or all of the estate would have to be sold off to pay the debts.

Robert set up his escape route in a conveyance dated 8 October 1914. The document is complex and elaborately detailed in its provisions, but at the centre of it is a simple transaction; Robert sold the corner plot at the Firle Road-Upper Belgrave Road junction to his wife Elizabeth. The London County & Westminster

Bank were signatories to this deal, though they required a stipulation that the transaction did not 'form part of a larger transaction or series of transactions'. But at least Robert was able to elicit the significant agreement that Elizabeth's ownership of the plot would be free 'from all claims and demands under the Mortgage and Transfer'. So, whatever happened to the rest of the estate, the Arlington House plot would remain Elizabeth's. She paid Seaford West £300 for the land.

Elizabeth almost immediately (on 2 December 1914) borrowed £1,000 from Mrs Sarah Hillman, Charles Flamen, Montague S. Blaker and Reginald Blaker, using the building plot as security. The Lambes were desperate to get their hands on cash in any way possible, still taking on new loans to pay off old ones. Elizabeth paid off this mortgage in January 1924, after Robert's death, and the property was reconveyanced to her.

During the next two years, Robert oversaw the building of Arlington House at the foot of Firle Road. He and Elizabeth were careful to document their claim to use the right of way that ran along the back of the property from Firle Road, though it is not clear why they wanted it. It was 8 feet wide and they and their heirs were to have the right to pass and re-pass along it, with or without horses, carts, carriages and other vehicles. It was one of several old access tracks connecting the village street with the fields on each side; it went right across Home Furlong, to the centre of the East Laines, though it post-dated the medieval strips which it crossed diagonally. It led from the roadside immediately opposite the front door of Blatchington House, which may explain both its location and Robert's 'connection' with it. The westernmost stretch of the track is still there, though it no longer leads to open farmland.

In August 1919, Elizabeth Lambe's cousin Hope Horne of West Tarring died intestate. Elizabeth was her next of kin and so inherited her estate. But it was £108, too small a sum to make any difference.

Arlington House has the look of an Edwardian mansion. It is elegant, roomy, with an imposing double-fronted façade and bay windows looking out onto what was once a sloping lawn. It even, initially, had the two entrance (or entrance and exit) drives arranged at right angles which Robert had organized at Blatchington Court in the early 1900s. This was Robert's third residence in Blatchington. The first had been Blatchington House, where he lived from 1850, the second Blatchington Court, where he lived from 1900, and the third Arlington House, where he lived from 1915 until his death – all three near the centre of the village.

On 27 May 1922 there was a reconveyance between Robert Lambe and his bank. The bank conveyed 'all the hereditaments and premises' back to Robert Lambe. The text mentions 13 acres, but a footnote added in 1923 refers to Blatchington Court amounting to about 8 acres. With fragments being sold off to keep the bank quiet, the estate was dwindling. But there was still money owing as it was stipulated that each quarter interest must be paid at 5% per annum.

In a will made on 7 June 1922, Robert appointed his sons Tom and Dick as executors (William had died in October 1920), along with his nephew Stephen Marchant of Brenchley and the family solicitor Harold M. Blaker of Lewes. Stephen Marchant was the son of Robert's brother-in-law, also named Stephen. After some specific bequests, Robert Lambe bequeathed the residue of his estate to the trustees with the instruction to convert it into money. Robert Lambe did not have long to live, and he recognized that there were going to be substantial debts to settle after his death. What he was handing on to the next generation was not just debt, but the destruction of the estate, including selling off Blatchington Court itself, in order to settle it, and the destruction of the village's historic rural setting.

On 19 September 1922 Robert Lambe died, at Arlington House. He was buried near the western edge of St Peter's churchyard, as if to be as close as possible to Blatchington Court. On 14 December 1922, probate was granted and the estate valued at £74,790 (£1,586,000 today). By agreements dated 1919 and 1920 properties with frontages of 68, 102 and 208 feet on Blatchington Street had already been sold off.

Margaret Palmer was a major creditor and in September 1923 the executors (Thomas and Richard Lambe, Stephen Marchant and Harold Blaker) agreed to pay the £4,000 that remained owing to her. In the same year the Seaford Company sold on to Charles Bravery some of the land Robert Lambe had bought back in 1875-77. Mr Bravery then in 1929 sold part of this land (a 15-acre piece abutting Seaford Golf Course on the south west side) to Arthur Hobbs of Croydon. Mr Hobbs divided the land into plots and immediately sold some of them to Mr C. H. Kirtlan, a builder. In 1932 Mr Hobbs sold the remaining plots to Kirtlan. In 1937 Mr Kirtlan entered an agreement with ESCC for the preservation of the area as open space under the Town and Country Planning Act of 1932.

Robert Lambe's estate at the time of his death, according to the probate papers, consisted of a rather odd assortment of properties.

There was Blatchington Court and its 8 acres of gardens, described as a freehold house used as a hotel, with Miss Bradley as its tenant. She was given the option, to be held open until 1924, to buy the property for £10,000. There was a freehold garden worth £160 adjoining, with a Miss Gorsey or Jersey as its tenant. This may be the walled peach garden now occupied by Four Walls. There were four freehold cottages, 1-4 Blatchington Street, occupied by four tenants, Mr Saunders, Mr Stevens, Mr Russell and Mrs Reed, and valued at £450.

Then there was a miscellaneous collection of properties including Lexden House, Roslyn and Hamsey Cottage in Salisbury Road, 17 Pelham Place, 1-6 Beach Cottages, 1-4 Edinburgh Cottages, 1-2 Field Cottages, a field close to St Peter's Church, 17 and 23 Chichester Road and Carlton Lodge in Claremont Road.

There were few specific bequests. He wanted his grandson Robert Eric Lambe, his eldest son William's son, to have his gold watch and chain, but all his other personal possessions he left to his wife. He had interesting comments to make about his legacy to his sons, and he seems to have been conscious that it could be negative legacy. 'During my lifetime I made considerable advances in money to each of my three sons. . . I do not wish the Trustees to require repayment from them, provided thay make no claim on my estate and provided Richard makes no claim to purchase Upper Lodge.' This last seems an odd condition; what difference would it make to the estate if Richard bought Upper Lodge?

Upper Lodge is a house on the east side of Firle Road, immediately below the junction between Firle Road and Firle Drive. At that time it stood in the middle of a large garden, but this was subsequently divided up to make plots for seven additional houses. Upper Lodge is still there, a very solid-looking late Victorian villa, now called Blatchington Lodge.

He left £1,000 to his son-in-law David Gregory Smith, the husband of his late daughter Bessie and who as a youth back in the 1880s had been the Richardsons' lodger. Amongst other bequests, he left small sums to longstanding servants: 'Thomas Stevens my Foreman £20, Frederick Saunders my Groom £20, my Nurse Mary Davidson £20.' He also left a house in Salisbury Road, Hamsey Cottage, to his widowed sister Ann Downs.

In March 1927, Stephen Marchant died. Another executor, Richard Lambe, asked to be discharged from his responsibilities as trustee. Richard Lambe was a local solicitor, with offices at 2 Clinton Place. This left only Thomas Lambe and Harold Blaker as trustees, burdened with the complicated task of selling off the remainder of the Blatchington Court estate to pay off the debts. The management of the Trust continued to be a headache. When chartered accountants carried out an audit in 1933 for the period autumn 1928 to December 1932, some errors surfaced.

1) Wakefield Corporation £800 4½% Stock. In the schedule of Dividends received is an entry 'Half year to 1 Sep 1929 – Gross £15. 12. 8.' Half year's interest on £800 at 4½% should normally be £18.

2) Queensland Government £983. 10. 9 4% Stock. Nothing is shown in respect of the half year to 4 Oct 1929.

3) India £3,000 3½% Stock. Similarly a dividend due on 5 Oct 1929 does not appear in the accounts. . .

But no-one was getting rich on the back of these small mistakes.

What went wrong? It is very hard, on the evidence we have, to understand why Robert made the blunder of purchasing Blatchington Court when it was clearly far beyond his resources. The best-guess scenario is that he was seduced by Tyler Smith's vision of a Seaford that would be transformed *imminently* into a thriving seaside resort. Tyler Smith himself had lived at Blatchington Court, and Robert may have aspired to be his successor as Seaford's leading light, with not only the same role but the same address. He was perhaps carried along by Tyler Smith's charisma and confidence into believing that Seaford and Blatchington land values were going to climb steeply in the near future and that all property in the area would prove a lucrative investment. But it was not to be.

A view that was evidently promoted within the family was that Robert Lambe had put himself in financial difficulties through public works. Fred Lambe believed that his grandfather had 'spent a fortune on <u>making the sea wall</u> as far as his land went and then had nothing left for development'. The underlining was added by Fred himself in a letter written near the end of his life in the 1980s. Another source, UU, similarly promotes the idea that Lambe 'spent large sums on the sea-wall. . . But for the venture he would have died a rich man.' UU also says Robert Lambe 'inherited a large fortune', though, if he had, he would surely not have been in debt from the moment he acquired Blatchington Court.

The idea that Robert Lambe bankrupted himself by building the sea-wall may be wrong; Fred Lambe and perhaps the rest of the family had been given a false impression about Robert Lambe's estate and where it had come from. Fred believed that his grandfather had inherited huge wealth and that it had 'come to our family through marriage with a Miss King.' Fred may have misheard the story in childhood and subsequently been under a misapprehension. There is no doubt that Blatchington Court and the Blatchington Estate had come to Robert *Dennis* though marriage with a Miss King. Nor is there any doubt that Robert *Lambe* bought the estate from the Dennises, because the conveyance survives. And when Robert Lambe bought the estate, he had not inherited anything from his father, because his father was still alive at the time. It looks as if the acquisition of the Blatchington Court Estate through an ill-judged purchase was being glossed over.

Robert Lambe was certainly involved in the building of the sea wall, and it is worth examining the true extent of his financial commitment. After the major storm causing sea-flooding at Seaford and Blatchington in 1865, a scheme was put forward to build a groyne at Splash Point to help retain beach material. An 1867 map showing the site of the groyne declared that this was 'to be erected by W. Tyler Smith on behalf of the Corporation'. The commercial extraction of beach sediment was halted at the same time and a sea-wall was discussed. In 1876 Seaford Corporation received a proposal from a firm called Goldberg & Creed to build a sea-wall. By June 1876 work had started on the eastern end, starting at Splash Point, but within the year Creed had abandoned it. In 1880 a Mr Gregory offered to resume the work. He was granted the concession (sold the land) in April 1881, with the condition that the sea-wall would be built. Work was to commence by February 1882 and completed to the Corporation's satisfaction by Februay 1884. Instead, Gregory sold the land, and the task of building of the sea-wall, on to John Lee. In May 1881, the *Sussex Advertiser* reported that great progress was being made; the excavations for the wall had almost reached the Assembly Rooms. The structure consisted of two parallel walls and the intention was to fill the space between them with chalk robbed from the cliffs at Seaford Head. By November 1882 the seawall was completed as far west as Pelham Road. Then Lee died and the land and the responsibility passed into the hands of the Seaford Bay Estate.

At about the same time, the London, Brighton & South Coast Railway Company built a sea-wall between Tide Mills and the Newhaven East Pier, together with six groynes near the pier and two at the Buckle. This was to protect the Newhaven-Seaford railway line. Robert Lambe's name is not mentioned in connection with any of these works, so there is no reason to suppose that he was involved or paying for any of them, at least at that stage. But in

1898 he did become involved in sea defence. The Newhaven and Seaford Sea Defences Act was passed in that year, and it specifically names Robert Lambe several times, as one of those who was to be responsible for paying for and carrying out the work. The Newhaven Company and the Brighton Company were jointly to bear five-eighths of the total cost. The list includes Seaford Council, the Estate Company, the Crook trustees, Lord Chichester, Alfred Hutchings and William Catt, who were collectively to pay £4,975. Robert Lambe was to pay the difference between that sum and three-eighths of the total cost. The Act stated that the anticipated total cost was £60,000, so Robert Lambe could have expected his required contribution to be £17,500. Curiously, Robert mentions nothing about the Act or its implications for his family in *Incidents of my Life*.

Robert Lambe was given the additional responsibility of forming a properly metalled seafront road 60 feet wide along his frontage, perhaps costing another £2,500.

This heavy financial burden was a reflection of Lambe's role as a landowner who was 'liable to sustain injury' as a result of encroachment by the sea. Conversely, he would be a major beneficiary of the sea defences. The general view was that flooding by the sea militated against the town's development, and it was natural for the Seaford Bay Estate Company to start work on the seawall in 1881 with a view to developing the seafront. The idea had been explicitly to create a conventional resort seafront that would attract visitors and boost the town's general development. The 1898 Act implies that the cost was being shared according to the likely benefits. Because Robert Lambe had bought so much land in Blatchington and Seaford, he owned a significant length of the coastline. It is strange that he did nothing to avoid this problem; in fact even as late as 1894 he was making his situation worse: in *Incidents of my Life* he notes under that year, 'Bought Chambers land on Front £1,250'.

It would have been better to sell off fields next to the sea rather than buy additional ones, in order to avoid the impending huge cost of sea defences, but he may have clung to the idea that Seaford would take off as a resort and that seafront property would one day be extremely valuable. He may have believed that building a sea-wall would generate confidence in coastal property and accelerate the development of the seafront. Certainly others were thinking in this way as the development got under way; the press commented, 'The town is evidently growing at as rapid a rate as even its best well wishers could hope for. The sea wall makes an admirable parade!'

By acquiring more seafront property, Robert was buying his way into further difficulty. His decision to move into Blatchington Court in 1900, just at the moment when he became liable for £20,000 worth of sea defences, is hard to understand. Most people would have seen this as the time to down-size, but not Robert Lambe. Was it bravado? Not only did Blatchington Court require renovation before he could move into it, he added a substantial north wing to the house as well.

Some time after the passing of the Act, Robert Lambe would have had to find £20,000 to meet his obligation. But this would have been in about 1900, not before, and he had by then been in serious debt for more than twenty years. To put the sea defence debt in context, the £20,000 represents one-third of Robert's total indebtedness in 1912. He sold £80,000 worth of land in 1901, and only a quarter of that sum would have been needed to meet his sea defence obligation. The cause of his financial problem went well beyond sea defence.

So, in spite of grandson Fred Lambe's comments, it is likelier that the ultimate source of Robert Lambe's financial difficulties was the purchase of the Blatchington Estate at a time when he did not have the funds to honour the transaction. He was in debt from that moment on - for the rest of his life. He may have expected to inherit property, as indeed he did. In 1916 he inherited The Fox beershop in Wilmington from Mary Lambe, who had inherited it from her father. By 1916 it was a village shop and post office. Robert Lambe sold it on. In 1881 he had inherited the Black Horse in Wilmington, which much later formed a plot in a sale of his estate some time after 1912. In 1913, Robert mortgaged an estate in Wilmington consisting of Gothic Cottage, Cyprus Lodge, Rose Cottage and a baker's shop. But selling these Wilmington properties seem to have made no difference to his fortunes.

Robert's tragedy was his ambition. Even as a young man he wanted to be the squire, the biggest landowner and the richest man in the parish. It was a self-image partly adopted from Tyler Smith, but perhaps partly inherited from his father. In the early nineteenth century Blatchington House was surrounded by farmyards, paddocks, barns and other outbuildings, a typical working farm-house. By the 1870s the large barn and another outbuilding beside it in front of the house had been demolished; the yard was developed into an open front garden with a turning circle for carriages. The paddock to the west was laid out with walkways lined with trees, fruit trees perhaps; again this was more like the walled garden of a gentleman's country house than a working farm, and suggests a retreat from agriculture as a way of life, a shift towards the lifestyle of the country gentleman. This was done while *William* Lambe, Robert's father, was still living there. But William had taken Robert into formal partnership as early as 1864, so the decision to turn Blatchington House into a minor mansion may, after all, have been Robert's.

The widow

Robert Lambe's widow, Elizabeth Sarah Lambe, lived on at Arlington House for another nine years after his death. The new house was designed to have some points in common with Blatchington Court. The double-fronted two-storey south elevation was the same length (20m) and had the same south-south-easterly aspect, no doubt to make the principal rooms as light and airy as possible, and give them a fine view across to Seaford Head. As at Blatchington Court, the windows were large, and there was a sun room built along the west elevation. The Lambes evidently wanted to feel at home at Arlington House.

Elizabeth Lambe's recipe books have survived, exercise books containing her own prized recipes, some collected from friends, and some handed down from earlier generations. They are written in several distinct hands and were evidently added to across more than a hundred years, starting in the late eighteenth century and continuing into the twentieth century. The writers of these recipes were farmers' wives, not highly educated, and writing very much as they spoke, which adds to the charm of the recipes. 'Wan it his boyl let it bee streand. . . than put your Jelly throw the Sive.' One of the writers writes 'brad' for 'bread', which shows her Sussex accent. A custard pudding recipe ends with the commendation, 'It is a verry Good pudden.'

Elizabeth Lambe's personality comes across strongly in her will, made in 1929; she died in 1931, appointing her two surviving sons, Tom and Dick Lambe, and Harold Blaker, the Lewes solicitor, as executors. Her belongings were to be divided up among the two sons and the grand-daughters. The major properties she left were the two houses she owned. One was Blatchington House, which she left to Tom. The other was Arlington House, which she left to her grand-daughters Joyce and Joan Gregory Smith.

The way some of the items are described suggests that she was

Arlington House

very aware of the personality of particular rooms in Arlington House. Rosanna Lambe (Tom's wife) was left 'wearing apparel. . . also my inlaid table in the Drawing Room with two flaps.' Tom was left the Sheraton sideboard 'in my Dining Room and the 6 chairs and 2 arm chairs to match, also the large painting of his great grandfather William Lambe of Wilmington in the same room. . . also one bracket clock in my Morning Room and one inlaid walnut cabinet in my Dining Room and two paintings after Morland in the Drawing Room.'

The qualifying '*after* Morland' shows her awareness of paintings, and the significant difference between paintings by Morland and paintings in the style of Morland. She was doubtless aware that the latter were less valuable. For some reason kept with her copy of the will was a memorandum she wrote to her bank explaining that she was moving money about. It is a revealing note, returned to her by the bank with 'Received' stamped on it, presumably after appropriate action had been taken. Written in a clear and confident hand, the memo is a model of succinct clarity and directness:

26ᵗʰ March 29

Memorandum - Westminster Bank
My account at this Date having over £900 to my credit I have transferred £800 to deposit a/c I have told the Manager to keep the deposit receipt for me on safe custody and transfer the interest when and as earned by the deposit to my current account. Elizabeth S. Lambe

Her will shows the same directness, when she reaches the money legacies. '. . . to each of them, Thomas Lambe, Richard

Frederic Lambe and Harold Montague Blaker, who shall accept the office of executor and trustee but not otherwise the sum of £100.' She was aware that Richard had resigned as Robert's executor, leaving Thomas and Mr Blaker to do all the work, and must have suspected that without incentive he would do the same again. This was a hard-headed manager of money at work. Perhaps she had more business sense than her husband.

Notes & sources

Arlington House Papers (Abstract of Title)

Castleden and Franks 2012 (Mrs Lambe's recipe books)

Conveyance for sale of Seaford West Company plots (1914)

Incidents of My Life. The precision of some of the detail suggests to me that this summary was developed from Robert Lambe's diaries, which unfortunately have never come to light.

Lowerson 1975 (Activities of Seaford Bay Estate Company)

Robert Lambe Papers

Provisional Agreement for sale and purchase of the Blatchington Estate (1877)

Wills of Robert and Elizabeth Lambe

Fred Lambe's letters to Mrs Davis 1980s

Newhaven and Seaford Sea Defences Act 1898

Sykes 1946 (sea defences)

Chapter 11
The first windmill

The village shepherd, the keeper and guardian of the common flock, was central to the success of the medieval sheep-and-corn economy. The miller who ground the parish corn was equally central, and his windmill was one of the village's two most important landmarks.

The post-mill

Bishopstone, a mile away, had a windmill in 1199, but Blatchington's windmill was referred to in 1324 by the name 'Peghemill', and this is said to be the earliest reference to any specific named mill in England.

Two hundred years later, in 1523, Blatchington mill reappears in the Blatchington Court Rolls. At that time, early in the reign of Henry VIII, the mill was owned or rented by Richard Frenche: 'Richard Frenche produces copy containing 1 acre of land called Mill acre with a certain windmill built thereon in Blachyngton dated 24 Sept 15 Henry VIII and rent yearly 11s.' This 'certain windmill' was the same structure as the Peghemill, and it is likely that the 'peg' was the king-post on which the mill swivelled to catch the day's wind. In comparable mills, the king-post was a hefty tree trunk 16 feet high, 30 inches in diameter at the base, mounted on an equally stout cross-shaped base. There were four diagonal quarterbars rising from the crosstrees to hold the king-post steady. It was a simple structure that ensured stability, the same structure that, turned upside down, held aloft the church roof. Mills of this design were often called post-mills.

Sometimes the timber substructure was left open to the weather, sometimes it was contained inside a roundhouse about nine feet high. To judge from H. H. Evans's drawings, at least by the late nineteenth century Blatchington mill's king-post had a protecting roundhouse built of flint, with a stable door on the south-east and a shallow window with a shutter on the south side. The little drawing of the mill (only 4mm tall) on Figg's map suggests that in 1818 there was no roundhouse, but Figg's drawing may be more symbolic than realistic.

The mill's superstructure was a wooden weatherboarded box about twenty feet high and free to revolve on top of the king-post.

Like other medieval mills, Blatchington mill was fitted with common sails: sailcloth furled round a cross of wooden ladders caught the wind. These were replaced in around 1850 by spring sails, which had wooden shutters that could be opened or closed like Venetian blinds. One account mentions two pairs of stones, another three; the mill was said to be large. Blatchington mill was also known as the Black Mill, a common name, which probably arose because the weatherboarded superstructure was daubed with pitch to waterproof it.

In 1572, the mill was owned or leased by Jeremiah French and in 1572 or 1573 he surrendered it to the use of Anthony Martin, who was given a licence to let the mill for the next three years, on payment of a fine (or fee) of 12 pence.

In 1594-5, the windmill was acquired by Humphry Rowe, who had a licence to let the mill for nine years, beginning that year. Three years later, Rowe let the mill to William Dunton. At the same time, and dealt with in the same manorial court, John Colvyll surrendered 'a messuage and 6½ acres to the use of Humphry Rowe'. Humphry Rowe moved to Blatchington in 1595, when he first acquired the windmill, and lived there for nineteen years. Then in 1614 he moved to Seaford, where he lived for nine years. By 1622 he was 72 and blind.

William Dunton, who had rented the mill since 1597, surrendered it to the use of John Hunnye 'late of Wilmington': 'he gives as heriot 40 shillings.' In 1620, John Hunnye died and his younger son and heir, Edward Hunny, was 'admitted to the mill and 1 acre.' Several of the old documents mention that the windmill stood in one acre of land, so the two were naturally bought, sold or let together. The mill and its one acre plot passed from owner to owner, miller to miller. There was a cottage for the miller to live in, standing in the same plot, as shown on the 1870s Ordnance Survey map.

A complication with young Edward Hunny's inheritance was that he was very young; the Court Book says that he was under age. 'There comes John Gilbert and married the widow of the said John, and he prays to be admitted to the guardianship of the land and body of Edward.' By marrying Edward's widowed mother, John Gilbert, the squire, became Edward's stepfather and guardian, and he was formally given stewardship of the mill. A 'fine' or fee of £6 was payable. This is strange, as the mill belonged to Blatchington manor, not Alciston, so Squire Gilbert was apparently paying the fine to himself; perhaps it was seen as fitting to follow the customary form for these transactions.

Once Edward was of age, he acquired the mill. Twenty-seven years on, on 31 May 1647, Edward Hunney ('of Ripe') was ready to hand the mill on. It was sold, with its trademark one acre, to Samuel Britredge of Eastbourne. Britredge sold to Edward Merriam. On 16 November 1675 Edward Merriam conditionally surrendered the mill to the use of Susan Seaman, widow. This sale seems to have collapsed, as three years later Edward Merriam was once again surrendering Blatchington Mill, messuage, garden, windmill and one acre, this time to Henry Beane. Henry Beane sold the mill to William Coombs.

On 18 April 1693, William Coombs attempted to sell the mill to Thomas Alchorne. A mortgage was involved and this transaction appears to have failed. The next day William Coombs sold Blatchington mill to someone else, William Brett of Friston. Only two years later, on 18 October 1695, William Brett conditionally sold the mill to Thomas Alchorne, who had tried to buy it before. Again the transaction failed. In 1696, Brett sold the mill (messuage, mill and one acre of land) back to William Coombs of Seaford. The pattern of transactions is complex and hard to understand; the mill was changing hands more frequently than might be expected. Yet after this episode we do not read of its changing hands again until 1757, sixty years later, when it was sold by a William Coombs who may have been the grandson of the miller in the 1690s. In 1757 the mill was remembered as having formerly been owned by Merriam, who was the miller in the 1670s.

The men who spent their lives aboard the old wooden sailing ships developed their own culture, their own character, their own way of talking and behaving. On land, the men who spent all their time aboard those beached sailing ships, the wooden windmills with their continually furling and unfurling sails, similarly developed their own distinctive character. It may have been because their way of life was peculiar, industrial in a world that was mainly agricultural, working in a confined, machine-driven space while nearly everyone else worked outdoors, and because of their special expertise. Millers were often different from other people in their village, independent-minded, quirky, eccentric. They even looked different; they were immediately identifiable because of the dusting of flour on their clothes.

Early in the eighteenth century, the mill made its first appearance on a map, showing prominently on Budgen's 1724 map. Windmills were major landmarks.

At the end of the eighteenth century, Blatchington had its eccentric miller in the person of William Coombs. His favourite boast was that Blatchington mill had been in the possession of his family, 'ever sin' the days of King Harry the Eighth'. He may have known that another William Coombs, possibly his grandfather, had the mill before him in the 1690s, and assumed from this that the mill had been in his family for many generations. But the sixteenth and early seventeenth century documents (the Blatchington Manor Court Book) clearly show that Blatchington mill passed through the hands of several other familes, named Frenche, Martin, Rowe, Dunton and Hunny. William Coombs had his own view of the past, and each of us sees the past differently.

It was said that William once swore that if something he had said proved to be untrue he would never set foot in his mill again. He was as good as his word. When he was proved to be wrong, he never again entered his mill. Instead he oversaw the work from the top of the mill steps, outside the mill door.

More eccentric still was his habit of not only painting his horse but painting it different colours. One week he would be seen riding down Blatchington Hill on a yellow horse, the next on a green horse. He even coloured his horse for visits to Lewes, where he might be seen on a horse of yellow, green or blue. Master Coombs used his horse to carry sacks of flour. Sometimes, if the horse was overburdened, Coombs would throw a sack over his own back to relieve the animal of some of the weight, though he stayed in the saddle. 'A merciful man is merciful to his beast,' he said.

Blatchington Mill in 1818 (Figg map)

Coombs was a kind and gentle man with a shrew for a wife. He sometimes reflected, 'Tis my own fault, for I had a warning. As I was a-going across Exceat laine for to be married at church, I heard a voice from heaven saying unto me, "Will-iam Coombs! Will-iam Coombs! If so be that you marry Mary you'll always be a miserable man!" And so I've always found it – and I be a miserable man.'

The mill was on the market once more in 1796, when William Standen was either the vendor or the purchaser. In the Defence Schedules of 1801 Blatchington Mill was said to be capable of producing three sacks of flour a day, although the miller was unable to get enough wheat to maintain that level of production.

Little is recorded after that, and the mill went out of use in about 1870. The building survived for many years, though in the end it had to be propped up to stop it from collapsing. It was demolished some time before 1900. There is no known photograph of it, though several survive of Sutton Mill. There are three slightly different drawings by H. H. Evans in Seaford Museum, all showing it in a state of ruin in 1873, but it is uncertain how accurate they are, or what information Evans was working from. It is assumed Evans worked from one or more photographs, but there are discrepancies among the three drawings suggesting the artist was using a certain amount of licence. There are even discrepancies between the captions of two of the pictures; one says 'pulled down as being dangerous 1878', the other 'pulled down 1860'.

Two of them show the miller's cottage to the east of the mill, which is correct according to the 1873 OS map. All three drawings show haystacks in the field on the west side of Mill Road, a field regularly used for stacks. The OS map dating from 1873 shows that the mill stood on a roughly rectangular plot that coincided with the plot now occupied by Firle Cottage. A group of four buildings stood on the footprint of the modern cottage. The mill was demolished during the twenty years after 1873; it does not appear on the 1898 map, though the miller's cottage and its outbuildings were still there. The 1873 map shows clearly that the mill stood on a specially built raised and level platform to the west of the miller's cottage, in other words in the middle of the square lawn in the front garden of Firle Cottage. The platform (still there) was presumably built to ensure that the sweeps were well up in the wind.

In 1763, the newspaper described an accident that may have happened at the mill. The *Sussex Weekly Advertiser* for 29 August reported,

'On Monday last a melancholy accident happened at Mr Farncomb's at Blatchington, a lad about thirteen years of age being drawing of water with a Jack-Ass in a large cog wheel, he was catched between the wheel and a post, which almost tore his head off, [he] lived about thirteen hours after, and then expired.'

The derelict mill (redrawn from H. H. Evans's picture)

The only boy who comes anywhere near fitting this description is Edward Carter, who was the son of Edward and Mary Carter, and he was fourteen years old, not thirteen. But he was buried at St Peter's on 9 May 1763, not in late August. So the boy must have been buried elsewhere, perhaps at Bishopstone or Seaford. Jack-ass wheels were more commonly known as donkey wheels. These were timber treadmills powered by donkeys to draw water up from deep wells. They were housed in small square timberframed buildings with pyramid-shaped roofs, and they were in common use from the fifteenth century onwards.

There were several wells in the village, for instance at the Well House, The Star House and Hog Plot, and it is possible that one of these had a donkey wheel, though both the Well House and the Hog Plot wells were identified on the 1872 survey as draw wells: wells that supplied water by the use of a bucket on a rope. It is most likely that a donkey wheel would be associated with the deepest well in the village, and that is likely to have been at the highest point, highest above the water table. That would have been at the windmill, and the small community working the mill would have required its own water supply. The mill stood on a land surface 45m above sea level, and about 32m above the summer water table. It is possible that one of the three small square buildings in the windmill complex was the wellhouse, and that this was where the fatal accident happened.

The building must have been a distinctive landmark in the village, so it is odd that there is no other known mention of a donkey wheel at Blatchington. A donkey wheel is known to have existed at Bishopstone and there were Farncombes who owned property at Bishopstone too; John Farncombe was the victim of a burglary at his stable at Bishopstone in March 1793. It is possible that the newspaper made a mistake, misreporting an accident that took place at Bishopstone, not Blatchington.

One of the few stories we have that can be definitely attached to Blatchington mill is a poignant story about an old blind horse (*The Times*, 14 September, 1810). It had been 'captured' in France during the Napoleonic Wars and brought to Sussex. Blind and in a foreign land, possibly bewildered by unfamiliar commands and not knowing where it was, in 1810 it wandered into the path of the sweeps of Blatchington Mill as they scythed round in the wind. It was struck on the head by the sweeps and killed.

When the mill was finally dismantled in the 1870s, one of its millstones was taken down and laid in the path through the churchyard, just outside the church door. It was as if the ancient mill was being laid finally to rest. The mill came down at the same time that the lands holden of Alciston manor were being enfranchised, and the Gage family's light but long-enduring grasp on Blatchington's affairs was released. The entire traditional rural way of life in Blatchington was coming to a close.

The Tower Mill

Another mill was built further up Firle Road in 1882. This was a loftier structure, six floors high, with staging round the outside. It was used to pump water up out of the chalk for the Newhaven and Seaford Water Company (on a site sold to them by Robert Lambe). The site, close to the golf course, was not well chosen. Being down in a dip it did not catch the wind very well. When it did work, and pumped the water up to the surface, the water turned out to be brackish.

The tower mill stopped working in 1914, and was taken down in 1920.

While the mill was still working, in 1907, Seaford Golf Club moved to its new course on Bullock Down at the top of Firle Road, the greens invading what had been the village's tenantry down, grazed for centuries by flocks of sheep. The club had been down on Seaford Head for the previous twenty years. The new clubhouse was built on the southern edge of the golf course, while the old tower mill was still working just to the west of the northern end of Firle Road. An unforeseen effect of moving the golf club here was the steady increase in traffic that it would draw through the old village, pumping unwanted vehicles up Blatchington Hill and Firle Road towards Bullock Down in the same way that the mill had pumped brackish water.

Notes & Sources

Blatchington Court Book (changes of ownership)
Deposition Books, 1580-1640.
Hopkins 1927 (windmills)
Water table. Assuming that the summer water table is two metres below the floor of the valley at the foot of Blatchington Hill, and extends roughly horizontally northwards into the Downs, the water level in the well at the Well House would only be 5m below the wellhead. The level in the well at the Star House, further up the slope, would be 12m down. Because the land rises steadily up Firle Road, the well at the windmill would have needed to be over 30m deep to reach water. In that situation a donkey wheel may have been considered necessary.

Chapter 12
The Great War

Grand old aeronaut

The history of Blatchington circles and revolves round St Peter's church, the oldest building in the village. Even the windmill has its symbolic grave there, beside the church porch, the millstone set in the path. A few residents, too, have conspicuous graves in the churchyard. Tyler Smith's double-width grave looks a shade ostentatious by today's standards. Robert Lambe's obelisk was intended to be imposing, but is lost now in *Briar Rose* undergrowth, its inscriptions unreachable, virtually impossible to read. Most villagers lie unrecorded, unmarked, in the churchyard, while a privileged few have memorials inside. Henry Tracey Coxwell is one of those.

On the west wall of the nave of St Peter's church there is a memorial to him in white marble. Coxwell's unusual career had its final phase in Blatchington, where he lived in semi-retirement. He trained as a dentist and became a dental assistant in Tottenham, but his main interest, his obsession, was ballooning. He made his first flight in 1844; within four years he had given up dentistry and turned professional balloonist, making ascents from many foreign cities.

Henry Coxwell made his balloons in a factory behind Seaford railway station. He died on 5 January, 1900, just too late to be buried in St Peter's churchyard, which was deemed to be full in 1899. He was buried instead in the Alfriston Road cemetery.

In the mid-nineteenth century, very little was known about the atmosphere above the mountain tops. The British Association for the Advancement of Science decided to fund a series of balloon flights to find out more about the upper atmosphere. One of the founder members of the British Meteorological Society, James Glaisher, volunteered to make the twenty-eight dangerous ascents between 1862 and 1866, and his usual pilot was Henry Coxwell.

In 1862 they made three ascents in a large new balloon specially designed to reach high altitudes. Coxwell called it the *Mammoth*.

The third and record-breaking ascent took place on 5 September, when they reached a height of about 7 miles, but almost died. Glaisher lost consciousness. Coxwell climbed up into the rigging to free a valve line that had become snagged. His hands were so numb with cold that he had to pull the cord with his teeth

Henry Coxwell to the rescue

in order to stop the balloon going any higher. If he had failed, they would have died of pneumonia, hypothermia or oxygen starvation.

The balloon landed in Shropshire after making the first journey up to the tropopause, the upper boundary of the lower layer of the atmosphere. The balloon journeys allowed Glaisher to observe and measure the decrease in temperature with altitude, which turned out to be a regular one degree Celsius for every 100m of ascent; they discovered the lapse rate.

Glaisher commented that Coxwell was always alive to the beauty of the earth beneath them. Whenever a landscape of surpassing beauty appeared, Coxwell invited him to admire it. Glaisher was the cold scientific observer.

The flights were made from the Midlands to avoid the possibility of coming down into the sea, but Coxwell had his balloon factory in Richmond Road in Seaford in the 1860s and 70s and he did some small-scale ballooning in Sussex. In 1876, the press reported a flight that nearly went wrong. 'Mr Coxwell made an ascent from Lewes, last Monday evening in the balloon *Jem*, with Mr A. T. Ashton, its owner. He left at 5.20, starting in the direction of Tunbridge Wells. The balloon landed safely shortly before 7 o'clock, about two miles from Seaford. The aeronauts descended because they found themselves drifting seawards.'

Henry Coxwell

Coxwell's last balloon ascent was in 1885, after which he settled down in Connaught Street to write his autobiography, *My Life and Balloon Experiences*, published in 1887. A journalist tracked Henry Coxwell down at East Blatchington in 1895. He found 'the grand old aeronaut amidst the cruisers of the air in the dry dockyard of a huge loft, where their supine forms lay, ready to be filled with gas . . . ."This is the car," said Mr Coxwell, laying his hand on the *Mammoth* car, "in which Mr Glaisher, the Great Scientist, and I ascended to an altitude which has never before or since been attained." '

Prelude to the Great War

The Edwardian era in Blatchington was in some ways the culmination of the activities of the nineteenth century landowning class. Early in the nineteenth century, John King had worked towards acquiring nearly all the land in the parish, to the point where he could be formally recognized as lord of the manor. The Dennises were unusual landowners, in that they acquired half of the parish almost inadvertently, Elizabeth by inheritance from her father and Robert by marrying Elizabeth. They decided in 1862 to move out of Blatchington Court and into the enlarged rectory, leaving the mansion available for tenants. When Robert Lambe bought the Blatchington estate with the mansion house, he may from the start have aspired to live in it, but decided to let it instead. It must have been with a sense of pride and fulfilment that he at last moved into Blatchington Court in 1900, even if he could not afford to remain there for much more than decade.

Edwardian Blatchington was a microscosm of England, with a peaceful and stable surface, but inwardly on the brink of cataclysm. Robert Lambe's mounting debts meant that soon there would be a terrible reckoning, and that followed his death in 1922. The national cataclysm that was to come was signalled by the tramp, tramp, tramp of thousands of soldiers' boots marching up and down Blatchington Hill, from 1902 onwards, on their way to and from the military training camp, Blatchington Camp (later called North Camp to distinguish it from the camp on the north flank of Seaford Head, South Camp).

Yet Blatchington at the turn of the twentieth century was still to all appearances a nineteenth century rural village. At the bottom of Blatchington Hill were the two ponds, each in a grassy hollow, one on each side of the road. The larger, Blatchington Pond, was overlooked to the north by a low steep scarp, so steep that the bare chalk rock was exposed, like a stranded sea-cliff.

Blatchington Hill, Sutton Drove and the Pond in 1914

Above that was a clutch of farm buildings, Bravery's farm. On each side of the pale metalled road and its flanking white chalk footway banks of tall trees ran up the hill towards the village. This was a natural ribbon of green belt – not that that phrase would be coined for several decades yet – a short stretch of open country clearly separating Blatchington from Seaford.

At the foot of the hill, banks of mature elms rose on each side: no houses, only the remains of some old cottages or cowsheds on

The southern end of the village in about 1902, with the bakehouse and Nos 4 & 3 Blatchington Street on the left, the Rectory in the centre and the two gables of Blatchington House in the distance, at the top of Blatchington Street. On the right are The Gables, Glebe Cottage, Rectory Cottage and The Star House (extreme right).

the west. Further up the hill, the southern edge of the village was well-defined, with the Widows' Cottages closely followed by Star House on the right and Nos 1 and 2 Blatchington Street, now Seagull Cottage, on the left. It was here that Blatchington Hill became the village street, Blatchington Street.

Today Seagull Cottage looks crisp with smart white-painted walls, white-painted windows and Mediterranean blue shutters, and two windows in the wall facing the street. In 1900, this pair of artisans' cottages looked less attractive, with cement render unpainted and one small window high on the otherwise blank gable-end facing the street. The next pair of cottages on the left, Nos 3 and 4 Blatchington Street, was also plain. These were the unpretentious cottages of ordinary working people. Fred Saunders, who lived at No 1, was Robert Lambe's groom. William Reed, who lived at No 4, was a gardener.

These cottages, together with the village bakehouse on the roadside between them, and the Star House and the Widows' Cottages opposite, marked the beginning of the village. A flint road wall continued northwards from The Star House to join the south wall of Rectory Cottage; behind it was a paddock, with a midden on the northern side. The wall was breached in 1902 to make way for the western part of Homefield Road as an entrance to Blatchington (later North) Camp.

Then came the pair of old flint cottages, Rectory Cottage and Glebe Cottage. Beyond that was a huddle of two or three small cottages, one of them with its front wall right on the street; The Cottage replaced them in 1908.

Further up Blatchington Street, and opposite St Peter's, was The Gables, looking much as it does today, except that the substantial outbuilding (now converted into a dwelling) had been a stable below with hay loft above, but for the past few years had functioned as a stalled cowshed below with fodder store above. Beyond The Gables was a barn and yard, and there was a further barn and yard to the north on the site of what is now Upper Belgrave Road, which then did not exist.

St Peter's Church looked then very much as it does today, its churchyard stocked with mature shrubs and trees. In 1900 the Old Rectory was still functioning as the home of the rector, the Revd Arthur Richardson, and beyond it to the west was a rather dilapidated Blatchington Court. Robert Lambe moved into it that year after having it repaired following a period of neglect.

A photograph was taken of the score of workmen brought in to

Renovating Blatchington Court in 1900. The same firm, Morlings, was later to build the Lambe family vault in the churchyard.

carry out the renovation; they are standing in the graceful pillared porch. One of the changes Robert Lambe made at this time was an extension to the drive. Until now visitors entered along a drive between the rectory and the churchyard, from Blatchington Hill to a turning circle in front of the pillared porch. Robert continued the drive past the south front of the house, then turned it north through ninety degrees to join Belgrave Road. This enabled a trap or carriage to drop people at the front door and continue on its way without turning round. To the north-west of the house, along Belgrave Road, there was a collection of farm buildings.

Going on up Firle Road, on the left was a substantial open space that had become the front garden of Blatchington House but, from its name, Hog Plot, had once been the site of a pigsty. Blatchington House had been the Lambe family home for fifty years. Now Robert Lambe was living at Blatchington Court, and had a house built for his son Dick further up Firle Road (Upper Lodge), while Tom (Dr Thomas Lambe) remained at Blatchington House, an old farmhouse rebuilt in the early nineteenth century. Several of the neighbouring buildings and paddocks were tied to it in some way.

Old thatched cottages at the bottom of Firle Road, looking south. The cottage on the left stood almost opposite Blatchington House. It was demolished in 1913. Not one of the houses in this picture is still standing.

Alces Place in 1914 or 1916, before its conversion, the barn with its big double-doors at the back, the bullock-shed on the right and the yard in the foreground. The boy is Fred Lambe.

Alces Place was one of the farmyards, with barns or byres on three sides. The yard was used as a bullock yard, and the range along the north side was an open-sided shed where the bullocks were fed: it provided them with shelter in winter. Fred Lambe had his photo taken there by his mother when his grandfather sold it. The large central building was a threshing barn. It had twin doors in the centre, opening right up to the eaves, and another set of doors on the other side (now the back). With the two sets of doors open, a westerly breeze passing through would blow the chaff through into the yard. Laid between the two sets of doors was a fine paved square of York stone (as Fred Lambe remembered it) for threshing the grain; it was worn smooth by the flails. It is still there.

On the right hand side of Firle Road, opposite Blatchington House and its walled front garden, was another walled garden, an orchard. Immediately to the north was a small thatched cottage, right beside the (later) entrance to Arlington House. It was demolished in about 1913, and the lower part became part of the road wall, but the window openings, blind and bricked-up for a hundred years, can still be made out under the ivy.

Further up Firle Road on the right, in a large garden, was Upper Lodge, the house built for Richard Lambe and his family at the northern edge of the village. To the north of Upper Lodge was the site of the windmill and its mill cottage, now destroyed. To the north of that, on the site of Dial House, there was a shepherd's cottage. On the opposite side of the road, just below the mill and in the forked junction with the old road to Bishopstone, lay a pond with a stack yard to the north.

This was Edwardian Blatchington, still looking like a classic English village. But it was not entirely a rural idyll. A 1912 photograph of the Sunday school, marked 'in Firle Road' shows two stone-faced men and a woman, presumably the Sunday school teachers, with seven glum and wary children, though they are at least holding croquet balls and mallets.

Blatchington was increasingly brought into Seaford's orbit, not least for entertainment. Typical fare in 1910 was an itinerant entertainment called Miss Doris Nelson's Concert Party. This featured Miss Doris Nelson (soprano), Miss Dorothy Greig (dancer), Mr Arthur Gale (baritone), Mr Ravenscroft (tenor) and Mr Alexander Mee (refined light comedian). Then, as now, not all light comedians were refined.

The Lambes and the War

By the outbreak of the First World War, Blatchington was well established as the site of a large army camp, one of two at Seaford. The fields immediately to the east of the village, which had been tentatively planned for housing development as a means of alleviating Robert Lambe's financial difficulties, were chosen as the main site for the army camp. St Peter's Road had recently been laid out parallel to Firle Road and some houses had already been built along it. The ends of their gardens marked the western edge of the army camp. From there, the camp stretched eastwards to Cradle Hill Road. The southern edge was marked by Vale Road, from which the camp extended up the slope towards The Holt, The Risings and Lexden Drive. This was a much less comfortable addition to the village than the old Napoleonic barracks, which had at least been separated from the village by several fields, and accommodated hundreds of soldiers: now there were thousands.

This large new temporary settlement, a township in itself, was Blatchington (later North) Camp. In the run-up to the Great War it had been used mainly seasonally, a summer encampment of bell tents, but, in year-round use during the war, it was fitted with orderly rows of wooden huts. Along the line that would later be Upper Belgrave Road and Quarry Lane four square parade grounds were laid out; a fifth, Parade No 5, lay about halfway along Homefield Road. Between there and Cradle Hill Road were the rows of tents, and later huts. The earliest photos of Blatchington

Camp show neat, formal rows of bell tents on open downland at the very beginning of the twentieth century, when it was a summer camp for volunteers. As early as 1902 there were 10,000 volunteers from London camping 'on the Downs just above East Blatchington village'. In 1903 the site was described as 'near Blatchington Church on land owned by Mr Lambe'. There was, even at that stage, a large YMCA Reading and Writing Tent, and gradually the site acquired more facilities.

An early air photograph shows the camp extending west of Firle Road as well, into the Carlton Road-Tudor Close area, so the camp eventually extended across a very large area, west as well as east of the village.

In 1903, the British Medical Journal praised Blatchington Camp.

'A new camping and manoeuvring ground for the London Volunteers has been discovered at Seaford. The 2nd, 3rd and 5th London Brigades went there this year for their annual week's training [in setting up and running field hospitals], and pitched their camp in two large fields north-east of the town, close to Blatchington Manor, the owner of which, Mr Lambe, not only allowed the use of his land, but gave every facility for making the week interesting, instructive and pleasant. . . One of the difficulties of the annual camps has always been the limited size and the distance of the manoeuvring ground, but at Seaford there is ample room in the immediate vicinity of the camp.'

*Tower Hamlets Volunteers marching down
Blatchington Hill in about 1903.*

Blatchington Camp was reckoned to be the best the brigades had attended, even though the volunteers had to dig their own rubbish pits and latrines, as 'the field was handed over just as it was'.

Blatchington Camp was for training recruits and, once the First World War began, for the transit of troops across to France. In September 1914 the camp was still mainly canvas, and the men needed plenty of warm clothing to keep them comfortable. It was clear that huts needed to be provided as soon as possible. Work on building the huts meant a huge increase in heavy traffic on the roads leading to the camp; by 1915 the roads were in a poor state.

On 3 October 1914, thirty ships set sail from Canada with 30,000 men, 7,000 horses and 600 vehicles on board. The following year thousands more men followed across the Atlantic, many from the USA. The War Diary for November 1916 notes, 'Many new Battalions arrived in camp direct from Canada during the month. A high rate of sickness developed among these new arrivals, due largely to the unaccustomed dampness of the English climate.' The Canadians arriving at the two Seaford camps nevertheless had a better time than those stationed on Salisbury Plain. They had access to local people and facilities, including sea-bathing. The soldiers were to an extent separated, with Canadians stationed in the South Camp and native British ('Imperials') in the North (Blatchington) Camp.

There were rivalries and jealousies, which came to a head when a hot-headed Canadian soldier resented being reprimanded by an Imperial N.C.O. The Canadian beat and injured the officer so badly that the officer died the next day. The incident was kept from the Press, but it nudged the authorities to decant the Imperials to Shorncliffe; after that, both the North and South Camps were for Canadians only. In August 1917, Private Joseph Wild was shot dead at the North Camp by Stanko Loyovitch, who said in his defence that he was the victim of sexual bullying.

The presence of the military, and all the equipment that came with it, was a source of temptation to the local people. In June 1917 a Seaford man was fined for stealing a wheel from a motor ambulance. There were incidents, there were accidents. A soldier was knocked down and killed in the village by a charabanc. The jury returned a verdict of accidental death, but thought the County should exercise some control over passenger vehicles, and over the age of drivers. The accident was blamed on a driver aged only seventeen.

But there was a positive side to the relationship between the village and the army. In January 1918, a child skating on Blatchington Pond fell through the ice, and was pulled out by two military policemen. Charles Bravery, who lived at Rosedale on Blatchington Hill, witnessed the rescue and was impressed. He wrote to the Royal Humane Society to try to gain some formal recognition for the two policemen, but the Society 'did not want to know'. So Mr Bravery organized a collection for the two men and in the Empire cinema, after the film show, he made a formal presentation on the stage. One man was given £10, the other £8.

Some of the North American soldiers were to die in the North Camp when the Spanish flu struck. The epidemic reached a peak in October 1918, when more than fifty men died in the camp in one month.

One of the entrances to the newly-built Arlington House, Robert Lambe's final home, was close to the Upper Belgrave Road entrance to North Camp. Robert Lambe insisted that the army put in a fence along the western edge of the camp, to separate it from the village. St Peter's Road was a new road with houses in the process of being built along it, and Robert Lambe wanted the army

Fred Lambe (left) with his sister Audrey (right) and their mother, Florence Hartung of Blatchington, who married Richard Frederic Lambe in 1900.

First World War telephone engineers in Blatchington Street. The Star House is behind them and in the distance on the left is Blatchington House.

camp kept separate from it; he pressed for a fence running along the eastern edge of the new housing development. Just beyond the fence, in the First World War, were the Signal Company and the Royal Engineers, billeted in over sixty wooden huts.

Robert Lambe's grandson, Fred, was a boy during the Great War. Letters written to him at boarding school by his parents living at Upper Lodge survive from this time. One is dated 4 July, but without the year. The first half is from Mother;

> *'As it was so hot I went to the 10 o'clock service this morning and sat near the door. Now we are sitting in the shade and enjoying the rest. . . Granp. Lambe has let Blatchington Court for some months to one of the Staff.'*

She meant that Robert Lambe was letting Blatchington Court to one of the North Camp officers. This is clarified in the second half of the letter, in Father's handwriting.

> *'Everyone here seems to be letting their house this year to the officers at the Camp. I have decided not to let as it is so much trouble and I am very busy with the farm. I have now hired about 100 acres so shall have plenty to do. It is great fun and we are getting a nice lot of hay. The steam plough should have been here but has been delayed. They will come next week I hope. I have 3*

Volunteers marching to Blatchington Camp, one summer afternoon in 1906. This is the southern end of Firle Road, looking south. The chimneys of the rectory can be seen in the tree-tops at the centre of the picture. Look how narrow Firle Road still was at that time.

horses now but am only working 2 of them full time at present.'

The church-going tells us that the letter was written on a Sunday. The only war year when 4 July fell on a Sunday was 1915. Another letter is dated 20 July. Again no year is given, but the Peace Day celebrations mentioned took place on 19 July 1919. The focus of the Peace Day celebrations was a Victory Parade of Allied troops through the streets of London.

'Dearest Boy, Peace Day is over. . . I am glad Audrey [Fred's sister] went off today with Gran for it. Dad & I will have our Peace time in October I think for yesterday Dad kept the pig-food going etc as his three old men went down to Old People's dinner at the Simmons' Institute. Grandpapa L. took the chair. I went to the dentist so not a gala time for me! Dad also washed Snuff!! The bonfires last night were very poor it was too foggy to see the fireworks anywhere about. The papers give full description of the Procession of our Allied troops. The rain came down just after 5 yesterday & I think was pretty general. Dad has covered up his last hay stack which is at the back of our Nursery, on the corner. You might find out from one of your friends who like yourself have to be careful [with money], where they get their blue serge suits. I shall wait for you at Victoria at 12 till 12.15 & then go to Odines, where you came before, a restaurant opposite Underground (Victoria). I have

drawn you a beautiful ! plan of same. . . If you want to send anything home to
be washed – do – I can also bring you up a clean shirt. All news when we meet.
Yr loving Mother.'

The impression is of a close and affectionate family, the mother sensible, sensitive, loving and good-humoured, the father enjoying working the farm. Farming was not his habitual work: he was a solicitor by profession, but that was not a reserved occupation and it may be why for the duration of the War he took up farming. Fred was evidently coming home from school for the summer holiday. He kept these letters for the rest of his life.

Fred's father Richard became a Special Constable in July 1915. As a Special he was issued with *Instructions* by the Chief Constable of East Sussex on 4 March 1916. They communicate a real sense of anxiety.

I wish these instructions kept quite secret as it is of so much importance that
the inhabitants should not be unnecessarily alarmed, and the probability of a
Zeppelin raid is very remote; at the same time it might be necessary owing to
information being received of their possible proximity to take all necessary
precautions.

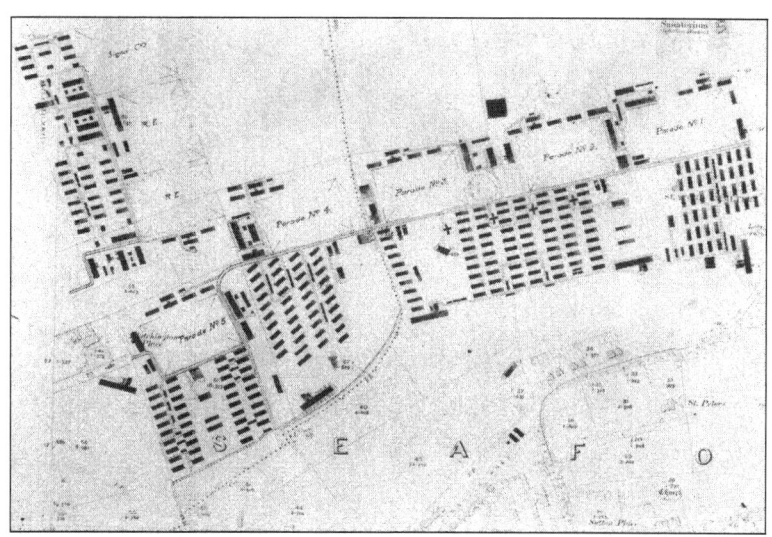

North Camp:
Blatchington Hill lies just to the left of the lower half of this map

Sholud [sic] occasion arise, you will at once be called by the Police, and I wish you to proceed at once as quietly and unostentatiously as possible to the Seaford Police Station where you will be served out with Warrant Card, Badge &c, and remain there awaiting instructions.

I cannot too firmly impress upon you in the interests of the town the great necessity for your acting throughout with the greatest secrecy. Do not mention this to a soul, and if you have to parade, do so promptly and above all as quietly as possible. The probability is, as I said before, that your services would not be actively required, and this being the case I do not wish to cause any unnecessaru [sic] excitement among the inhabitants, but want to be fully prepared as far as possible should the emergency arise.

Hugh Lang

The soldiers arrived by train, disembarked at the station and marched along Clinton Place, down Blatchington Road to the Pond, and from there either along Sutton Drove or up Blatchington Hill to reach the North Camp. When the training was over and the time came for the men to be shipped to France, they marched back again – like the grand old Duke of York, who had ten thousand men, marched them up to the top of the hill and marched them down again. The real-life soldiers marched in their tens of thousands too. They marched six abreast down Blatchington Hill, filling the road. The roads between the camps and the station could not withstand this much traffic: they disintegrated and had to be rebuilt by Welsh roadmenders.

During the First World War, the tents were replaced by rows of huts. Access was by way of Cradle Hill Road in the east, the lower end of Vale Road in the south, and in the west Homefield Road and Upper Belgrave Road. The main entrance was outside Blatchington Place in Homefield Road; from there the spinal road ran through the camp, linking the five parade grounds together.

One of the officers of the North Staffs Regiment stationed at North Camp wrote to a friend on 31 October 1914:

Above you have my address and 'd. v.' it will be so for many months! You might send me a copy or two of 'How to form fours' down here, when it is published! Very few of the men here have much idea of the noble art of – forming fours; they are as much handicapped by only having 100 rifles and no equipment between them. All this does not seem to damp their ardour for saluting, and as there are 60,000 soldiers here and all salutes have to be returned a walk into the town is very hard work!!!

I must say the atmosphere is rather too military for me, and I long for some quiet retreat where one can be at peace & cease from the endless struggle to be the absolute - it - . Swank is the art of the officer & must be cultivated as quickly as possible. One must always be dressed to the nines, never acknowledge (except officially) the existence of an inferior, and throw as many 'd---ns & bl---dys' into every command as possible . . .

Best wishes. Yours ever,

B. L. Lawrence

The New Pontodrome
Opening Night Saturday Dec 22

7 pm: Chunks from Chu Chin Chow

Chu Chin Chow. An Eastern Story Teller	*Lt Smith*
Sitooya	*Harper*
Tchinka. A Merchant	*Sgt Sowerby*
Nanooya. His Favourite Wife	*Weston*
The Cobbler	*Lt Smith*

10 pm: The Living Cinema

The Lady	*Sgt Sowerby*
The Lover	*A. N. Poole*
The Jealous Husband	*A. M. Burdock*

God Save the King

But, as this programme for a camp entertainment shows, life at North Camp was not all rifle drill and bayonet practice. There was an amphitheatre made of tiered wooden benches, for religious services, boxing matches and light entertainment.

Notes & sources

British Medical Journal, 22 August 1903, pp 441-2. (The London Volunteer Camp at Seaford)

Carter 1917 (life at North Camp)

Contemporary newspapers.

Newhaven & Seaford Telegraph, 16 May 1910

Letters to Fred Lambe from Mr and Mrs Richard Frederic Lambe in 1915 and 1919

Letters to Mrs Davis from Fred Lambe written in 1987, 1988 and 1989
Letter to Ogden from B. L. Lawrence written in 1914
Penny Illustrated Newspaper, 3 June 1876 (ballooning)
Penny Illustrated Newspaper, 26 October 1895. A veteran aeronaut; a chat
 with Mr Henry Coxwell, author of *A Knight of the Air*.
UU (Edwardian Blatchington)

Chapter 13
Pleased as Punch

Two men, one grave

The story circles back once more to St Peter's. Buried in the churchyard are the ashes of 'F. Anstey', the pen name of Thomas Anstey Guthrie. He was born in 1856, the year of George Meredith's unhappy stay with his wife at the house on the beach. Anstey too was a man of letters, though of a far less serious sort. He was born in Kensington, educated at King's College School in the Strand and Trinity Hall, Cambridge, and called to the bar in 1880.

The huge popular success of his story *Vice Versa*, published in 1882, made his reputation instantly as a humourist, and an original one at that. In 1883 he published a serious novel, *The Giant's Robe*, but in spite of its quality he was seen by readers as a comic writer. His reputation in this lighter genre was confirmed by *The Black Poodle* in 1884, *The Tinted Venus* in 1885 and *A Fallen Idol* in 1886.

Guthrie became a major figure on the staff of the magazine *Punch*, and particularly well-known for his humorous parodies of a reciter's stock-piece. Perhaps the best of these is *Burglar Bill*.

Through a window in the attic
Brawny Burglar Bill has crept;
Seeking stealthily a chamber
Where the jewellery is kept. . .

Several of his stories were adapted for the stage or cinema; *Vice Versa* has been filmed several times.

In his autobiography, Guthrie described himself as an 'uncomely, undersized Cockney youth'. In spite of these several handicaps, he met an interesting selection of literary late Victorians: Browning, Tennyson, Swinburne and Meredith. He went to parties with the likes of William Morris, Edward Poynter and Burne-Jones. At one of these he met Meredith, then an old man who expected to deliver monologues uninterrupted. He was privileged, he thought, to be invited to visit Meredith on his own at the old man's house, but when he called, and told the maid who he was, he heard Meredith inside saying, 'Guthrie? Guthrie? Never heard of him.' Guthrie not surprisingly took fright and left.

J. K. Stephen, known to Guthrie as Jim, amused himself by writ-

Thomas Anstey Guthrie

ing his friends facetious epitaphs. Guthrie challenged him, knowing that he would be unable to find a rhyme for 'Guthrie'. 'Perfectly easy,' said Jim. ' Here you are!' And there it was in an instant:

> *Here lies all that doth re-*
> *Main of Mr Guthrie.*

He felt that, when the time came, he could want no better epitaph.

Until recently both Mr Guthrie and his epitaph were hard to find. He lived in Holland Park Road in London, which is where he died on 5 March 1934, yet his ashes are buried in St Peter's churchyard. To the west of the tower is the grave of George Millar of Lincolns Inn. The headstone tells us that George was a barrister who died in 1889 at the age of 34. His widow added the famous line from Shelley's *Adonais* - about Keats, who also died young - 'He has outsoared the shadow of our night'. But at the foot of the grave, hidden under an overgrowing hydrangea until I cleared it, is an additional stone which reads, 'Also his friend and brother-in-law Thomas Anstey Guthrie ('F. Anstey') b. 8th August 1856 d. 10th March 1934.' Instead of the J. K. Stephen witticism, Eric - I assume it was Eric - added the comment that his uncle had 'A nature whose love was unselfish and chivalrous.' This was a quote from the closing sentence of *The Giant's Robe*. In spite of the long interval between their deaths, Millar and Guthrie were contemporaries. The shared grave nevertheless invites further explanation. Two schoolfriends who died 45 years apart?

George Millar was not only at school with Guthrie: they studied law together at Cambridge and shared chambers in Carey Street as young barristers. It was Millar who, in a spirit of true friendship, encouraged Guthrie to follow his muse. Guthrie had his novel *Vice Versa* accepted by a publisher just at the time when he was called to the bar. As an undergraduate, Guthrie had discovered he had a flair for comic writing and he wanted above all to write. He was beset by an irrepressible facetiousness, and the law was not the best arena for this. George Millar encouraged him to face down his family's expectations - and ditch law in favour of writing. The decision was vindicated almost immediately by the huge success of *Vice Versa*. It became, as Guthrie playfully commented, 'a best seller – the kind of book it does not do not to have read.'

Millar and Guthrie remained friends and Millar married Guthrie's younger sister Edith. In the spring of 1889 they were staying in Marlow to-gether, the three of them, for the rowing, when Guthrie suddenly noticed how ill Millar looked. He had to leave George and Edith to go on *Punch* business to the Paris Exhibition, and when he returned it seemed that Millar had recovered. But later that summer it became obvious that Millar was seriously ill. Guthrie's brother Leonard was a medic, and he diagnosed a tumour. Millar was taken down to Seaford by Guthrie and his brothers, and they were visited there by a specialist who confirmed Leonard's diagnosis.

That summer, Guthrie and Millar walked for the last time together to 'the beautiful churchyard at Blatchington', doubtless both knowing that this was where George was shortly to be laid to rest. George Millar died just a week later in Edith's arms, and he was buried in the beautiful churchyard. Old Cambridge friends gathered with Guthrie and his sister beside his grave. 'We all felt that we were saying farewell to the truest friend, the noblest and most lovable nature, we had been privileged to know.'

George died leaving a two-year-old son called Eric. Eric was not only fatherless: he had no real opportunity to get to know his father. Guthrie, who had no children and remained unmarried, assumed a very special role in his nephew's life. He introduced Eric to many of his literary friends and suggested to M. R. James, one of his cycling companions, that James might use his influence to get Eric a job at the British Museum. When this was achieved, Guthrie marked the occasion by giving Eric enough money to buy a fourteenth century manuscript.

A 1947 film of Guthrie's book

Eric was deeply interested in manuscripts, and already had a collection of his uncle's work. He went on to become Keeper of Manuscripts at the British Museum in the 1940s.

In his last years, Guthrie poured all of his affection into his dog, a Cairn called Mac. His great hope was that he would not outlive Mac. Anstey Guthrie died of pneumonia at Holland Park in London on 10 March 1934 – and the dog lived on for a year. When Guthrie died, what could be more natural than for Eric to arrange for the ashes of the surrogate father who had done so much for him to be buried with the natural father whom he had never known? Eric had two fathers, two fathers who belonged in the same grave.

Cheer up, everybody

Another comic writer who worked in London but developed a Blatchington connection was F. W. Thomas, a prolific contributor to *The Star*. From 1912 until 1945 he produced a stream of sparklingly inventive humorous stories and poems. Born in Hackney in 1882, he first worked as a commercial clerk, trying his hand at writing while out of work in 1905. He sent off some pieces for publication, his first being *On Getting the Sack*, published in the *Morning Leader* on 28 October 1905. His second, with equal appropriateness, was *On Looking for Work*. His pieces were witty but honest portrayals of the plight of the ordinary working man, and still recognizable a hundred years later.

He joined the staff of *The Star* in Bouverie Street in London in May 1912. He produced a book containing a selection of his stories in 1917, *Extra Turns*, which was very successful. His early stories are drawn from everyday life in London, with recognizable stock city characters, like Mr Grindle the cobbler and Pamela the society girl with an affected way of speaking. Later he set nearly all his stories in the countryside, in a rural England that was vanishing and about village rustics that no longer exist. Another collection of his stories followed in 1932, *Windfalls*. He managed to make his observations funny, without ever repeating jokes, always managing to surprise. Out of the blue he commented that some singers' high notes are so high that they have snow on them all year round.

In 1922, he started collaborating with the cartoonist David Low in the series *Low and I*. It was a weekly column about their visits to various London tourist attractions. There was a good deal of tension between the two, as Low considered himself an underrated genius, while Thomas was nine years older, a native Londoner, and naturally expected to take the lead in these assignments. But a friendship gradually developed as they both approached their work with 'boyish glee', as Low described it. If Low was off sick or on holiday, Thomas produced his own cartoons. This collaboration led to two collections in book form. The collaboration ended when Low went to work for the *Evening Standard*. Thomas was invited too, but decided to stay with *The Star*.

Some of his pieces were more serious. He wrote a piece called *At Sea with Kipling* in 1936, a reminiscence of a voyage with Kipling to Buenos Aires. They were not friends; Thomas had stumbled onto the passenger list by chance. The voyage was arranged by *The Star* as a sabbatical leave to help him get over the death of his eleven-year-old son Peter; he was also ill with overwork. Kipling was initially irritated to find himself button-holed by a journalist, but later relaxed and they had several conversations as they travelled the length of the Atlantic.

Thomas did not take the classic English rural idyll very seriously. He was a Londoner and he thought a great many villages were too pretty-pretty, with their 'Ye Olde' village shops. But he was a lover of open spaces, gardens, birds and country pubs.

In spite of the enormous popularity of his writings, F. W. Thomas was a very private man, keeping his family life to himself. In an interview he said, 'People come to the office to see me sometimes and are disappointed. I believe they have expected to see a man with a red nose and a humorous cast of countenance - a sort of cross between Harry Lauder and George Robey - and instead of that have found a serious-looking young gentleman. It takes quite a serious man to be a humourist.' J. B. Priestley was a great admirer of Thomas. He said in 1925, 'The phonetic spelling itself is a triumph of observation. Writing of this kind needs something more than a comic fancy, it needs a man who keeps his eyes and ears open and has observation and memory at the service of his calling. It needs, in short, a serious writer. That, I think, is the secret of Mr. Thomas's success as a humorous journalist. He is seriously occupied with the business of writing. He gives his work, however light it may be, however extravagant, the flavour of literature. He is, like all successful humorists, a sober craftsman and a serious man.' Priestley's piece was entitled *The Gravity of Mr F. W. Thomas*.

Thomas's family originally came from East Sussex, and he always felt the pull of Sussex as a place to live. Even some of the early writings hint at what he described as 'the call of the Downs'. In 1929, and now in his fifties, he stopped resisting the pull and moved to East Blatchington, where he was able to enjoy walking up into the Downs and along the coast. And he was able to work at home, writing in his country retreat and mailing his copy to *The Star* and the *Daily News* in London.

In 1939, Thomas took a break from writing stories for *The Star* to write a series with illustrator Leslie Grimes, *F. W. Thomas and Grimes at Home with the Militia*. They visited a different army barracks

F. W. Thomas

each week, falling in with the troops and sharing the daily routine. This series was stopped on the outbreak of war. Then a collaboration with *The Star*'s sports cartoonist Roy Ullyett, in *Low and I* style, started and just as abruptly stopped when Ullyett was called up. In 1940, Thomas used his *Cock-Eyed-Corner* column to comment on the false information given out by the Nazis. He had visited Germany in 1938 and saw for himself the persecution of the Jews. He was working for a paper that had taken a firmly anti-Hitler stance, and as early as 1933. Thomas was not afraid to ridicule Goebbels and consequently found that like David Low he, Thomas, was on Hitler's extermination list.

Thomas's series *Coastal Zone* was his swan song with *The Star*. These were stories set in and round East Blatchington. With his usual humour, Thomas depicted the feel of a country community suddenly caught up in war - the interplay between local residents and billeted troops: a new world of sentries, army bases, barbed-wire, bunkers, coastal defences, rationing, queuing for meat. As usual, it is hard to be sure which bits are real-life observation and which are invented. Made-up names were used for both people and places, because of the war-time obsession with security, but this was Thomas's style anyway. The last *Coastal Zone* story was *Miss Pringle and the Major* (2 March 1945), a serious piece in which Thomas gently rebuked the British for being pessimistic. Some of H. G. Wells's predictions had come true, but many had not. 'So cheer up, everybody.' He was right. The war was almost over. So was his association with *The Star*. He left quietly, without leave-taking, and with typical modesty and privacy.

He went on writing, reviews and articles for *John O'London's Weekly*, at Rosecroft in Firle Road, his home for over 30 years. After his wife died in 1961, he moved to Old Heathfield where he died in 1966 at the age of 84.

Notes & sources

Guthrie 1936 (Guthrie)
Kelly's Directories, 1934, 1951 (Thomas's address)
Simms 2010 (Thomas)
Vice Versa was dramatized and made into a film, and more than once. The 1947 World Films production by Peter Ustinov had a cast that included Roger Livesey and Anthony Newley as the role-reversing father and son, as well as Kay Walsh, James Robertson Justice, Petula Clark, Kynaston Reeves, James Hayter, Peter Jones and Alfie Bass.

Chapter 14
Old cottages on Blatchington Hill

Development

At the turn of the twentieth century, several of the local farming families were making money by asset-stripping. At nearby Sutton, the Harison family sold their land in 1897 to a Mr Hutchings, who promptly developed it into a housing estate. And Robert Lambe, as we saw in Chapter 10, was doing the same thing over a period in Blatchington, partly through his Seaford West Company. This development company encouraged people to buy plots for building by posting ads in the local press. This one from the *Newhaven & Seaford Telegraph* of 1910 is typical:

> *The Seaford West Estate. Applications invited for all classes of private residences, schools, boarding houses and shops, which will be erected to tenant's requirements. Freehold plots for sale. Land on building lease, near golf links [ie in Blatchington], on Marine Parade, near Station. Apply, stating require- ments, the Secretary, The Seaford West Co., Ltd, Seaford, Sussex.*

Blatchington village was engulfed by the northward expansion of Seaford in the twentieth century, yet it retained its identity largely because many of the old village houses and cottages survived, clustered round St Peter's church. They continue to give the village its character and show its original linear shape. Every village had its pub, and Blatchington's was The Star Inn. It is still there, though no longer a pub, on the corner of Homefield Road and Blatchington Hill.

The Star House

The flint and brick building dates from the late seventeenth or early eighteenth century, but like the other houses on Blatchington Hill it may replace an earlier building on the site. The present building has been converted into a private house, comprising the flint-walled inn and two adjoining semi-detached cottages. The 1913 plan of the East Blatchington Estate shows The Star House and the two adjacent square cottages as separate but adjoining properties, but by then the map was already out of date; the conversion was carried out in 1910.

The garden and south aspect of The Star House.

The original Star Inn, built in or before 1723, is a well-built flint structure with red brick dressings; it has a small cellar. The weather-boarded section with conspicuous gables is the conversion of the two cottages. These were bought early in the twentieth century and joined to The Star to make a single large house, which it has remained for the last hundred years. This was done shortly after Homefield Road was created. The entrance to the pub and the cottages was on the south side, as shown on the cover picture.

The inn originally had a red brick chimney running up its north wall, four large sash windows on the upper floor fronting Blatchington Hill, and floors at different levels from today. The two adjacent cottages originally had only a ridge roof with no gables. In 1910, the Homefield Road frontage was redesigned, with gables added to the two cottages, the north chimney removed, and the fenestration on the Blatchington Hill end changed; the ghosts of the original four upstairs windows can still be seen.

The panelled front door dates from the eighteenth century. There was a well about two metres from the house in the garden to the south, an area that was originally a cobbled courtyard, and the cobbles are still there, underneath a foot of soil.

There are three plaques cemented into The Star House walls, representing landmarks in the building's history. The one over the front door (the exterior of the inner front door lintel, not visible from the street) reads 'WSA 1723'. Between 1580 and 1800 it was common to put a plaque with the date and the house-owner's initials on the wall of a house, to commemorate the building or some other important stage in the life of a house.

On the south wall of The Star Inn is another plaque, which reads 'WM 1789'. This appears to be a plaque that has been rescued and re-located. My guess is that it originally belonged on the pair of cottages. There was a court case regarding a house that was built illegally somewhere on the east side of Blatchington Hill – in 1788. A 1789 plaque would be what one might expect if the illicit building work took place in 1788, perhaps after compensation had been settled. A third plaque marks the most recent transformation of the three properties in 1910.

The Star Inn was the scene of one of many turbulent episodes in Seaford's past as a 'rotten borough': and it was a night of what must have been exceptional trade. In the 1747 election, the Pelham family's (Whig) candidates were William Pitt and William Hay. A feast was laid on by the Pelhamites at Bishopstone Place for William Pitt, and for all the local gentlemen and farmers who might be persuaded to vote for him. After being wined and dined, at daybreak the guests were taken in carriages to Seaford town hall to vote. The Gages' (Tory) candidates were William Gage and the Earl of Middlesex. The Gages canvassed and entertained the lesser householders who were eligible to vote. They were excluded from the Flag & Gun and other Pelhamite pubs in Seaford, and resorted to going out to Blatchington to buy their prospective voters drinks at the Star Inn; the drinks were taken to a barn rented from the bailiff, John Fletcher, for consumption. Pitt and Hay won the election. The Gages complained about unfair practices, but their complaint was voted down in the House of Commons 247 votes to 96.

A 1920s reference to The Star House cellar seems to be the origin of the indestructible legend that a tunnel connects the house to the rectory. The connection is made by the sentence structure: 'there have been rumours that in the early nineteenth century this cellar and that at the rectory were more than once used by smugglers.' The two separate cellars are mentioned in the same sentence and joined by a common purpose. From there it was a

The garden and south aspect of The Star House. The two cottages.

short step to imagining that the two cellars were physically connected. In the 1970s the boys of Blatchington Court School picked up a variation on the story, in which a tunnel joined The Star House and St Peter's, and decided to dig for it in the school drive (now a footpath) between the church and the Old Rectory. They did not find it.

Just to the west of the church tower is a row of three headstones. The first is for John Washer, who died at 76 in 1794, together with his wife Sarah, who died five years before him. The second is for Elizabeth Washer, who died aged 70 in 1830. The third reads, 'In memory of William Washer, departed this life Sept 17th, 1809 aged 61 years.'

William Washer was a victualler, who lived and worked at East Blatchington; he was the landlord of The Star Inn and a churchwarden. He was also in a small way a man of property, with a house and a workshop in Lewes. The day after William Washer died, on 17 September 1809, *The Sussex Weekly Advertiser* described the circumstances of his death.

'On Thursday last as Mr Washer, master of the public house in Bletchington Street, was returning home from Alfriston, on a blind pony which had safely carried him for many years, he missed his road on Hindover Hill and rode over the brink of a chalk pit, at the bottom of which the unfortunate

man was, on Sunday morning, found alive and apparently sensible, but without the power of speech or motion, having lain in that dreadful situation 36 hours.

He was taken up and conveyed home, where he languished till yesterday morning and then expired. Being enabled to speak before he died, he was sensible to the situation; he called out for assistance, but could make no one hear him. The pony, though he escaped unhurt, did not quit the pit, but took his post at the entrance of it, and there remained stationary, as the signal of his master's distress, until he was in consequence discovered, as above stated; but unhappily too late to be of any avail.'

On 21 May 1832 The Star Inn was put up for sale. The press notice gives details of the outbuildings.

The Star Inn: a copyhold house with stable, chaise house, outhouse, well, pighouse, large yard, large garden and freehold field, about ½ acre, large carpenter's shop, a roomy yard.'

The Star House from Homefield Road

On the south side of The Star House was an entrance to the large cobbled yard, which in turn gave access to the original front doors of the pub and the two cottages beyond. It also gave access to the Widows' Cottages, a double-square single-storey building on the south side of the yard. In the nineteenth century these were the last buildings in the village on the east side Blatchington Hill – apart from what was later called 'Bravery's farm' on the site of La Soldanelle, No 2 Blatchington Hill.

The outbuilding in the centre of the back garden of The Star House is the inner one of the two Widows' Cottages. In the road wall it is possible to see the outline of a blocked window and the corners of the outer cottage. This represents the original end wall of the Widows' Cottages. Each cottage was a perch square.

Glebe Cottage and Rectory Cottage

Glebe Cottage and Rectory Cottage, two more flint and brick buildings, were run as a single property in the nineteenth century. Although the fronts of the two cottages now look quite different from each other; Rectory Cottage has been altered, and the style would originally have been like that of Glebe Cottage. Both are built of well-coursed flint cobbles from the beach, with red brick quoining. Both originally had corniced gables that extended just above the roof. This design feature had a practical purpose - to prevent the wind from getting under the roof and tearing it off. It was removed from Glebe Cottage during a twentieth century re-roofing. Allowing for these changes, the style of the façades is so similar to that of The Gables and The Star House as to imply that they are all of similar date, 1690-1730.

Two blocked doorways on the ground floor show how the Glebe Cottage entrance passage was connected with the front and back rooms of Rectory Cottage. Another blocked doorway on the first floor connected the landings. The joint property accommodated two households. This may be when the property was run as an alehouse.

The name Glebe Cottage has it origins in 1892. When the rector, Revd Robert Dennis, made his will in 1860, he bequeathed all his property to Elizabeth Dennis. Nearly everything he had, after all, had come to him through his marriage to Elizabeth. After he died on 17 February 1892, she decided to provide a glebe to augment the rectory and benefice.

In November 1892 Elizabeth Dennis signed an agreement with her husband's successor, the Revd Arthur Richardson, and the Bishop of Chichester to create a glebe. Elizabeth inherited the cottage from her father, John King, who is known to have owned it in the 1840s. Elizabeth and her husband sold it to Robert Lambe in December 1877 - and bought it back from him the same day.

The 1892 conveyance transferred to the Rector 'that cottage in two tenements'. The implication is that William Reed and his large family lived in Glebe Cottage and first James Kennard, then Thomas Stevens, lived in Rectory Cottage.

But village families changed through time. By 1881, William and Elizabeth Reed, then in their mid-sixties, had only one of their twelve children still living with them, their 28-year-old son Leonard. Instead they had three other people either living or staying with them. One was the Reeds' 9-year-old grandson, Charles Collet. Another was Easter Arnald, a visiting schoolteacher. The third, hardest of all to understand, was the 2-year-old James Glidden, who was a visitor from London; there are many things a census does not explain.

Glebe Cottage & Rectory Cottage

The Kennards next door were a younger and smaller family. James was 35 and his wife Harriet was 38, he born at Firle, she at Fairlight. They had five young children, George, Mabel, Harriett, Charles and Charlotte, aged from 8 months to 12 years.

The building as a whole was given to the diocese to generate rent income for the Rectory. But Elizabeth Dennis's generous gift was sold on. In July 1924, the Bishop and Richardson's successor as rector, Revd Henry Martley, sold Glebe Cottage to Dick Paterson for £750.

The cottage was immediately sold on to Henry William Drew, a surgeon and property speculator.

The ground floor Rectory Cottage consists of two square rooms, separated by a small square lobby and a transverse staircase.

Blatchington Street in 1960, with Glebe Cottage and Rectory Cottage on the right. The Old Rectory was covered in Virginia creeper at that time. The young woman appears to be heading for Rectory Cottage.

The Gables

The Gables is the fourth of the flint and brick houses dating from 1690-1730. In the 1840s the building belonged to John King, who let it to William Catt. Whether at that time the building was a single residence, or two or three cottages is not known. At one time it was used as a village smithy. After John King's death, ownership passed to Elizabeth Dennis, who decided on her husband's death to give the property to the diocese, along with Glebe and Rectory Cottages and a three-acre meadow at the bottom of Blatchington Hill.

Robert Lambe bought the entire Blatchington Court Estate from Robert and Elizabeth Dennis in 1877 but, as we have seen, Robert Lambe had insufficient funds for the transaction. He had to mortgage and borrow, and he had to sell some of the estate on as quickly as possible. One odd thing that happened is that he immediately sold back bits of the estate to the vendors, Robert and Elizabeth Dennis. He must also have sold them back the lower part of The Lawn, in effect the garden of Blatchington Court, otherwise it could not have been in Elizabeth's gift in 1892, though it is not clear why the Dennises would have wanted it, other than to save it from building development. The 1892 indenture states that Robert Lambe sold Rectory and Glebe Cottages back to the Dennises – on the *same day* that he bought the estate as a whole from them, 20

The Gables from the courtyard

December 1877.

The Dennises evidently let The Gables, as they also let Glebe and Rectory Cottages. One in a series of tenants was Mary Shelton, and in 1892 the tenants were William Jordan and Thomas Williams, implying that the house was then divided into two cottages. The design of the building is puzzling. The three gables suggest three separate cottages, each with two bedrooms above and a living room and kitchen below. The first gable, next to the road, has this two-up, two-down layout, though there is no sign of the staircase. It also has a cellar beneath what was once the living room, with trap-door access from the original kitchen. The rest of the house has been altered to a point where it is hard to reconstruct the original layout. The second gable has a fine big inglenook fireplace that appears to be original. The third gable has a smaller fireplace in a similar position, with a substantial bread oven beside it.

The middle gable is one perch wide, the flanking gables slightly narrower. The early eighteenth century building we see today replaces an earlier building on the site. The chalk-floored cellar beneath the first gable, next to the road, is 16 feet long and 7 feet 6 inches wide, and none of its walls match the walls of the house above. The cellar has only 5 feet of headroom and its wall-tops are broken off 6 inches below that. There are the remains of the lower part of a blocked window in the north wall of the cellar; this must have been the outer wall of the building, yet it is 7 feet in from the present external wall. The cellar belongs to an older and smaller building than the present house.

Three cottages? Two? Or one? It may be that the building was once a farmhouse. A predecessor on the site stood at the roadside end of a medieval cultivation strip a chain wide and running out roughly at right angles to Blatchington Hill across Home Furlong, parallel with The Star Inn strip. William Figg's 1818 map implies this, though by then three neighbouring strips (those running east from behind The Gables, The Cottage and Glebe and Rectory Cottages) had been run together to make a single broad strip. So, by 1818, the consolidation of holdings was well under way.

The outbuilding, facing the road across the paved courtyard, is brick-built in Flemish bond with dark headers. This contrasts with the main building, which is coursed beach flint with brick corners. The outbuilding was apparently built in the nineteenth century as a stable, with horses below and hayloft above. At the turn of the twentieth century it was a stalled cowshed with fodder store above. Both buildings seem to have changed their use several times. The Gables was a village shop for a time.

The Church did not keep Mrs Dennis's gift for long. Only six years later, in December 1898, the diocese sold The Gables on for £600 to two sisters, Emma and Ethel de St Croix, who happened to be Arthur Richardson's sisters-in-law.

Just behind The Gables is the School House, which has its present-day entrance on Upper Belgrave Road. The original single-

The path to the School House

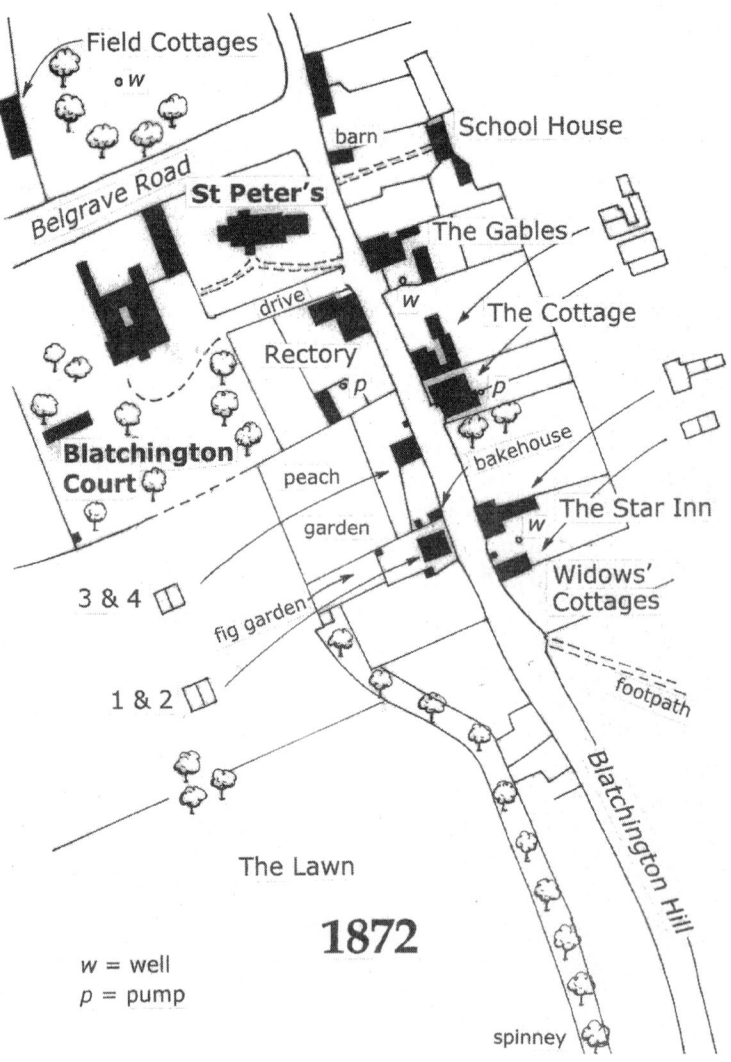

Field Cottages
w

barn

School House

Belgrave Road

St Peter's

The Gables

drive

The Cottage

w

Rectory

p

p

Blatchington Court

bakehouse

peach

garden

The Star Inn

w

3 & 4

fig garden

Widows' Cottages

1 & 2

footpath

Blatchington Hill

The Lawn

1872

w = well
p = pump

spinney

The older buildings on Blatchington Hill and Belgrave Road, as they stood in 1872. The white outlines show how some of the buildings were divided into more than one property or tenement, as in 1, 2, 3 & 4 Blatchington Street. Blatchington Street began at the Widows' Cottages and continued up past the church into Firle Road. The peach garden, fig garden and probably the next enclosure to the south were walled gardens attached to Blatchington Court; they were linked by interconnecting doors.

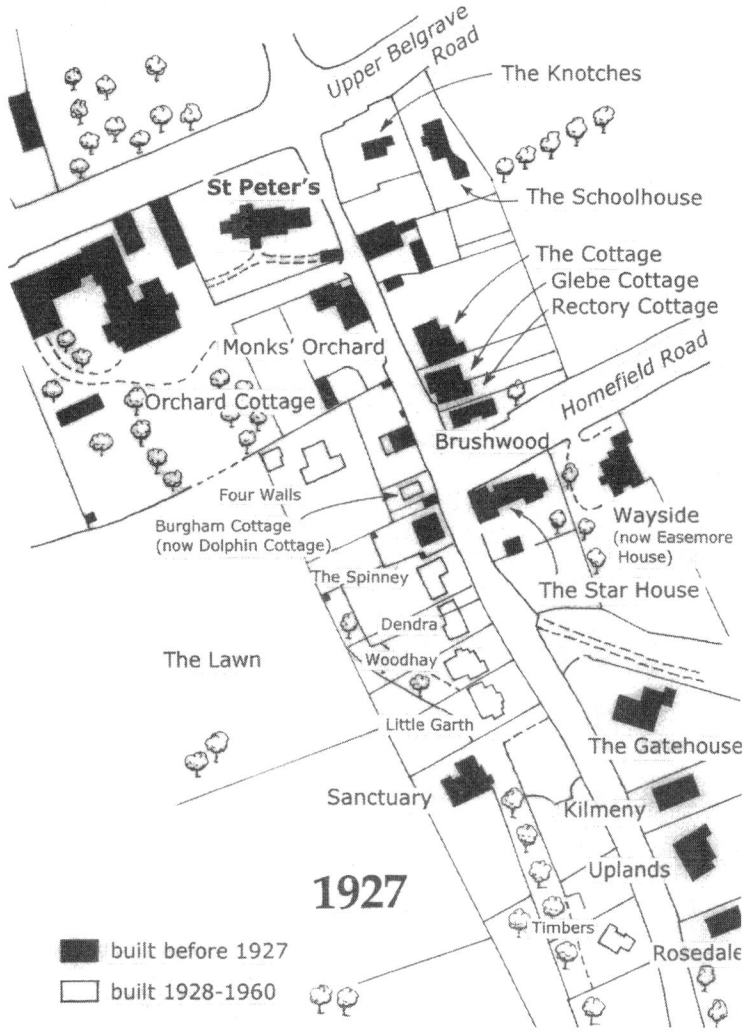

Blatchington Hill as built up in 1927. The Knotches, Wayside and five sub-stantial houses on the Hill have been added. The white-outlined properties show infilling and suburbanization in the 1930s, 50s and 60s. Bryn and The Well House were subsequently added between Sanctuary and Timbers.

storey building has been preserved and ingeniously modified to turn it into a dwelling. The Old School House was formerly the village hall and school room. It has 18-inch-thick flint walls with brick quoins and a tiled roof. Until a hundred years ago, access to the School House was from the west, from near the top of Blatchington Hill, and by way of a path across a paddock.

The Cottage

The Cottage, 30 Blatchington Hill, stands close to the centre of the village, a stone's throw from the church. It was built in 1908 on the site of a cluster of older dwellings.

At the northern end of the flint road wall in front of the property there is a sandstone plaque about 15cm long and 10cm high, with the date 1677 carved in relief. It has a raised border and numerals in authentic seventeenth century style. Near the southern end of the wall there is a second stone plaque, slightly smaller, but carved in the same style with the letters GW. No doubt these formed a pair, dating from the late seventeenth century, and origin-

ally mortared into the front of one of the earlier cottages on the site. The only person living in the village at the time with the right initials was George Wood, who was in his forties and likely to be the occupier and possibly owner.

George Wood, the son of George Wood, was born and baptized in Blatchington in 1629 and was married twice. By Anne, his first wife, he had a son and a daughter, William and Anne, who died in infancy in 1659 and 1663. His wife died in 1665 and he re-married immediately. By his second wife, Jone or Jane, he had five children. Of these, three daughters, Elizabeth, Ann and Mary, died in infancy in 1667, 1669 and 1671, and another was stillborn in 1672. Joane, who was born in 1674, survived. George was 48 years old in 1677, when he had the Cottage built (or rebuilt) and it is probable that he died there at the age of 56 in 1685, after losing two wives and six children. He was buried in St Peter's churchyard. The land George Wood was working in Blatchington was holden of the Manor of Alciston, so he was the successor of those Alciston tenants and copyholders of the middle ages.

'GW 1677' is likely to record the building or making-over of one in the sequence of cottages that have been built on this plot. When the 1677 cottage was demolished, perhaps in the nineteenth century, the materials were recycled, and built into the walls of new houses or boundary walls. Probably some of the flint and brick in the road wall came from George Wood's cottage.

On the inside of the same road wall is a third plaque, dated 1726. This is incised instead of embossed, and carved (less skilfully) in a different style. The upper part of the plaque has three symbols, a carefully inscribed equilateral triangle at the top, an indecipherable symbol that may be a kind of swastika on the left and a flower on the right, and possibly another symbol to the right of that. The triangle could be a Christian symbol, representing the Trinity, or

The 1726 plaque

an alchemical symbol, representing Ignis, fire. If the latter, the 'flower' symbol might represent Mercury. Alternatively, the flower may be a decoration between two degraded letters, the owner's initials.

This 1726 plaque with its strange ciphers would seem to be all that recognizably remains of another early cottage standing on the site. As with the 1677 cottage, some of its wall flints may have found their way into the road wall, and into the fabric of the new house. The date plaques were evidently rescued when the two earlier cottages were pulled down. Someone with a feeling for the past saved the date plaques and incorporated them, for posterity, in a rebuilding of the road wall.

The ownership history of the plot, so far as we have it, is unusual. In 1881 Lydia Pelham was described as a widow of 86, living at Blatchington with an 83-year-old nurse called Easter Geering. The Cottage plot was said in 1892 to be owned by Lydia Pelham, but she had died eight years earlier at the age of 89, so that information was out of date. Putting that to one side, Lydia was said to be the owner of The Cottage plot, while the properties to north and south (The Gables and the joint property consisting of Glebe and Rectory Cottages) were owned by Mr and Mrs Dennis. How did Lydia Pelham come to own this, when everything else in the area was owned by either Robert Lambe or the Dennises?

The plot was an ownership anomaly fifty years earlier. The Tithe Map of 1843 shows distinct blocks of property ownership in the village. John King owned the northern half and let it; he owned the south-west quadrant, Blatchington Court and its gardens, and occupied that himself. That left the south-east quadrant, which was owned by John King and let to the Catts. The rector was regarded as owning the church and rectory. That left just one property, The Cottage. The Tithe Map described it loosely as 'cottage and garden' (which could as easily mean 'cottages and gardens') owned and occupied by the 61-year-old William Alce Junior.

William was baptized at St Peter's in September 1782, but there is no record of his marrying or dying in the village. Just two other things are known about him. One is that his parents were Abraham and Sarah Alce; the other is that they died at the same time, and were buried in the same grave on the same day, 11 December 1803, perhaps of an infectious disease, perhaps in some sort of accident: the parish register does not tell us. If William Alce inherited this substantial property near the centre of the village from his parents, he did so at the age of 21.

The independent ownership of this plot may help to explain the marked difference in the style of building that took place on it. To each side were built substantial flint-and-brick cottages in the early eighteenth century, and they were maintained as such with minor alterations right through the next 200 years. The Cottage plot seems to have been developed with varying numbers of small cottages on it that were knocked down and replaced from time to time, suggesting that the standard of design and building may have been low. The final replacement happened in 1908.

A very small cottage stood on the site of the front garden of the present house in 1873, at which time there was a second building of equal size immediately behind it, presumably another cottage, though positioned awkwardly. The UU manuscript describes 'two or three very small cottages abutting onto the street'. The Tithe Map of 1843 shows these buildings as a single block, though this may not be accurate; in another part of the map the building that contained the pair of cottages, Farm Cottage and Rookery Cottage, is shown several metres too long.

An undated map, probably based on a 1900 survey, has a different arrangement. This shows, in more detail than any of the other maps, a rectangular house at the back, parallel to the road and with either a second cottage or an outbuilding built onto it. It also shows two cottages side by side on the road and a connecting structure between the back and front properties on the Glebe Cottage side. The detailing of this map implies that the structures really did exist as shown, but it is hard to believe that as many as three or even four dwellings were packed into the space today occupied by one house and its small front garden. The 1913 Plan of the East Blatchington Estate shows the overall footprint of the buildings in the same way as the undated plan, but without the property divisions. Whether these changes represent actual changes to the property or variations in surveying accuracy is hard to tell.

The two, three or four tiny cottages crammed into the plot had in any case by then been demolished, as a single substantial new house, the present one, was built on the site in 1908.

A similar property ownership anomaly is visible in the 1867 Kelly's directory, where the 'principal residents' were listed as the Revd Robert Dennis, Dr Tyler Smith, William Lambe and - *James Alce*. Robert Dennis was a major landowner - he owned Blatchington Court as well as the rectory – and Tyler Smith was his tenant. William Lambe was the principal tenant farmer in the parish. This leaves James Alce who, although described as 'shoemaker and farmer', was apparently a landowner. He was also the parish clerk. The implication is that he had inherited The Cottage from William Alce, though I have not been able to establish their relationship. James Alce was born in 1802, the son of James and Catherine Alce, and died in 1875 at the age of 73. He appears in the 1851 census return as 49 years old, unmarried, and living with his 55-year-old single housekeeper, a woman called Siddy Pelham. The Pelham connection is interesting, as in the 1890s the property is described as *Lydia* Pelham's.

Farm Cottage and Rookery Cottage

Farm Cottage and Rookery Cottage originally formed a symmetrical pair of semi-detached cottages with a pyramid-shaped roof sloping up to a central chimney stack. All the existing photographs of the two cottages, going back to 1890, show the walls rendered. The render may be original, put on when the cottages were new in the eighteenth century, or it may have been added in the nineteenth century – as at Twyn House – to cover up a flint building with red brick dressings that either needed repointing or was considered unfashionable. The cottages may therefore once have looked more like Glebe Cottage in terms of materials and finish. The render

Blatchington Hill in 1931. Rookery Cottage (Caroline Reed's home) and Farm Cottage (Robert Russell's) on the left, five years before Underdown's make-over. In the distance on the right, The Gables (home of Ethel and Emma de St Croix).

was probably added to Twyn House in 1810, which gives an indication of a possible early nineteenth century date for the rendering of Farm and Rookery Cottages.

The front doors were near the outer corners of the south wall, with living-room windows between. There was one window upstairs, front and back, in each cottage, each to light a bedroom. The original windows were sideways sash windows.

A pair of semi-detached privies stood in the back garden, one for each cottage; the building is still there. The original gardens were generous in size, but both front and back gardens were truncated by developments in the 1930s, when the cottages were owned by George and Amelia Woolgar. Farm Cottage remains very much in its original condition, but Rookery Cottage was doubled in size. The extension was done in a late English vernacular style, with red-brick ground floor and clay tile-hung upper floor. At the front the upper floor jetties over the ground floor. At the same time a new chimney was added, in the centre of the new house, and the roof over the two cottages was completely reshaped in the spring of 1937 (April 1937 was inscribed on one of the roof timbers). Over the jetty is a half-hip gable, Sussex barn style.

The remodelling was done by the local architect, Alwyn Underdown, who designed many houses in the Eastbourne-Seaford area in the 1920s and 1930s, mostly in this style.

In the 1840s, Farm Cottage and Rookery Cottage were owned by John King and let to Edward and William Catt, who probably sublet them to Tide Mill workers. Later in the nineteenth century they reverted, and became tied cottages for employees of Blatchington Court, as they presumably had been in the eighteenth century. Farm Cottage and Rookery Cottage were Nos 3 and 4 of the four cottages, 1-4 Blatchington Street, owned by the squire, Robert Lambe, and subject to probate valuation in 1922 following Lambe's death. The four cottages together were valued at £450.

During the long, slow sell-off of Lambe's estate, George Woolgar bought Rookery Cottage on 1 April 1930.

In 1938-39 George Woolgar had a cottage built on the southern half of the front garden. On 3rd June 1940 he sold the new cottage, Burgham Cottage, later renamed Dolphin Cottage, to Miss Florence Mary Wilcock.

The 58-year-old gardener William Reed was living in Rookery Cottage in 1901. He had been born in Blatchington and his father was William Reed senior, then aged 83 and still living across the road at Glebe Cottage. The father was listed in the 1861 census as a domestic gardener, with his wife Elizabeth and twelve children.

Born in 1818, he was Robert Dennis's gardener and later sexton. William Reed junior was listed in 1861 as born in Blatchington, unmarried, 18 years old and an agricultural labourer; he was one of Mr Dennis's bird-boys. Also living at Rookery Cottage in 1901 was William junior's wife, Caroline, who was 52 and had been born in Hastings. The cottage consisted of just four rooms, two up, two down. The Reeds had Henry Towner living with them, Caroline's 82-year-old widowed uncle, a farm labourer who had lived in Blatchington all his life.

William and Caroline had evidently been living in Rookery Cottage as far back as 1881 – just the two of them – while the next 1881 census entry, which by implication is for Farm Cottage, has Henry Towner, then a 61-year-old agricultural labourer, taking in a lodger, a 16-year-old fireman called James Newton. Many villagers took in lodgers to fill empty beds and bring in additional income. The Knights, William and Miriam, had several children and also four unmarried labourers as lodgers. These were young men aged between 17 and 26, all from Dorset, where the Knights' two youngest children had been born. The Knights moved to Blatchington from Dorset, bringing this small labour force with them. Unfortunately it is not clear which house they were living in. As Henry Towner grew old, he too became a lodger, moving from Farm Cottage next door to Rookery Cottage, to be looked after by his niece.

William Reed senior died in January 1904, aged 86, and some time between then and the outbreak of the First World War William junior died too, as Caroline Reed is recorded as living at Rookery Cottage alone from then on. Mrs Reed was still living at Rookery Cottage in 1930 when Robert Lambe's executors succeeded in selling it to George Woolgar. The documents indicated that Mrs Reed's sitting tenancy was to be respected.

Mrs Reed probably died in 1935. In 1936 Rookery Cottage was empty with Alwyn Underdown undertaking a great deal of work enlarging and improving it, in preparation for the Woolgars moving into it. This was when oak panelling was added to the dining room and the extension was added, doubling the size of the cottage. In the spring of 1937, the roof was reshaped, completing the conversion.

Seagull Cottage

Directly opposite the Homefield Road junction is a small building that looks like a garage, and became one in 1971, but was built as

Seagull Cottage & the bakehouse (now a garage)

the village bakehouse. According to one account of the village the bakehouse, or parish oven, dates from the sixteenth century, but it is not clear from pre-1971 photos why it should be given this very early date. It is assumed that the ovens were used for communal baking – of cakes and loaves. It originally stood in the corner of the front garden of Farm Cottage, with a street door for public access. Building Dolphin Cottage separated the bakehouse from Rookery and Farm Cottages, and the strip of land it stands on has been added to Seagull Cottage.

By the 1960s the village bakehouse was in disrepair; Jean and Bernard Mote, who owned Nos 1 and 2 from 1968, decided to have it made six feet longer and a foot higher, to turn it into a garage. All that survived of the contents are a doorbell on a spring, a peel for sliding loaves into the oven, and a clay pipe. The pipe is a three-inch nose-warmer of a bird's claw design, and probably dates from the late nineteenth century.

The bakehouse, 1936

In 1843 the two cottages were owned by the squire, John King, with the nominal occupiers, William and Edward Catt, in reality sub-letting. The cottages were later acquired by Robert Lambe. The probate valuation following Robert Lambe's death in 1922 groups the cottages with the next pair along the road: 'Freehold cottages. 1, 2, 3 & 4 Blatchington Street, Seaford, Sussex. F. Saunders, T. Stevens, R. H. Russell, Mrs Reed.' In his Will, Robert Lambe left Mr Stevens, his 'late foreman', £20 and Mr Saunders, his groom, the same amount. Robert's widow Elizabeth continued to employ both men. In her will dated 1929, Frederick Saunders (still tenant of No 1) is described as 'my manservant' and Thomas Stephens (tenant of No 2) as 'my late manservant'.

In September 1930, 1 & 2 Blatchington Street were offered for sale, together with the walled lower garden, for £941. There is no sign of a purchaser among the documents, so presumably the cottages were unsold. It took a long time for the executors to sell off the whole of the Lambe estate, and the cottages were overpriced. Eventually, in October 1935, they achieved a sale. Mrs Woolgar, then living at Four Walls, bought the pair of cottages for £500. The cottages were sold with their sitting tenants, Mrs Saunders and Mr Heasman, who paid their rent weekly. The agreement was that Mrs Saunders was to remain tenant of No 1 for her lifetime, so long as she went on paying her three shillings a week rent. An obligation was placed on Mrs Woolgar to maintain the tall western boundary wall to its existing height. This was a stipulation by the proprietresses of the girls' school at Blatchington Court, who were concerned about their school's security.

Mrs Saunders' unmarried daughter took on the tenancy when her mother died, and stayed there until her own death in 1968.

On 10 November 1950, Mrs Woolgar, who was by then living at Rookery Cottage, sold the two cottages for £750 to Mrs Elizabeth Miller of Wakefield, with their sitting tenants, Miss Saunders in No 1 and now Mr Hawley in No 2. Mrs Miller agreed to brick up the door in the north wall of the lower garden through to Four Walls. While Mrs Woolgar owned the two cottages and lived at Four Walls it had presumably been useful for her to retain the door for her own access.

Seaford Town Council decided to rename the street and renumber the houses. Blatchington *Street* had been the village street, beginning where the houses began, with Seagull Cottage, while the tree-lined lane up from the Pond was Blatchington *Hill*. With houses built all down both sides, the distinction in road names was no longer real. It all became Blatchington Hill. Instead of the Motes' cottage being No 2 Blatchington Street, it became No 31 Blatchington Hill. The following year, 1968, Bernard Mote was at last able to buy the house next door, No 1 Blatchington Street or No 29 Blatchington Hill, from Mrs Miller. The original 1 and 2 Blatchington Street were joined to make a single house, Seagull Cottage.

Notes & sources

Dimensions of houses. The following were laid out in units of one chain (4 perches): Blatchington Court (N-S), the older part of Blatchington Court School Chapel (N-S), The Pound (N-S), Field Cottage (N-S). The west side of the churchyard (N-S) is 2 chains. The following were laid out in units of 2 perches: The Star Inn (N-S), Blatchington House (W gable), Old Rectory (E-W), Glebe Cottage plot (N-S). The following were laid out in units of 1 perch: The Star House (E-W), Widows' Cottages (N-S), church tower (N-S).

Wills of Robert and Elizabeth Lambe.

1892 Conveyance for Rectory Cottage.

1892 & 1898 Conveyances for The Gables.

Title deeds for The Gables, Glebe Cottage and Seagull Cottage.

Newhaven & Seaford Telegraph, 26 May 1910.

William Washer's tombstone is unusual; because of the favourable angle of the floodlighting, it can be read most clearly *at night*.

Chapter 15
Village of peace:
Arts & Crafts in Blatchington

From rurality to suburbia

The village remained about the same size through the first three-quarters of the nineteenth century. At the beginning there were 150 people living there, and in 1871 there were 130. But its character was about to change. As neighbouring Seaford expanded, building development increasingly encroached into East Blatchington parish. The population of the parish had grown to 740 by 1901 and this was the moment when the population density of the parish for the first time passed that of England and Wales as a whole. In 1881 there were 0.25 people per acre in the parish, compared with 0.75 for the country as a whole; in 1901 the density was one person per acre for the parish, slightly above that for the country. We can see 1901 as a watershed. Before 1901, East Blatchington was a rural village. From 1901 onwards, it became increasingly suburbanized; we might call it an urban village. The old village at the centre of the parish retained much of its visual character, but it became increasingly surrounded – and invaded – by housing development. By 1921, the population density of the parish reached 2.4 per acre, well over twice the national average density. Blatchington was becoming absorbed in the general growth of Seaford, and it was from then on in danger of losing its separate identity.

The shift from rural to urban can be seen in the changing seasonal patterns in marriages at St Peter's Church. Typically, in a traditional rural community, marriages were fitted round the rural calendar. Marriages did not take place until after Lent, so usually not in March: May was a popular month. The summer was a busy time so people waited until the harvest was in, with very few marriages in August. Then there was a second peak, with many weddings in October and November, after the harvest. In Blatchington's parish registers there was a shift in the second half of the nineteenth century, with a noticeable increase in March and August weddings. The change in March and August is from around 2% (in each of those months) in the sixteenth and early seventeenth centuries to 10% in the late nineteenth century. Blatchington gradually freed itself of the demands of the rural economy.

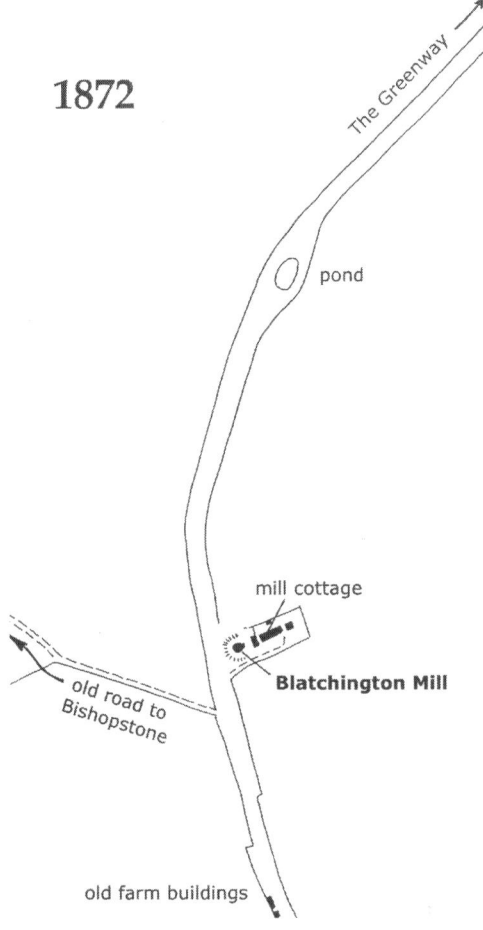

1872

The Greenway

pond

mill cottage

Blatchington Mill

old road to Bishopstone

old farm buildings

Upper Firle Road in 1872: still in its medieval rural state.

When the great jolt of World War One was over, North Camp was dismantled, though not all at once. Parade Grounds 1-4 and all the army huts to the south and north of them were done away with. Most of the huts along the western edge of the camp were demolished – though not all. Nine years after the war had ended, there were still over a dozen large huts left, including a row of six huts close to Hilltop Court School, and the southern half of Parade Ground No 5. There was a scatter of huts surviving along North Camp Lane and North Way. Two huts along North Way were adapted to make a Jewish School.

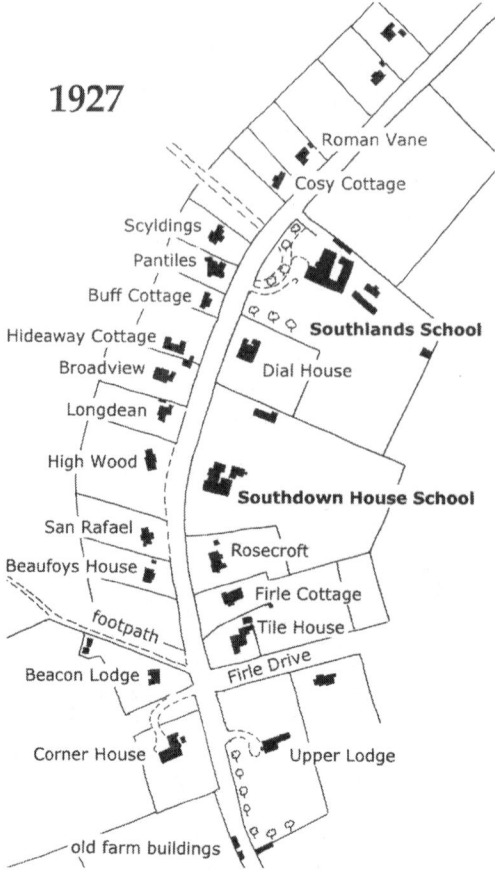

1927

Roman Vane

Cosy Cottage

Scyldings

Pantiles

Buff Cottage

Hideaway Cottage

Broadview

Longdean

High Wood

San Rafael

Beaufoys House

footpath

Beacon Lodge

Corner House

old farm buildings

Southlands School

Dial House

Southdown House School

Rosecroft

Firle Cottage

Tile House

Firle Drive

Upper Lodge

Upper Firle Road in 1927: suburbanized.

Education, education, education

Seaford and Blatchington were flooded with private schools. Many of the private schools set up at the end of the nineteenth century were dame schools, little schools catering for maybe ten pupils and run by one or two teachers. These were mostly wound up at the onset of the First World War because the owners were preoccupied with the war effort. But in any case they were dwindling from 1905 onwards because of competition from larger schools.

The dame school phase was important in establishing Blatchington and Seaford as a centre for education. It paved the way for
the larger, custom-built schools that would cater for the greater
demands of the newly prosperous middle class. By the 1920s the
two settlements had consolidated their reputation.

In 1930 there were twenty-seven private boarding schools in
Seaford as a whole. By 1984 there were only two. This was partly

SCHOOL	STREET	DURATION	GIRLS/BOYS
Pelham House	Belgrave Road	1902 - 1939	G
Gladleigh		1928 - 1939	G
Flint House		1924 - 1939	Co-ed
St Mawes		1902 - 1924	B
Blatchington Coll. for Boys		1927 - 1933	B
King's Mead		1911 - 1968	B
Cliff Girls		1932 - 1936	G
Blatchington Court		1886 - 1926 1951 - 1985	B
Kenwood	Upper Belgrave Road	1924 - 1938	B
Jewish Free	North Way	1922 - 1952	
Blatchington Place	Homefield Road	1906 - 1924	B
Hilltop Court		1924 - 1938	B
Hamilton House		1924 - 1939	B
St Michaels; Belvedere Coll.		1938 - 1947 1947 - 1950	B B
Hartfield House		1934 - 1939	B
Southdown House	Firle Road	1915 - 1958	B
Southlands		1924 - 1938	G
Pilgrims; St John's		1946 - 1975 1999 -	B
Bowden House		1907 -	B

because parents demanded more and more sophisticated facilities, more and more choice in terms of subjects and extras. Really only the largest schools could survive. Because of the site constraints, schools might extend a certain amount, but there was a limit. This contraction in numbers of private schools was much more severe here than in Sussex generally; in the county as a whole the contraction of the independent sector between 1930 and 1980 was only 2.5%, but in Seaford it was 93%.

During the post-war period, Seaford (with Blatchington) became a different sort of focus. It became a residential focus for people of retirement age. The demand for housing meant that there was a ready and profitable market for the playing fields and the sites of the school buildings.

The schools took a lot of land, an average of 12-15 acres each, and they gave the town significant areas of open green space. A lot of Seaford's (and Blatchington's) twentieth century character came from this aspect of the school craze. Equally, the closure of the schools meant a surge of residential development across their abandoned playing fields. As someone remarked, 'The town is going to end up wall-to-wall walls.' But, while the education craze lasted, Blatchington was a particular magnet for schools. An impressive twenty schools were attached to one small village.

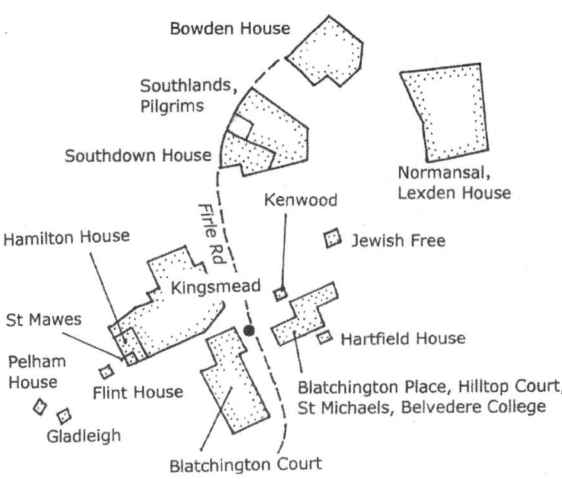

Blatchington's schools. Lexden House School was just outside the parish, but the boundary runs along its western edge and access was from Firle Road. The black dot is St Peter's church.

St Michael's School at what is now Homefield Place had a complex history, with its beginnings in the decanting of Blatchington Court School out of the manor house. In 1895, Robert Lambe built Blatchington Place, in effect as a custom-built school, on a piece of farmland to the east of the village, and sold it to Mr Warwick Wyatt Crouch, the schoolmaster who had previously run Blatchington Court School with Cecil Hand. This killed two birds with one stone for Robert Lambe; he developed and sold a piece of farmland for profit and also emptied his manor house of the school that had occupied it since January 1886. It had then been advertized as offering a workshop, playground, tennis lawns, cricket field, detached sanatorium – and a resident drill sergeant. But now Robert Lambe had decided he wanted to live in Blatchington Court. By 1900, he had emptied, renovated and extended it - and moved in.

Partially sighted girls at Blatchington Court:
a later phase in the school's history.

Initially Mr Crouch was headmaster as well as owner of Blatchington Place School, but from 1899 he appointed Mr W. R. Morton Clarke as headmaster. It was still a small school, with only 17 boys boarding at the time of the 1901 census. In 1920, Mr Crouch sold the school to the Revd G. Winlow and Revd A. Postance, and the following year Winlow sold his share in the school to Postance. From 1920 to 1937 the school, still in the same building, was known as Hilltop Court School and described as 'a school for gentlemen'.

In 1933, Postance took a £10,000 mortgage on the premises; the mortgagees were M. and J. Bower, and by 1937 they had become the owners. In that year, the Bowers put the school up for auction and it was bought by Charles Bravery. From 1936 to 1938 St Michael's School was in Hartfield Road. Then it moved to the Homefield Road site, which it occupied until 1947.

In 1938, the joint Heads of St Michael's were Captain F. W. Bedford and Bernard Ince and the school catered for about 40 boys. St Michael's had a fine chapel, an indoor swimming pool and a squash court. There were PT displays on the extensive playing fields. The prospectus reads, 'St Michael's School receives boys between the ages of 5 and 14 to prepare for the Public Schools and the Royal Navy. St Michael's stands in its own grounds overlooking the Downs, Seaford Head golf course and the sea . . . there is a flourishing Scout Troop and Wolf Cub Pack. Fees 30 guineas a term.'

In 1947, Mr Bravery sold St Michael's to Frederick Grunder, who continued the school under the name Belvedere College, but only three years later sold it to the trustees of the Society of All Saints Sisters of the Poor. They turned the building into St Elizabeth's, a convalescence home for the elderly. In 1968 the orchard was sold for development and eight houses were built on it, to make what is now Homefield Close. In 1969 St Elizabeth's was leased to East Sussex County Council, who bought it in 1986 and demolished it in 1987. The building was then replaced by Homefield Place, a custom-built ESCC care home for the elderly.

To the north, up Firle Road, was Pilgrims School. This had run from 1946 to 1954 as Southlands Girls School, after which the school equipment was sold off, including a grand piano and the chapel organ. The buildings were acquired at once by the Invalid Children's Aid Association so that it could be used as a residential school for fifty 'delicate' boys between the ages of 7 and 15. The prospectus released by the new Headmaster, Mr J. W. Davy, expressed anticipation that most of the boys would be asthmatic. In October 1955 Princess Margaret arrived by helicopter to open the new school.

There were advantages in having many schools together. It was possible, for instance, to share, swap or borrow equipment. The Headmasters of Blatchington Court School and Pilgrims School were on friendly terms, and it was possible for Ray and Ivan to ask one another for help of this kind.

Further up Firle Road was Bowden House, which started in 1907 as a boys' preparatory school which moved here from Harrow. It ran under a succession of Headmasters, Price (1907-18), Reiss and Verry (1918-1932), Quiney and Hole (1932-39) and Colley (1948-78). During the Second World War it was occupied by Canadian troops. Bowden House closed as an independent school in 1970, but was reopened by the London borough of Tower Hamlets.

King's Mead School was founded in 1912, when it was known as St David's and occupied Hamilton House. The main building of King's Mead School was custom-built on a large campus to the north of Belgrave Road, and in 1914 the nucleus of the school moved into it from Hamilton House. The new premises were expressly designed to take as boarders 60 boys of preparatory school age (8-14). The design is said to have been based on that of King's College Choir School, Cambridge, where King's Mead's first headmaster, Mr Whelon, had taught.

Additions were made as the years passed and the number of pupils increased. These included the library, a dining room extension, a gymnasium with a stage, and a chapel. Many extra facilities were added as well, such as a tuck shop, a swimming pool, two cricket pavilions, a hard tennis court, a rifle range, boys' gardens and a music room. The school grounds were quite extensive, amounting to 10 acres.

In 1918 Mr Whelon retired, handing over the school to Douglas Shilcock, under whose headship the school went from strength to strength right up to the outbreak of the Second World War, when it was evacuated to Bideford in Devon. The buildings were occupied by a convent until the school returned in 1945. Douglas Shilcock retired in 1951 after 33 years as headmaster. He was succeeded by Mr E. Barrett and Mr P. Holme as joint Heads. Mr Holme resigned in 1961 in order to take a similar post at Horns Hill School near Newbury. Mr Barrett appointed Mr Rawlins, one of his staff, as Assistant Headmaster.

The pattern from 1960 to 1980 was that, one by one, most of the independent schools in Seaford fell into financial difficulties and were forced to close. The smaller the school, the greater the difficulty. It was no longer possible for a small school like King's Mead, with only 80 boys in 1960, to pay its way. The decision was made, reluctantly, to amalgamate with a school in a more favourable location. In September 1968 a number of King's

Mead boys joined Stoke Brunswick School near East Grinstead, and the site in Blatchington was sold.

The school then became a nursing home for 79 residents, and for a long time it seemd that the whole building complex might be preserved. The King's Mead Chapel had a peculiarly medieval character, partly because of the use of recycled materials. In 1926 a seventeenth century barn at Ripe was purchased, demolished by the boys, the materials loaded onto a lorry and transported to King's Mead. The boys spent long hours cleaning and preparing the bricks for re-use, helped by Pettitts the builders. The aisled chapel had three-bayed arcades made of old oak timbers from the barn. The choirstalls were made by the staff and boys out of oak floorboards from the barn. A peculiarity of the chapel was that the chancel was in the west, its walls carrying on up to make a squat tower topped with a Sussex cap. In 1949 the stone windows were put in, with the names of the 43 old boys of King's Mead killed in action carved into the sills. The outside of the chapel was brick up to window sill level, then above that half-timbered. The roof was made of old clay tiles.

This beautiful barn-like building was dedicated in March 1927.

King's Mead School Chapel

The panelling in the 'medieval' dining-room carried the names of all the boys who attended King's Mead School. They included the show-jumper Harry Llewellyn, Geoffrey Keys, VC, MC, J. V. Fisher, DSC, the son of Admiral Lord Fisher, Prince Ronald Mutebi, the son of King Freddie, the Kabaka of Buganda, and Vajiralongkorn Mahidol, the Crown Prince of Thailand. King's Mead had more than its share of royal visitors: King Bhumiphol and Queen Sirikit of Thailand in 1966, and the Kabaka of Buganda in 1967. King George V and Queen Mary made an impromptu visit to their godson Peter Beck in 1935, while they were staying at Compton Place in Eastbourne. The unscheduled visit went awry as the school was virtually deserted when they arrived. It was a Thursday afternoon, and all the boys were scouting over at Bishopstone. Worse, while the boys were out, the masters traditionally relaxed with a drink or two, and the King was surprised to find evidence of this in the dining room. The boys were hastily recalled from Bishopstone, while the Queen inspected the flower beds.

In due course, the owners of the St Mary's nursing home, Westminster Health Care Ltd, decided to redevelop the site for housing, because the existing buildings did not meet new government guidelines. Suddenly it looked as if everything, including the chapel, would be destroyed. In 2001-2 a campaign was launched to save the chapel and the main building by having them listed, but English Heritage declined. 'These circa 1914 purpose-built Prep School buildings would originally have been of marginal architectural quality and have been too altered externally to be recommended for Listing and as the best internal features have been brought into the building. . . these buildings do not meet the listing criteria.' The Chapel did not warrant listing as it was not an archaeological re-creation of the seventeenth century barn; it had been subjected to too many changes. There were further problems arising from its inadequate foundations. In 2002, developers applied to build 24 houses, but within the year that had changed to 47 flats. There were objections that this was not only over-developing the site, but adding significantly to the density of traffic in the area. Planning consent eventually came for 23 new homes.

In 2003, the school buildings were demolished. The developers offered to erect a memorial to the boys of King's Mead School who had lost their lives in the Second World War. The granite obelisk, now standing in its own Memorial Garden, with access from Carlton Road along Kingsmead Lane, was dedicated in May 2004.

The demise of King's Mead School looks with hindsight to have been an economic inevitability, but it was a school of great character and charm – backward-looking perhaps in its architectural references, but that was like much of Blatchington village, and it had a solid and heart-warming Englishness about it. The names of the boys' dormitories tell all: Drake, Baden Powell, Roberts, Beatty, Haig, Scott, Kitchener, Churchill, Wellington, Nelson.

The Merrie England make-over

There was a lot of new building in Blatchington in the 1920s and 30s. But there was a lot of 'making-over' as well, with old cottages restored to make them appear even older. As the rural past was left behind, there was a pining for it, and an attempt to re-create it. The building of King's Mead Chapel was typical of this movement. Eighteenth or nineteenth century barns were converted to make them into imitation fifteenth century yeoman farmhouses. The rustication process going on between 1910 and 1940 represents an expression of an intensely nostalgic vision of traditional English village life, a nostalgia that had begun even in the eighteenth century.

In Goldsmith's 'The Deserted Village', rural holidays in this bygone neverland were rosy idylls,

When toil remitting lent its turn to play,
And all the village train, from labour free,
Led up their sports beneath the spreading tree;
While many a pastime circled in the shade,
The young contesting as the old survey'd.

But in reality there was little remission from work and precious little play. Thomas Hardy commented that in the old days even Morris dancing was performed as if it was just one more task that had to be done. Even fun was work.

The nostalgia movement had its detractors, and there were many, even a hundred years ago, who were sure that the Merrie England of Good Queen Bess was a fiction. The detractors poked gentle fun at the arts and crafts architecture that celebrated Merrie England too. Peter Simple wrote in the *Morning Post*: 'The new fashion in domestic architecture is a mixture of Tudor and Rustic, with a dash of Hollywood added. Thatched roofs, latticed windows, and oak cocktail bars are now *de rigeur* all the way from Eastbourne to Selsey Bill, and the Best People are replacing their garden gates by rustic stiles.' They weren't quite doing that, of course, but there was a lot of fake half-timbering, and a fair number of new antique-looking oak plank doors with antique-looking wrought-iron latches. Peter Simple hammed it up, but there was some truth in the picture. A medieval-cum-Tudor vernacular style did break out.

The revamping of Rookery Cottage in 1937, with its tile-hung walls and jettied first floor, was typical. It represents part of a late flowering of the arts & crafts style that was a speciality of not one but two inventive local architects, Rowland Hawke Halls and Alwyn Underdown.

Underdown (1897-1976) was a Seaford architect whose work included some ambitious and fine houses in English vernacular style, designs realized in the 1920s and 30s.

Underdown's distinctive style resulted from his use of a particular range of materials - variable-coloured stock bricks, a small amount of sandstone, hand-made clay tiles and recycled oak - and assembling a repertoire of characterful details. He used a lot of recycled oak beams rescued from old buildings; some came from Laughton Place, which was demolished in the 1930s, others from demolished farm buildings. He used these old timbers to great effect internally as exposed ceiling beams, and externally to simulate a timber-frame structure. The exposed edges of the ceiling beams were chamfered and given a signature double nick at each end. The doors were oak plank doors fitted with wrought-iron latches. There were carefully crafted brick fireplaces with heavy timber mantel-pieces. Often there was a recessed bedroom window. Rosemary Cottage has a recessed bedroom window with a curved, almost vaulted, plaster ceiling. Rookery Cottage has one based on flat planes of plaster, and with an oak window seat set into the thickness of the cottage wall. The roofs were typically made of slightly uneven clay tiles that gave a strong Wealden look. Usually he mortared a signature beer bottle into the apex of a gable or dormer window.

The houses were all sorts of shapes and layouts, but the way Underdown fitted them out with the same array of quaint detailing ensured that they all had the required olde worlde look, a look of having been built centuries before and bearing the authentic patina of age.

The lack of documentation makes it hard to be certain which houses are Underdown's, but it looks as if he was busy; there are scores of Underdown-designed houses in Blatchington and Seaford. Often there are clues in the house date. Underdown extended and reshaped Rookery Cottage in 1937 for George and

Four Walls

Amelia Woolgar. The Woolgars owned the large square walled garden next to it as well and they had just had a new house built on that plot in the same style in 1931 – initially for themselves. It is likely that Woolgar used the same architect, Underdown, for the two houses. Four Walls, a fine detached house, stands in what was once the high-walled peach garden belonging to Blatchington Court.

Field Cottage in Belgrave Road was originally a pair of dwellings, a smaller, square cottage to the south and larger cottage to the north with two rooms on the ground floor. This asymmetry is still visible in the arrangement of the chimneys, in spite of Alwyn Underdown's extensive 1937 make-over. The enlarged cottage Underdown created was intended as a home for his second wife, Vera Robertson, whom he married in 1937, though she spent her final years at Knowle next door.

Underdown switched the position of the Field Cottage front door from the east side to the west, adding the rustic porch and dormer windows, all with beer bottles cemented into their gables. He also added six substantial flint buttresses to the façade, making a very picturesque Snow White's cottage effect overall.

In front of the original cottages on the western side he added a new exterior wall; between the walls a passage connected the original ground-floor rooms. He also incorporated into the structure some of the roof timbers from the barn that formerly

Field Cottage from the walled rose garden

stood to the west, to create a house with a strong vernacular character. The truncated flint walls of the dismantled barn still exist as a pleasant walled garden which began with a formal Tudor-style design by Underdown. His pen-and-wash drawings for the design of house and garden still survive.

The Pound and Alces Place

The Pound in Firle Road was a very plain barn until the turn of the twentieth century. The original building was a simple box in rendered brick, one chain long, with a pitched slate roof. At 'ground-floor' level there were two large apertures, double-doorways, one with a lintel, the other with a shallow arch, and there were two small windows. It is said that the barn and yard on the site were where Robert Lambe's cattle were housed.

In about 1930, the barn was virtually rebuilt for Mr A. T. Redgewell to make it look like a fifteenth century yeoman farmer's house. The original door and window apertures completely vanished. There is a fine gabled jut above the front door, which was not part of the original building at all. It is fitted with finely weathered heavy pale grey timbers infilled with herringbone red-brick nogging. The back of the house is even more picturesque, with two juts and a feature brick chimney running up the full height of the building at one corner.

South of Alces Place is the plain white-rendered double-gable of

The Pound

Blatchington House. This was the home of William Lambe, and of the young Robert Lambe. Later it was the home of Dr Tom Lambe, Robert's son. It was a farmhouse, with some outbuildings, including the roadside buildings which still exist. What is now Alces Place was in later years one of its farmyards, though earlier it may have existed as an independent farm. On old maps the land opposite Alces Place is shown as Alces Fields. The sheep-folds were where Barn House is now, the stables at Lambes Cottage, the horse troughs in the garden of Field Cottage (in Firle Road) and the cattle pound where the Pound is now.

In Bruce Ottley's conveyance of 1914 Alces Place is described as 'a dwelling house, barn, outbuildings, forge at Alces Hall', an arrangement similar to that of 1774.

Bruce Ottley, an equerry to George V, created a fine house with accommodation built round three sides of the large square courtyard, which he had paved with cobbles - and some flagstones from Buckingham Palace. There were also a swimming bath, squash court and fine gardens.

The *Sussex Weekly Advertiser* for 5 September 1774 contained an advertisement; 'To be sold in one lot copyhold, an estate consisting of a messuage, barn, blacksmiths shop, yard and garden all lying in Blatchington street (near Seaford) in this County in the possession of Mrs Jane Alce and others and 4 acres of valuable arable land lying in three pieces dispersed in the common laynes of Blatchington now occupied by Mr Joseph Goldsmith, the whole of which may be viewed by applying to Mrs Alce at the House. Particulars thereof had of Mr Sinnick attorney at Hailsham.'

The result of that advertisement was that Alces Place was sold to Major Boarder. By 1798 a Mrs Boarder owned the place, perhaps the major's widow. In 1805 James Boarder owned it and a Mr Horner occupied it, presumably as a tenant. By 1820 the owner was Miss Boarder, and Mrs Horner was her tenant but by 1821 Mrs Horner had become the owner and Mr King was the occupier. Mr King remained the owner of Alces Place from 1821 through to 1843 and beyond. The King family were followed at some date by the Lambe family, possibly from 1850, when William Lambe came to Blatchington and moved into adjacent Blatchington House. By the time Bruce Ottley bought Alces Place, it had had many owners.

It was originally a modest group of farm buildings dating from the early seventeenth century. The main building was a barn. According to an old-time resident of Blatchington, 'Robert Lambe's sheep were shorn there.' The two wings were byres. The abstract of title refers to a conveyance of September 1905, which may represent Robert Lambe's acquisition of Alces Place. But Robert Lambe's finances were so stressed that in August 1912 Robert Lambe and his sons, William, Thomas and Richard Frederic mortgaged the property to Seaford West Company and Barclays Bank. In 1913 the mortgage was transferred to London County and Westminster Bank.

Alces Place

In July 1914, the property was sold by Seaford West Company to Richard Bruce Hamilton Ottley, to create a dwelling (Alces Hall) with outbuildings. Mr Ottley paid £775 for the property. In October the same year land to the north, the site of the Firle Close development, was sold by Seaford West Co to Arthur Clovell Salter. In April 1916 there was a further conveyance from Seaford West Co to Bruce Ottley, by which Mr Ottley acquired the remainder of the Alces Place property, the all-important eastern frontage bounded by a flint wall and the 9-feet wide strip of land bordering the road. By this transaction, Bruce Ottley now had the entire square of land that makes up the buildings and gardens of Alces Place, the access from Firle Road and land for a kitchen garden on the far side of Firle Road. Now the property could be converted into a grand house with gardens front and back.

Before the work began, Robert Lambe's son Fred went down from Upper Lodge to the abandoned farm yard with his mother, and she took photographs of him standing in the open byre forming the north range and in front of the big barn along the western side of the farm yard. Fred Lambe remembered in later years that the barn and yard went as one of the lots in one of the auctions. The complex was altered in 1916 in the prevailing arts and crafts style. The Conservation Area appraisal rather patronizingly describes 'the charmingly contrived quaintness of this group of buildings and their setting', but also says that it exemplifies the character of this part of the Conservation Area. It is hard to understand why the building has not been listed.

Bruce Ottley's executors sold Alces Place in 1948 to Commander W. A. Dunderdale for £12,500. In 1956, Commander Dunderdale sold the outbuildings flanking the front quadrangle to Bertram Clayton Adams' development company, Architectural Developments Ltd, for £8,500. Bertram Adams commissioned his architect, Roy Clare, to produce detailed architectural designs for the conversion of Alces Place into six dwellings. The concept was Adams', the detail Clare's. The main building, the old barn, became two dwellings, and there were two dwellings in each of the north and south ranges. The development was completed in 1957, each dwelling selling on for £3,000 or more. A great selling point in the brochure was that each house was 'a charming old Sussex Style Home of exceptional character standing in beautifully cultivated and matured grounds. . . It is built of local flint and brick with a mellow tile roof.' Great emphasis was placed on 'old world features' and 'exterior charm and dignity'. And the properties still have these qualities.

The fine wrought-iron gates hung on lofty red brick piers are a Roy Clare addition, replacing lower and more modest predecessors. Bruce Ottley's entrance had brick pillars that rose only about three courses above the wall. They were topped by small stone balls, which Bertram Adams hated; he replaced them with the present urns, which are far more elegant.

When Mr Adams acquired Alces Place, he also acquired the kitchen garden opposite. There he built two properties, Featherstones, a chalet bungalow sporting one of Adams' trade-mark eyebrow windows, and Littlegate House. Littlegate was a larger house, three storeys high with an artist's studio at the top. This was designed specifically to house Adams' three unmarried sisters-in-law, Eileen, Doris and Iris Hamilton: it was Iris who was the artist.

Two more projects of Bertram Adams were the division of The Corner House into three dwellings and the building of Little Glebe. Little Glebe, initially named Lindens, was a cottage designed by Roy Clare as a home for Mr Adams and his family.

A large rectangular plot 300 feet by over 200 feet behind Alces Place, part of the old cricket ground, was much coveted for building development in the 1950s. This plot was owned in the 1950s by Alfred Blenkarn, who offered it for sale at £5,000 with planning consent claimed for 6 or 7 houses or bungalows to the acre, and a 36-feet-wide right of way as access. But the claim was a false one. Although a building contractor offered £5,000 in November 1959, it was conditional on the alleged right of way being proved and acknowledged by the occupiers of adjoining properties.

But the neighbours did not approve and by the time Mr Blenkarn died in January 1964, planning consent had been refused owing to the narrow access along Robin Post Lane. Because it was claimed that the land now had only agricultural value, it was given a provisional probate value of only £500. The District Valuer was expected not to agree this, as planning permission for housing might be given, and then the value of the land would be much higher; the Valuer in fact proposed £1000, which Mr Blenkarn's widow accepted. Then the plot was put on the market for £5,000. A new property developer came along, seeking planning consent to build 31 houses on the rectangular plot behind Alces Place together with two adjacent plots to north and west, in effect filling the open space between Alces Place to the east and King's Mead School to the west. In February 1965 permission was refused 'on the grounds that the standard of development would not be in keeping with the high standard of existing development and would be detrimental to the residential and visual amenities of the locality'.

By this stage a new plan had been put forward to develop the cricket field to the north of Alces Place. Guildford architect Roy Clare had produced the design for this for Bertram Adams as early as 1959: a banjo with fifteen houses on 30-metre-long plots ranged round it. The design also included a track running south, providing access to two building plots occupying the northern half of the (so far) inaccessible rectangle behind Alces Place. Planning consent was given to this low-density scheme, which now exists as Firle Close, a very pleasant development of Underdown-style houses by Adams and Clare, all different from one another, very much in the Blatchington style – and five of them with eyebrow windows.

Rowland Hawke Halls

Beacon Lodge in Firle Road is a substantial house with a half-timbered porch and a balcony. It looks as if it might be an Alwyn Underdown design, but in fact it was by Rowland Hawke Halls, a local architect born in 1879. He was a surveyor's assistant in Lewes, where he was later an architect and surveyor with an office in Seveirg Chambers until his early death at the age of 40 in 1919. He was cycling across a level crossing when he was hit by a train.

Originally Beacon Lodge stood on a very large plot which included the open space to the south with lawn and the L-shaped drive leading to The Corner House. Opposite Beacon Lodge are three more large detached houses designed by Rowland Hawke Halls just before the First World War, The Tile House, Firle Cottage and Rosecroft. These are built in arts and crafts style, with varied fenestration and form, incorporating loggias, balconies, mullioned windows and local materials such as oak timbers and clay tiles.

The Gatehouse halfway up Blatchington Hill and the next two houses, Kilmeny and Uplands, were also designed by Rowland Hawke Halls. The Gatehouse was built by Halls for himself, and he named it Rowlands. After his death the house was sold and the new owner, Austin Harrison, changed the name to Lychgate House. Later it was changed again to The Gatehouse. In the 1980s, it became the home of Sir George and Lady Coldstream. Sir George was a lawyer and, as a member of an inner circle of top civil servants, he was described as one of the ten men who ran Britain. In 1960, he was instrumental in advising the Queen to adopt Mountbatten-Windsor as her family name. He also helped draft the Peerage Act 1963, which allowed Alec Douglas-Home to become Prime Minister and Lord Stansgate to become Tony Benn. Sir George lived at The Gatehouse until his death in 1994; Lady Coldstream, Sir George's second wife, lived there until she died in the autumn of 2011.

Dignity and good taste

At the foot of Blatchington Hill where Blatchington Road, the old road into Seaford, curves round to the right, most of the traffic now carries straight on up Avondale Road. This is a new route into Seaford made in the twentieth century, though its western pavement follows the line of an old footpath, which can be seen on the Tithe Map. On the west side of this lies just one more property that has been included in the East Blatchington Conservation Area, in spite of being just outside the parish. This is Norlington House, a fine flint-built house with two big gables and a recessed central bay. It has an air of having been there for hundreds of years, an air that is deceptive.

In fact it was once somewhere else altogether. It was originally Place House on the corner of Broad Street and Place Lane, facing east. It was built in 1603 for the Gratwicke family and demolished in 1935. A former Seaford headmistress, Amy Chambers, acquired the materials and recycled them to build Norlington House, which has the same general shape as Place House, but scaled down. The central bay is narrower, with only one window, whereas Place House had a row of three. The building is two storeys high instead of the original three. It is perhaps the most unusual of the early twentieth century experiments at Blatchington, this scaled-down Jacobean flint mansion, but architecturally very successful.

As a developer, Robert Lambe went in for clean-cut Edwardian 'modernism'. Upper Lodge was built in this style. Then there was Easemore House, a slightly unexpected creation in Homefield Road, just beside The Star House and the two adjacent cottages. Lambe was building, speculatively, on his own farmland next to the village, and he put up an imposing house - initially called Wayside, then Green Hedges, and today known as Easemore House.

This fine, solid, Edwardian villa (ground plan below) was designed for Robert Lambe by William Cooper & Coussens of Seaford in 1902 and built the following year. The five lofty chim-

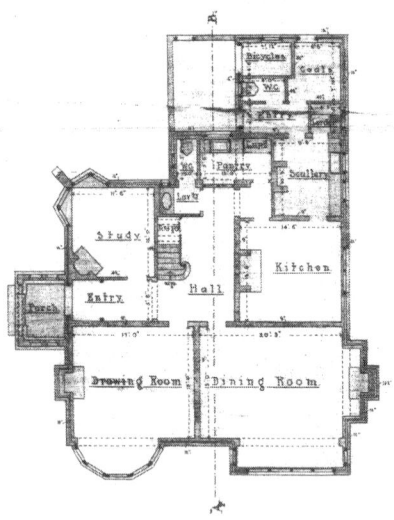

GROUND FLOOR.

neys rising from the eaves are a major feature, with their white-painted render and red-brick collars, and two of them bearing eye-catching crosses in red brick, like banners of St George.

The windows are a special feature. The lower sash, which is over half the window, is a single pane designed to give an uninterrupted view. The upper sash is made of four, six or eight panes: unusual, but visually very effective. This feature - large single pane below, several small panes above - was borrowed from Blatchington Court. Robert Lambe must have had a particular liking for it as he later commissioned the same window design again for Arlington House.

More unusual still is the fact that Easemore House has its back to the road. The south elevation is the 'front', looking down from a terrace across what was open farmland towards Seaford Head. This is just like Blatchington Court, into which Robert Lambe had just moved; the big house too turned its back to the road and its face towards the sun and the view of Seaford Head. Robert Lambe's instructions to the architect would have been made with this pleasing feature of Blatchington Court in mind.

In the midst of all of this tasteful early twentieth century development, there was one lapse of taste, in the building of the Elm Court Centre. This began as a small hotel at the bottom of the Hill in the 1920s, and later became a youth centre. It was built on

The south front of Easemore House

the site of the Water Lily Pond, which lay in the floor of a grassy hollow lined by trees on its northern edge. Until it was built on it was a local beauty spot. The land had belonged to the Blatchington Court estate, and therefore belonged to Robert and Elizabeth Dennis. Like Glebe and Rectory Cottages, the Water Lily Pool was left to the diocese. And, as with Glebe and Rectory Cottages, the diocese decided fairly soon to sell on. The sale of the Water Lily Pool was particularly unfortunate, in that it seems to have been regarded as building land, for which it was (and still is) unsuitable. It is low-lying, shaded by high ground to the south, cold, damp, and the Environment Agency's flood map shows it as liable to flooding. It was, even so, ear-marked for the building of a small hotel, in a style not seen anywhere else in Blatchington village.

The new building, Redcourts, was flat-roofed with rendered white-painted walls, with one wall on the curve, and it was fitted with Crittall windows. It was an art deco design, but a poor one, and out of character for the area. The rear elevation, facing Blatchington Pond, had a random asymmetric arrangement of windows and a large number of black-painted drainpipes, soil pipes and ventilation stacks – an unsatisfactory design for a wall on public view. It is another building with its back to the road, but in a far less satisfactory way than either Blatchington Court or Easemore house. The front elevation faced west, onto its two tennis courts.

Redcourts was designed to be a country and sports club, with 5 bedrooms, 2 bathrooms, a sitting room, a dining room and a large oak-floored lounge. It was sold in 1956 for only £3,000 and its final phase was as a youth centre, the Elm Court Centre. It was derelict for several years at the end of its life, and was then demolished. I watched – a solitary witness – as the last of it came down on 22 March 2011.

Notes & sources

Anon 1970 (Alces Place)
Clare 1959 (plan for Firle Close development)
Holland 2011 (Bertram Adams-Roy Clare developments)
Letter from English Heritage to Mrs Hubbard in response to application
  for listing of Kings Mead School and Chapel (8 Feb 2002)
Ridley 1984 (schools in Seaford)

Chapter 16
Conservation and campaigns

The battle for Britain

In 1939, just as the Second World War was about to begin, Seaford Urban District Council published its arrangements for evacuees. These were a response to the government's scheme to evacuate children from London to places of safety. In the early days of the war, the Sussex coast was seen as safe, though that perception quickly changed. Meanwhile, the town council listed billeting officers, each with up to six helpers. Each officer was to find billets in private houses for up to a hundred evacuees. Some billeting was voluntary, some compulsory.

Blatchington Road, Blatchington Street and Firle Road were treated as a single area, and its billeting officer was Miss D. H. Goodwin, who lived in Chyngton Road. She had four helpers, none of whom lived in Blatchington.

This arrangement for evacuees was short-lived. Once the Battle of Britain with its attendant threat of invasion had begun, this stretch of the Sussex coast no longer looked safe; in fact, the German high command had decided on nearby Cuckmere Haven as one of seven projected East Sussex landing places for Operation Sealion, the German invasion of England. By July 1940, in anticipation of the arrival of thousands of enemy troops, children living in Seaford and Blatchington were themselves being evacuated to other parts of the country.

Seaford became a significant target for German air attack. By November 1944, the local Civil Defence had counted 1,051 alerts and 42 incidents. 142 high-explosive bombs had been dropped on Seaford (including Blatchington), and more than 10,000 incendiary bombs. 22 people had been killed and 100 injured, 82 properties had been destroyed or damaged beyond repair, and another 1,600 properties damaged and repaired.

Most of the damage was to Seaford, though Blatchington did not go entirely unscathed. In September 1940, two high-explosive bombs were dropped in a field close to Firle Road, though without damaging any buildings. In January 1941, bombs damaged houses in Belgrave and Chichester Roads. Then on 10 April 1941 a Heinkel was shot down, crash-landing on the golf course, where the pilot was captured. Three of the crew successfully bailed out before the plane crashed and were captured on landing. On the same day, two bombs fell on properties in Firle Road and garden sheds were destroyed. On 16 April 1941, two bombs hit Pilgrims School, injuring four people, and a month later Bowden House also suffered bomb damage. Seaford was not bombed as intensively as Newhaven or Eastbourne, though more intensively than Brighton. Even so, Blatchington came through the Second World War almost unscathed.

The northward expansion of Seaford meant more and more new housing appeared to the east and west of Blatchington and, increasingly, to the north as well.

Firle Road was becoming more and more built up over the years. The number of addresses along Firle Road increased from 12 in 1914 to 22 in 1924, to 27 in 1927, 33 in 1936, to 64 in 1967. In other words, one new dwelling was being added every year through the first half of the twentieth century. By 2010 the number of homes had increased to 155, so the average rate of growth in the second half of the twentieth century had increased to 1.5 new dwellings every year. This shows how Blatchington village has been surrounded by suburban development, and has itself been sub-urbanized, at an accelerating rate.

Return to Eden

As Blatchington was surrounded by housing, the character of the village came increasingly under threat. There was a steady increase in the volume of traffic passing through the village. In 1913, apparently in response to Robert Lambe's building developments in Firle Road and St Peter's Road, Seaford Urban District proposed to widen the southern end of Firle Road. Robert Lambe agreed that, as and when required, the road wall boundaries would be moved back. At Alces Place, the roadway at that time was only 17 feet wide. The Council drew attention to the irregular width of Firle Road, proposing to widen the southern end from 20 to 40 feet, evidently to encourage traffic through at higher speeds. The flint road wall from the Belgrave Road junction up to Blatchington House was taken down and rebuilt 10-20 feet further back. By 1931 the council was even intending to pare off the eastern road wall of Firle Road, which would have meant demolishing both Lambs Cottage and the old entrance gates to Arlington House, to create a road 50 feet wide, the same as Upper Belgrave Road. Fortunately, that was never done but, with hindsight, the ancient bottleneck might have been better left as a deterrent to race-track driving.

With the nostalgic English vernacular movement in architecture, and with it the creation of Alces Place, The Pound and Sanctuary, came an awareness that this was an illusion that had to be protected and nurtured. In 1925 there was a piece in the local press describing the need for conservation. It was headed 'Village of peace gets conservation itch' and opened with an alluring word picture: 'Leafy trees overhang the narrow footway and the gable of a house peers round a hedge – a vision of rural peace in the heart of built-up Seaford is Blatchington. Long before semi-detached suburbia came to the south coast, Blatchington was a self-contained community high on its hill a mile from the centre of Seaford.' This echoed a description of Blatchington before the First World War: 'East Blatchington is seen embowered in a mass of foliage. The situation is a pleasant one, commanding a pleasant sea-view.'

The character of Blatchington has been threatened and changed by Seaford, but the village has also had a counteracting effect on Seaford, by stubbornly remaining a distinctive area within it, a positive attraction in the town. In its quiet way, Blatchington reaches out into the surrounding area, sharing its air of rural calm and permanence. We can see this outreach effect in the catchment area of St Peter's church. Its congregation might be expected to come entirely from within the parish, yet significant numbers live in Seaford, some even in Bishopstone.

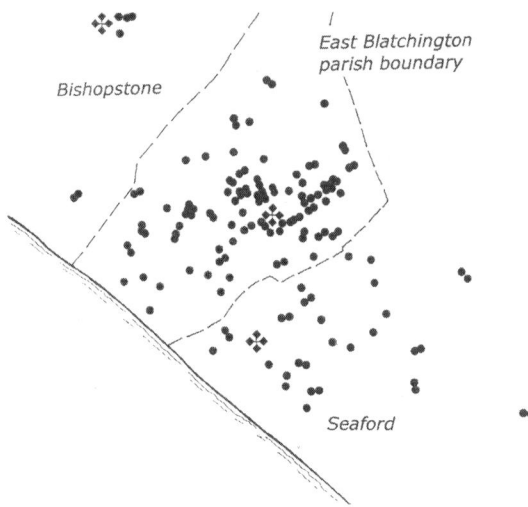

The St Peter's congregation in the 1980s (home addresses)

In 1937, the *Southern Weekly News* ran an article featuring the rector and his verger, and describing the village a hundred years before as 'a little parish with a few old cottages round the ancient church. A cosy inn stabled horses drawing the coach on the last stage of its journey to cross-channel boats'. Stagecoaches passed up and down Blatchington Hill, but whether The Star catered for them was never documented.

The coaching inn became an integral part of the twentieth century folk memory of Olde England, like gentleman-highwaymen. But was The Star really a coaching inn? A 1792 news-paper announcement suggests that it was not. A Seaford and Lewes post coach service was to commence in March that year, running on Mondays, Wednesdays and Saturdays (and then daily from June). It set out from the New Inn in Seaford at 5 in the morning; there was no mention of stopping at Blatchington on the way and there would certainly have been no need to change horses after such a short distance. Another notice in June 1792 advertized the Seaford and Newhaven *Diligence*, which set out from the Pelham Arms in Seaford at 6, to arrive in Lewes in time for the London coach; again there was no mention of stopping at Blatchington, though we can be sure that the stage coaches ran through the village. In the nineteenth century horses were changed at The Star in *Alfriston* on the coach service between Eastbourne and Brighton, and this may be where the perception (or misperception) came from that The Star at *Blatchington* was a coaching inn.

The 1937 *Southern Weekly News* article was on firmer ground when it described 'Blatchington today' - that is, in 1937 - as a suburb of Seaford and a refuge for retired people.

The reporter found the new rector, the Revd Ernest Winter, in the study of his modern rectory, some distance from the church. Ernest Winter wondered whether there was anywhere else in England a parish of nearly two thousand people without a pub or a petrol station. 'No means for filling up for man or car. It doesn't seem to do any harm because the neighbouring parish attends to these spiritual needs. Still, I sometimes wonder if the world would be a much happier and better place if man had never discovered strong drink and never invented the internal combustion engine. So perhaps Blatchington is the first step in a return to Eden.' But this rector chose not to remain in Eden; he left after only two years.

The verger, Joseph Abrahams, a neatly dressed retired civil servant, guided the reporter round St Peter's. He pointed to a patch on the wall plaster in the church. It resembled a crude figure of a man, but the reporter thought it looked like a damp patch. 'No,' said Mr Abrahams, 'It's not damp. I discovered it when I was spring cleaning. I wondered whether there are any paintings beneath. Once I discovered some beautiful medieval paintings hidden in the wall of a church . . .'

The reporter also visited The Gables to see 'the elderly Miss de St Croix', who showed him her watercolours illustrating Blatchington's history. 'Did you notice the pulpit?' she asked. 'There are some fine carvings of flowers – lilies, passion flowers, snowdrops. That was the work of a Pole. He did it on condition that he might smoke all the time.'

1970s: creating the Conservation Area

Some later owners of The Gables, Richard and Norma Good, were among the strong supporters of conservation forty years later.

The East Blatchington Conservation Area was set up by Lewes District Council's Chief Planning Officer, Michael Francis. This was announced in February 1976 and defined on a map. The Planning Committee set out seven policies relating to the area;

1) The existing character of the area should be preserved and, wherever possible, enhanced. The existing uses of the area should remain undisturbed and substantial new development should not be permitted.

2) Any alterations to existing buildings should be sympathetic, and be constructed in materials similar to those existing, to harmonize with and enhance the historic character of the Conservation Area.

3) Any new building should respect the character of the environment, especially in form, scale and materials, and should not prejudice the dominance of the existing buildings.

4) Schemes for the treatment of spaces round the buildings, for example hard surfaces, walls and planting, must accord with the character of the Conservation Area in terms of materials and design.

5) Trees within and around the area should be retained and improved where necessary with careful surgery. All trees within the area should be protected, not only for their importance to the visual amenity of the immediate surroundings, but also for their important contribution to the whole locality. New planting will usually be required when existing trees are removed or die, to maintain existing coverage and provide established trees for the future.

6) The District Council will encourage the undergrounding of existing overhead wires and will resist any proposal to extend existing overhead wires or install new ones.

7) To prevent the proliferation of advertising and assertive signing, there will be a presumption against illuminated advertising and efforts will be made to restrict the size, siting and number of all other advertisements.

Those who had supported the creation of the conservation area were thanked, with the hope that 'this co-operation can be continued to the benefit of the community'. Later, after the Millennium, when it appeared the authorities had lost interest in the Conservation Area, residents made two attempts at forming a residents association to foster its interests.

The East Blatchington Conservation Area, as set up in 1976 and subsequently extended. The outlines show buildings. The buildings in solid black are those considered to make a positive contribution to the character of the CA. They include buildings adjacent to as well as within the CA, which suggests that the Conservation Area might benefit from further expansion, so that architecturally interesting houses like Beacon Lodge and Easemore House come within it. It certainly looks as though the CA might be extended further up the western side of Firle Road. Asterisks show Grade 2 Listed Buildings.

1985: a church hall in the churchyard?

One day in 1985, the rector, the Revd Simon Crittall, proposed to his congregation that a church hall should be built in the churchyard. It was a proposal that tested the loyalties of the congregation and divided the local community. The episode shows how the need for conservation sometimes sharply conflicts with the perceived current need of the community. It shows how the interests of the village's past, present and future may appear to clash with each other – and also the mechanisms that may resolve such clashes.

In the parish newsletter the rector discussed three possible sites: the churchyard (which he favoured), the chapel of Blatchington Court School (which would be more expensive) and the kitchen garden of the Old Rectory (for which he did not want to ask Mrs Lewis).

A campaign to get the planning application to build in the churchyard rejected was co-ordinated by Thérèse Horner and Charles Pearsall-Horner, who lived at The Star House. Their leaflet drew attention to the fact that the scheme would disturb seventeen graves with headstones and many more that were unmarked, and destroy seven mature trees.

Richard Good engaged the rector directly, writing to say that he thought it would have been polite and politic to discuss the idea with neighbours. He reminded the rector that the community had decided that the area should be a Conservation Area. Mr Good could not believe that the rector was willing to despoil a graveyard. The rector wrote back immediately with the reassurance that the PCC's discussions were only at an exploratory stage. If they could find a way of achieving extra space without disturbing the churchyard they would certainly do so.

The move to build in the churchyard was perhaps mis-timed. A report from the Royal Fine Art Commission and the Historic Buildings Council that year explicitly *condemned* building in churchyards and urged church authorities 'to find the required spaces elsewhere.' The PCC informed parishioners that the Archdeacon and the Diocesan Advisory Committee did not favour an application to use the churchyard but advised giving priority to acquiring the school chapel.

The *Daily Telegraph* of 9 September noted a similar plan to build a parish room in the churchyard at Compton near Guildford. Although there were many objections from local residents, the planning committee of Guildford Borough Council had voted in its favour, by nine votes to seven. It seemed that Blatchington residents could not rely on the local planning office to reject a churchyard development.

The *Evening Argus* for 21 Oct 1985 carried an article entitled 'Grave objections to a church hall'. It explained that Mr Crittall was insistent that great care had been taken in designing a church hall in keeping with its surroundings: 'I value the conservation area as much as anyone, but the church has no facilities and is now too small for the congregation. It was built to serve a 200-strong population and now we have a parish of about 8,000 people. We have nowhere to run a Sunday school and have to fit 23 children into a tiny vestry. Many elderly people are staying away from services because there are no toilets nearby. There is no suitable alternative site, because a church hall has to be nearby to cater for the overspill of people wishing to take communion. Ours is a living community, not just a museum, and there is a lot of work we cannot do because of lack of facilities.'

One Seaford councillor accused critics of the scheme of failing to get their facts right; the statement that the church hall was going to be bigger than the church was 'absolute poppycock'. But the surviving plans show that the church hall *was* going to be larger in area than the church – ten percent larger. Readers noticed the mistake. They also drew attention to the Planning Committee's implicit undertaking in the terms of the Conservation Area to protect trees; 'all trees within the area should be protected.'

Simon Crittall admitted that gravestones would be moved, but denied that human remains would be dug up, adding that he believed 'that the important part of the buried bodies, the souls, are not below ground anyway.' A decision about the application was anticipated at the next meeting of the development committee at Lewes Town Hall. Meanwhile, letters of both objection and support were arriving on the desk of Michael Francis at the Planning Office in Lewes.

On 20 November the press announced that Lewes District had rejected the churchyard plan. The campaigners published an ad thanking everyone who wrote to LDC to save the churchyard. 'Despite the overwhelming decision shown by the congregation and residents and the LDC that they do not want this new hall in the churchyard, it is still most likely that an appeal will be made by the Rector to the Dept of Environment to overturn this decision.' This was followed by a contact number for those concerned to block an appeal.

On 24 November 1985 the St Peter's newsletter included a notice of a meeting to be held on 12 December of a Special Parochial Church meeting. The main agenda item was to consider a range of options:

1) to appeal against the rejection of the PCC's application for consent to build in the churchyard. (costing £30,000)
2) to negotiate with Trustees of Blatchington Court School to buy land within the school grounds to build a church hall. (£80,000)
3) to negotiate with Trustees to buy the school chapel. (£30,000)
4) to negotiate with Mrs Lewis for a plot of land within the walled garden of the Old Rectory and seek planning permission to build there. (£10,000)
5) to seek a faculty to build a gallery at the back of the church, and toilets adjoining. (£10,000)
6) to remove the parish centre to Wilmington Road, seeking consent to erect a new church with all necessary accommodation on the site of St John's. (costing over £250,000)

On 27 November, Max Godden, Archdeacon of Lewes and Hastings, wrote to Charles Pearsall-Horner. He confirmed that it was foreseen from the beginning that there would be widespread opposition to the churchyard scheme, voiced through the local planning authority. He added that this was emphasized to the PCC, but also that the Diocesan Authorities could do no more than advise, and in this case the rector, churchwardens and PCC exercised their undoubted right to go ahead with their application despite the advice given. He did not know whether the PCC would pursue the matter to appeal, 'though the grounds for refusal do seem to me to be very substantial and formidable ones. One must, I think, hope that appeal would be very unlikely to succeed. . .'

The *Sussex Express* for 20 Dec 1985 reported that a special meeting of parishioners had reached no firm decision on the next step after the plan for the hall in the churchyard had been refused. The rector said the voting had still to be assessed, but Thérèse Horner's poll - she had approached members of the congregation on the Electoral Roll - showed clearly that acquiring the chapel was what most members of his congregation wanted.

The St Peter's newsletter of 19 January 1986 reported that the PCC reluctantly agreed that the cost of mounting an appeal could not be justified; there were doubts about whether an appeal would succeed, and whether the subsequent application for a faculty would succeed. The newsletter of 22 July 1990 contained a PCC report, noting that the Blatchington Court School chapel was on the market. The PCC decided to pursue the possibility of buying it, alongside the plan to build in the churchyard. 'Should we aim to build in the churchyard or buy the chapel?' The cost of building in the churchyard was going to be £100,000; the chapel would give 50% more space, but cost twice as much.

On 22 December 1990 Simon Crittall sent a letter to his congregation to say that 'after beginning the year insisting that they would not sell the former Blatchington Court School Chapel for less than £150,000, Clarke Homes Ltd put the property on the market again' that summer. The guide price was still £150,000, but it appeared there might be flexibility. A new valuation was commissioned, which produced a figure of £100,000, significantly different from the 1988 figure, so an offer of £105,000 was made to Clarke Homes. The offer was not accepted, but Clarke Homes had no other offers, so the developer invited the PCC to make a final (higher) offer, one to which they could agree.

This story of conflict has a happy ending. The outcome was that the PCC *did* acquire the chapel and after conversion it has made a fine multi-purpose church room. Securing the chapel for the church also saved it from demolition, as its alternative fate was almost certain demolition and the insertion of yet another house. It is one of the few surviving remnants of Blatchington Court.

Blatchington Court School redevelopment

Blatchington Court was a school founded and refounded several times over. When Robert Lambe owned it at the end of the nineteenth century, he let it to Mr Crouch for a boys' boarding school called Court House School.

Blatchington Court from Belgrave Road. The original house, to the right, has a pale slate roof; the north wing added by Robert Lambe, centre, has a darker roof. Blatchington Court's chapel stands to the left of the church tower.

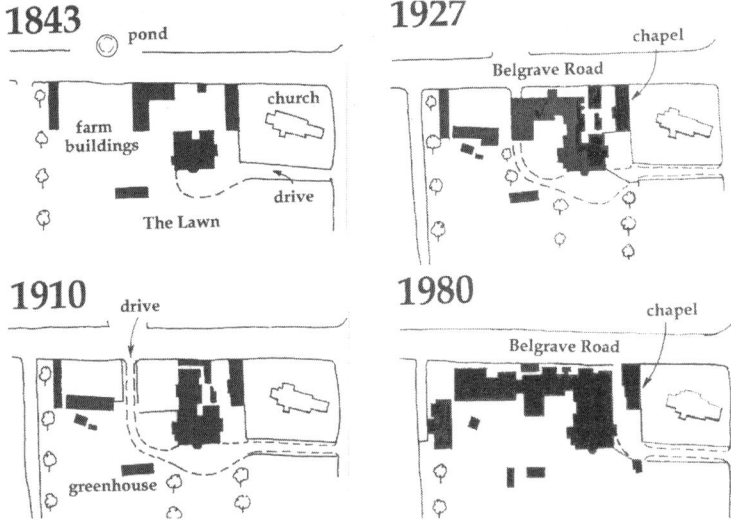

Stages in Blatchington Court's development. 1843: John King's mansion. 1910: Robert Lambe's mansion, with north wing and double drive. 1927: Cliff School, with classrooms added. 1980: Blatchington Court School, with more classrooms.

Later, after an interval when Robert Lambe decided to live there (1900-1915), Blatchington Court became a girls' boarding school.

From September 1951 Blatchington Court, the last school to occupy the building, was a school for 70 partially sighted boys. This transferred from a site in Eastern Road in Brighton to the 11-acre Blatchington Court site. Extensions were added to accommodate 105 boys.

The new school doctor was Dr Reg Sutton, a powerful swimmer who had captained the British water polo team at the 1936 Berlin Olympics. The new chaplain was the Revd C. K. W. Thorn, rector of St Peter's. In 1960 the school left behind its pejorative name 'Asylum', officially adopting the name Blatchington Court School for Partially Sighted Boys. The teaching rooms comprised 11 classrooms, 6 special rooms for Art and Craft, Science, Woodwork, Home Economics, Typing and Visual Aids. These were housed in a new block extending westwards along Belgrave Road; it included an assembly hall and a gymnasium equipped with stage and lighting. There were gardens, greenhouses, a chapel to the east of the old mansion and a covered heated swimming pool on the Lawn down the slope.

The living accommodation included a dining room, two sitting rooms, a games room, a hobbies room, three TV rooms and boarding accommodation for the boys. Most of this was housed in the old manor house. The Head's office was in the ground-floor reception room in the south-east corner and the library in what may originally have been a drawing room in the south-west corner. Between the two, inside the semi-circular porch, was a spacious hall that was partitioned to make an office for the Head's secretary, Mrs Chamberlain. Mr and Mrs Naylor and their children lived on the first floor, enjoying the wonderful views down the Lawn towards Seaford Head and east onto the churchyard. Three dormer windows were inserted into the attics to give them a couple of extra bedrooms.

The Naylors woke every morning at 6 to the sound of their loyal troupe of cleaning ladies arriving. As the cleaners approached on foot up the drive between the Old Rectory and the Church they chatted loudly; they explained to Mrs Naylor that this was to frighten off the foxes gathering round the bins outside the kitchens. But the early morning call suited the Naylors; it gave Ray the time he needed to sort the boys' post.

The Naylors enjoyed their sixteen years working at Blatchington Court - and the social life of the village too. They knew Hubert and Jill Martin, who lived opposite, at Field Cottage. They knew Madge Lewis, who lived at Monk's Orchard, Sir George and Lady Cold-

Ray Naylor, Headmaster of Blatchington Court School

Towards the end, Blatchington Court School took girls as well as boys. Here is a mixed class, reading.

stream at The Gatehouse, and David and Valerie Cairns at The Spinney. Reg Sutton at Robin Post was their school doctor, and Rex Hillman at Brushwood was one of their governors.

With improvements in peri-natal care, more children were surviving with multiple disabilities, and Mr Naylor and his staff were increasingly faced with educating children who were not only partially sighted but had other disabilities as well. The work became harder. With a national shift in policy towards educating disabled children in mainstream schools, there was a drop in numbers of handicapped children being sent to special schools, and this drove Blatchington Court School towards closure.

Ray Naylor had a close and friendly working relationship with his Chairman of Governors, Sir George Coldstream, who had grown up at The Corner House in Firle Road and been a pupil at Southdown School, and it was Sir George who recommended Ray to retire at 60 rather than trying to continue to 65. The job was demanding and Sir George thought Ray had a better chance of enjoying a long and useful retirement if he retired early. It was probably sound advice, as Ray lived to 95. Ray left Blatchington

Court to spend a year in Ghana, setting up a course to train teachers of the blind; this was at the request of Sir John Wilson, his friend and mentor, who was Director of the Royal Commonwealth Society for the Blind (now Sight Savers International). After Ray Naylor's retirement, John Wilkinson took over as Blatchington Court's Headmaster for its final eight years.

At the same time as the church hall controversy, an equally thorny controversy developed over the future of the Blatchington School site. The first intention was to turn part of it into an old people's home, but there were also plans to demolish and replace it with a housing estate. On 11 October 1985, applications for planning consent for both of these schemes, and the scheme to build a church hall in the churchyard, were published in the local paper.

The Revd Crittall wrote in St Peter's News for November 1985 about the proposal for housing development. He was concerned about the effect it might have on the character of East Blatchington. 'Housing at 8 units per acre might be felt to conflict with that character, especially in such quantity. At least the proposed plans allow for the trees on the estate to remain untouched.' Without any evident sense of irony, his letter was followed by an extract from the Homeland guidebook of 1916, which describes St Peter's churchyard as a flowery idyll, rich in hollies and yews, passion flower, clematis and wisteria, much of which would be destroyed if the *rector's* planning application went through.

As it became increasingly likely that the entire Blatchington Court site would be cleared for housing, Bernard Mote made an attempt to rescue it as a school. Living at Seagull Cottage, which backed onto the playing field of Blatchington Court School, he was naturally concerned about possible development. He also felt that the school was well-equipped, well-situated, full of character, and deserving of preservation. From late 1984 onwards, Bernard tried to interest various children's charities in taking the site on as a school or children's home: Barnado's, National Children's Home, Church of England Childrens Society, the Spastics Society. Unfortunately none of them wanted the premises.

A problem was that the Charities Commission insisted on the site being sold for the maximum price, a problem for any of the charities who might have been interested. Bernard proposed an ingenious scheme by which the Trustees might take out insurance to indemnify themselves in the event of an accusation that they had sold for less than market price. But it seemed unlikely that any insurance company would insure under these conditions, and the Charities Commission would probably in any case have objected to a sale at a figure below market value. Demolition seemed inevitable.

On 20 November 1985, at the same session as the rejection of the churchyard plan, the Planning Committee approved the plans to convert the old school buildings (including the chapel) into a nursing home. The plans to build houses on the Blatchington Court School site were refused. But the developer, Clarke Homes, appealed against the refusal.

Michael Francis, the Director of Planning, prepared an internal report in 1987 explaining that the developer was about to appeal, and outlining a strategy. He was aware that the Education Authority was keen to set up a primary school in the area, and the site was ideal for this use. He was also aware that there was limited provision of public open space, and that this had become significant with the progressive sell-off of private open space (the sale and development of the grounds of one private school after another). He proposed that the end result of the decision-making should include a primary school and playing field, some informal public open space and, if there was space left, a community use of some kind and some residential development. In fact this package is exactly what he achieved.

In the middle of this wrenching transformation of the heart of the village, a name from the past reappeared. It was Fred Lambe, the Frederick John Lambe who was Richard Frederic Lambe's son and Robert Lambe's grandson. In 1988 he was an old man looking back. He had known Blatchington Court as his grandfather's mansion in 1905-10, when he, Fred, was an impressionable small boy, as young and impressionable as his grandfather had been when *he* had watched Seaford Head being blown up. His earliest recollection of Blatchington Court would have been that short time when his grandfather had lived there. He thought it would be pleasant to come and have a last look at the house before it disappeared for ever. But then he had second thoughts. In May 1988, he wrote from Spring Cottage at Blackboys;

Dear Mrs Davies,
I feel I owe you an apology over the viewing of Blatchington Court. I certainly had the idea I would like to see it but really I expect after 50 or 60 years as a school it must be a bit tatty inside and out, and I thought I should be disappointed. . .
Fred Lambe

The Cheese House at Blatchington Court.
Even this quaint little flint-and-brick outbuilding had to go.

At about the same time Fred Lambe gave to Seaford Museum a photocopy of a nostalgic view up Blatchington Hill, and other items to the East Sussex Record Office. One was 'a mass of papers' relating to Robert Lambe's estate at Blatchington. Another was Robert Lambe's manuscript, *Incidents of my Life*. Perhaps after Robert's death or when her own approached Elizabeth handed the skeleton autobiography on to their son Richard Frederic, and he in turn left it to his son Fred. Fred died in the winter of 1989-90. In February 1990 a letter went to Mr Jakers of Twyn House from Wynne, Baxter, Godfree of Lewes High Street, allowing Mr Jakers to visit Spring Cottage to see if he could identify anything else that might be of interest to Seaford Museum.

That marked the end of the Lambe connection with Blatchington Court, and within a few months Blatchington Court was pulled down. The manor house had had a long and chequered history. In the middle ages its predecessor was in the hands of several generations of the Peverel family, In the sixteenth century, it passed eventually into the hands of the Gage family, and from there to the Gilbert family and the Fermor family. It was rebuilt in the 1780s by John Sherley Fermor, then bought by the Chambers family. In 1818 it was bought by John King, who left it to his daughter Elizabeth in 1853. She and her husband sold it to Robert

Lambe in 1877. One of the men commented as he worked on demolishing the fine old building, with its beautiful panelled rooms, 'This house doesn't want to be pulled down.'

The Pond

Once there were five ponds in and round the village, Blatchington Pond the largest of them. They had a practical function, to provide drinking water for passing herds of cattle, draft animals and travellers' horses, and in each case at a meeting of the ways. Blatchington Pond lay in the dell at the bottom of the village, at the junction of Blatchington Road, Blatchington Hill and Sutton Drove. Old maps show that in the nineteenth century people and livestock passed along both north and south sides of the pond. The northern route became Sutton Drove; the southern route is followed still by the footpath under the trees.

Over the centuries, the big pond was an important focus of the rural life of the area. Herds and flocks were watered there as they passed from Blatchington to Seaford or Sutton. Villagers regularly fished in it, caught waterfowl, and boys used to try to catch birds; it was a source of free food and a focus for recreation.

But the dark waters of the Pond represented a focus for despair. In the seventeenth century a young woman was found drowned in the pond, presumed to have committed suicide; this was where Sarah Reynolds 'came to an untimely end' on May Day in 1653. Again, in the nineteenth century, a woman 'came to drown herself' in the Pond, but she was prevented from doing herself any harm by bystanders and taken home.

Blatchington Pond was substantially larger and deeper than it is today, a favourite haunt for the bird-loving and bird-slaying rector, Robert Dennis. It was there that he saw a grey phalarope swimming in October 1846, and shot it. On another visit he shot a carrion-crow perched in the elm tree above the Pond. In 1861 he saw a beautiful hoopoe over the Pond; on May Day in 1869, one of his bird-children, Will Reed, reported seeing another in the same place.

By then there was already an interest in enhancing the area round the Pond. In 1877, Mr Cullingford gave an ornamental seat to be placed beside it. With the encroachment of building development, it became less attractive as a focus for wildlife. And then, as if losing heart, the pond itself began to shrink and disappear. It is thought that during some dry summers in the early

Adding the liner along the north side of the pond

twentieth century the pond's clay lining was exposed for too long, drying out and cracking, so that it was no longer watertight. The water drained away into the underlying chalk.

Residents, led by Richard Good of The Gables and Madge Lewis of the Old Rectory, saw the formation of the Conservation Area in the 1970s as a good moment to restore the pond. The Council owned the site and looked into the possibility of restoration, but decided it would be beyond the Council's budget.

Blatchington Pond in 1930

When a meeting was held to explore the possibility of a DIY restoration, the residents' response was enthusiastic and £2000 was raised to undertake the work. A committee was set up, chaired by Mrs Lewis.

The first task, in the winter of 1980, was to make a waterproof lining to prevent the water from draining away into the chalk. The lining was made by sticking together several large sheets of heavy-duty polythene. The accumulated silt and the remains of the old clay lining were dredged out and banked up round the site to form a high rim; then the polythene sheeting was laid in the excavated hollow and held in place with turf. Then the final knee-deep layer of clay was put back in. An island was created at one end, using several large pipes standing on end as a foundation. They were covered with wire netting, then soil.

Remaking Blatchington Pond was a major undertaking for a team of fewer than ten people, and it shows what local residents can do if they put their minds to it. The pond that today looks so natural is the result of 75 man-days of work and the shifting of a thousand tonnes of soil. It continues to need a lot of maintenance, which is overseen by the current Pond Manager, the indefatigable

Madge Lewis

Cedric Trenfield. The pond is kept in immaculate condition. In his programme of planting and maintenance, Cedric's intention has been 'to bring a little piece of the country into the town'.

What Cedric and the other volunteers have achieved is exactly that – a wonderful restoration of the rusticity that once saturated the life of the village. But he and they have achieved something more. In a world of diminishing open space, they have created a miniature green belt between Seaford and Blatchington. It helps to define, if not the separateness of Blatchington from Seaford, at least its *differentness*.

The demolition of the Elm Court Centre created an opportunity to restore a second pond, the Water Lily Pool, within its own little patch of tree-lined meadow. This would accentuate the green belt effect, and greatly enhance the provision of open space, but it seems unlikely it will happen. Councils are greedy for cash, which development generates, and greedy for additional council tax, which they can get from new home-owners. The drive is, as it has been for decades, to cram as many dwellings as possible into every available space, with decreasing regard for local identities, and scant respect for the local histories behind those identities.

The overwhelming change over the last century or so has been the engulfment of the village by Seaford's urban expansion. This can easily be seen in the population figures. From 1801 to 1871, there was, apart from the barracks, only the village, which was inhabited by around 150 people. After the closure of the barracks, this was also the population of the parish, but in the following decades while the village remained stable the population of the parish soared: to 740 in 1901, 1,750 in 1921, 2,448 in 1951, 9,467 in 2001. Today the parish is home to 10,000 people, yet the village at its core still has a population of around 150. The threat to the identity of Blatchington village is clear, just from these statistics, as is the need for its Conservation Area status to be taken seriously.

Bishopstone was threatened with massive residential development but, thanks to articulate local opposition, it was able to defend itself successfully and maintain its separate identity. Blatchington was unable to do so, partly because of its proximity to Seaford, partly because of a lack of co-ordinated local opposition, partly because the village was in effect betrayed by its principal landowner. The demarcation of the South Downs National Park boundary has, it may be hoped, guaranteed Bishopstone's future; Bishopstone village is firmly embedded in and surrounded on all

The Water Lily Pool as it was in 1900, a lost local beauty spot.

sides by the National Park. Although the Park boundary should effectively prevent Seaford from growing any further northwards, it seems to be impossible to stop infilling (such as the Bowden House School development) continuing within that limiting boundary. Bishopstone shows what might have been achieved but, as far as Blatchington is concerned, the horse has bolted; a great deal of the damage that has been done is irreversible.

Some of the changes have been for the better. The village is more prosperous now than it was. People once attempted to label social groups according to a simple class system – upper, middle or lower class – but that ceased to satisfy long ago. The new Acorn system consists of a spectrum of 56 socio-economic types. Most medieval villagers would have found themselves in the Hard Pressed category, around type 44: Low-Income Larger Families. According to Acorn, the twenty-first century residents of Blatchington village belong to the Wealthy Achievers category, the so-called Affluent Greys (types 5-8). So Blatchington has seen a shift right across most of the socio-economic spectrum. A survey run by Lewes District Council shows East Blatchington parish as a whole to be one of the least deprived areas in the district, where men have a life expectancy of 81 and women a life expectancy of 85. Not surprisingly, the place has an air of well-being about it.

East Blatchington was once a tiny village on the southerly slope of the Downs, cringing from the Channel gales behind its wind-break belts of trees. It is *still* that village, even though it is surrounded by Seaford's invading suburbs. And the single street is still there too, the lane worn ever-downwards into the chalk hillside by the iron-shod wheels of farmers' carts, stagecoaches and squires' carriages, the hoofs of horses, sheep and cattle, the blakeyed boots of soldiers and labourers and the trotters of runaway ringless pigs - the sunken lane etched into the land by the everyday existence of the village. A line scored across the landscape, the street is itself an expression of Blatchington's long history.

Exploring the past

This is a first attempt at telling Blatchington's story, but I am acutely aware that as I develop a greater understanding of its past I appreciate more the value of what I see around me. A walk up Firle Road is pleasant enough without knowing anything at all, but it is doubly pleasurable to notice things and understand their historic meaning: to stand, for example, at the Firle Drive junction and notice the dip in the lawn on the opposite side of the road, between Beacon Lodge and The Corner House, and know that 200 years ago that dip was a pond for watering livestock. There was once another pond further up, in the broad grass verge outside St John's School, again shown by a tell-tale hollow; the old Greenway used to pass round it on both sides. And between the two one-time ponds is the raised garden in front of Firle Cottage; it catches our attention once we realise it is the level plinth made long ago for Blatchington's windmill, a long-enduring landmark and focal point in the village.

Further down, Alces Place was once a barn with a threshing floor and its elegant courtyard garden was a farmyard; Blatchington House, now a care home, was once the main farmhouse in the village, owned by the lords of Alciston manor and in the nineteenth and early twentieth centuries home to three generations of the Lambe family: William, then Robert, then Thomas Lambe lived there.

Upper Belgrave Road is a late addition to the landscape, made initially to provide access to Robert Lambe's housing development in St Peter's Road and then to provide access, via North Camp Lane, to North Camp. Lambe laid out the housing so that the back gardens on the east side of St Peter's Road ran across to the field boundary of Home Furlong. That boundary was originally the grassy balk marking the eastern end of the furrow-long strips running eastwards from Firle Road – another line from the medieval rural landscape subtly preserved in the modern suburban landscape. And in an exactly similar way, the eastern ends of the back gardens on the east side of Kedale Road form a straight line that is one furlong (220 yards) west of Blatchington Hill. This tells us that medieval cultivation strips ran west from Blatchington Hill to *that* line. Another furlong to the west takes us to the long straight footpath that runs from the Trek Club to Belgrave Road and continues, straight as a die, in the pavement on the east side of Carlton Road; this is not just an alleyway left by chance, nor a chance alignment, but a centuries-old medieval headland footpath that once passed, unfenced, across the open fields between the furlongs, heading for Bishopstone.

On Belgrave Road, we can see the flint-walled church hall of St Peter's, neatly converted from the chapel of Blatchington Court School, and which in its turn was converted from the stables for the old manor house. Next to it, we have to use our imaginations to see the modern rectory and the house next to it as standing on the cleared site of the north wing of Blatchington Court, which was built in 1900 by Robert Lambe and demolished in 1991 by Clarke Homes. Of Blatchington Court itself, the manor house rebuilt in the 1780s, virtually nothing remains except its original drive, which survives as the unusually wide footpath between the churchyard and the Old Rectory. At its entrance are some overgrown pillars, rebuilt in the nineteenth century; on the northern pillar it is still possible to make out in peeling paint the word 'Court'. On the southern pillar, still less visible, is the cryptic syllable 'ching'. Nothing else is left.

On Blatchington Hill, in late morning sunlight, we may see a slight unevenness high up the wall of the Old Rectory, which shows where the Victorian rector, Robert Dennis, took off the Georgian roof in 1862 and added an extra storey – a reminder that he married an heiress. Passing down the road, we see on the corner of Homefield Road the flint building that was once The Star Inn, and just below it in the roadwall the ghost of a window in what was once the end wall of Widows' Cottages. Lower down are the descendants of the trees that made up 'Mr King's plantations', the spinneys that were maintained as windbreaks by successive squires, and which now help give Blatchington its distinctive village-in-a-wood character.

Even the brand-new, all-at-once development of the Princess Drive estate preserves traces of the landscape that was there before.

There is no sign now of the open arable land of the West and North Laines that existed from Anglo-Saxon times on, and the suburban road system is all new. And yet, if we compare old maps with new, we can see that the old road from Blatchington to Bishopstone *is* still there. It survives as a sequence of discreetly preserved footpaths running from Beacon Lodge across to Costcutter, and then on across Katherine Way and Clementine Avenue, finally resuming its identity as an open way across the fields to Grand Avenue and the Wall Walk to Bishopstone. The old coach road is still there.

This is the living history of the village, the different pasts that conjure themselves up in different places as we notice the surviving tell-tale clues. Sometimes it can seem as if all of those pasts continue to exist and to co-exist in the present. It is not possible for any of us to know all the history of a place like this, but the more we know, the richer our experience becomes - whether we are residents or visitors - and the more we appreciate how important it is to conserve what we have.

Notes & sources

Blatchington Court School Annual Report 1951-52.
Blatchington Pond Conservation Society.
Carol Chamberlain (Blatchington Court School)
Castleden 2011 (Robert Dennis)
Cedric Trenfield (Blatchington Pond)
Arlington House Papers (proposed removal of Firle Road east roadwall)
Deed of covenant between Viscount Gage and John King (1818)
Seaford West Company & Mrs E. S. Lambe and Seaford Urban District
    Council 1913 (widening of southern end of Firle Road)
Lewes District Council 2011 (deprivation level).
Morgan, F. 1933 *Letter to Blakers (Lewes) regarding Arlington House.*
    (width of Upper Belgrave Road and Firle Road)
Robert Lambe Papers
Southern Weekly News 1937 (lack of pub and petrol station)
UU
Valerie Naylor (Blatchington Court School)

References

Abbreviations:
CBA = Council for British Archaeology
ESRO = East Sussex Record Office
SAC = Sussex Archaeological Collections
SCM = Sussex County Magazine
SNQ = Sussex Notes & Queries

Alciston Manor court book. *ESRO*.

André, J. L., Keyser, C. E., Johnston, P. M. and Whittey, H. M. 1900 Mural paintings in Sussex churches. *SAC* 43, 220-51.

Anon 1832 Memoir of Rear-Admiral James Walker, C. B. *United Service Journal and Naval and Military Magazine* (1832) 1, 201-8.

Anon 1903 The London Volunteer Camp at Seaford. *British Medical Journal,* 22 August, 441-2.

Anon 1937 The parish without a pub or petrol station. *Southern Weekly News* (23 January).

Anon 1942 Sussex Archaeological Society. *SNQ* 8, 174-7.

Anon 1963 Report of the the Council. *SAC* 101, xlii.

Anon 1970 or later *Alces Place*. Typescript in Lambe Papers, Seaford Museum.

Arlington House Papers (in the possession Mr Robert Moore).

Banks, W. 1905 *Affidavit* regarding the Greenway.

Barrett, E. P. S. undated *King's Mead School, Seaford: brief ouline of the history of the school*. Unpublished ms.

Bell, B. 1977 Excavations at Bishopstone. *SAC* 115.

Bell, M. 1978 Saxon Sussex in Drewett, P. (ed) *Archaeology in Sussex to AD 1500*. CBA Research Report 29.

Blatchington Manor court book. *ESRO*.

Blaauw, W. H. 1839 Remarks on the Nonae of 1340 as relating to Sussex. *SAC* 1, 58-64.

Blencowe, R. W. 1851 Extracts from the parish registers. *SAC* 4, 241-90.

Brandon, P. *Development of the South-East 1100-1900*.

Brandon, P. 1998 *The South Downs*. Chichester: Phillimore.

Brent, C. E. 1976 Rural employment and population in Sussex between 1550 and 1640. *SAC* 114, 27-48.

Brent, J. A. 1968 Alciston manor in the later middle ages. *SAC* 106, 89-102.

Budgen, W. 1931 The Black Death in Sussex. *SNQ* 3, 124-5.

Budgen, W. 1944 Wists and virgates of land. *SNQ* 10, 73-6.

Budgen, W. 1946 The acreage of the Sussex hide of land. *SNQ* 11, 73-6.

Burleigh, G. R. 1973 An introduction to deserted medieval villages in East Sussex. *SAC* 111, 45-83.

Butler, C. 2009 *Desk-based assessment at land adjacent to Blatchington House, Seaford, East Sussex*. Chris Butler Archaeological Services.

Carter, Agnes 1917 *A canteen in a Canadian Camp*. Seaford Museum.

Castleden, R. 2000 *King Arthur: the truth behind the legend*. London and New York: Routledge.

Castleden, R. 2011 *The Bird Man of Blatchington*. Seaford: Blatchington Press.

Castleden, R. and Franks, B. 2012 *Mrs Lambe's Cook Book*. Seaford: Blatchington Press.

Challen, W. H. 1963 Elphick family of Seaford. *SNQ* 15, 28-9.

Clare, A. R. 1959 *Proposed development at Seaford*.

Cleveland, Duchess of 1889 *The Battle Abbey Roll*. 3 vols. London: John Murray.

Cline, C. L. (ed) 1970 *The letters of George Meredith*. Oxford.

Combes, P. 2002 Bishopstone, a pre-Conquest minster church. *SAC* 140, 49-56.

Cooper, J. 1879 On some recently discovered Ancient British urns. *SAC* 29, 238-9.

Cooper, R. M. 1998 *The literary guide and companion England*. Athens, Ohio: Ohio University Press.

Cooper, W. D. 1866 Participation of Sussex in Cade's rising, 1450. *SAC* 18, 17-86.

Cope, W. 1877 *The Rifle Brigade*. London: Spottiswoode.

Corner, G. R. 1853 On the custom of Borough English, as existing in the County of Sussex. *SAC* 6, 164-189.

Custumal of Alciston Manor, in *Custumals of Battle Abbey* (1897).

Deed of Covenant between Viscount Gage and John King (4 December 1818). *ESRO*.

Dennis, R. N. 1861a Monumental inscriptions, East Blatchington. *SAC* 13, 302.

Dennis, R. N. 1861b Urns found in East Blatchington Church. *SAC* 13, 309.

Dickins, K. W. 1956 The muniments of the Sussex Archaeological Trust: Guide to the calendars. *SAC* 94, 144-57.

Ellis, S. M. 1920 *George Meredith: his life and friends in relation to his work*. London: Grant Richards.

Ellman, E. B. 2004 *Recollections of a Sussex parson*. Bakewell: Country Books.

Gardner, M. 1995 Aspects of the history and archaeology of medieval Seaford. *SAC* 133, 189-212.

Gardner, M. 2003 Economy and landscape change in post-Roman and early medieval Sussex, 450-1175, in Rudling, D. (ed) *The archaeology of Sussex to AD 2000*. Kings Lynn: Heritage Marketing & Publications.

Garwood, P. 1985 The Cuckmere Valley Project fieldwalking programme 1982-3. *Institute of Archaeology Bulletin* 22, 62.

Godfrey, W. H. 1940 Axial towers in Sussex churches. *SAC* 81, 97-120.

Gray, H. L. 1915 *English field systems*. Harvard University Press.

Grinsell, L. V. 1931 Sussex in the bronze age. *SAC* 72, 66.

Guthrie, T. A. 1936 *A long retrospect*. Oxford: Oxford University Press.

Halliwell, 1904 *Dictionary of archaic and provincial words*. London: Routledge.

Holden, E. W. 1963 Excavations at the deserted medieval village of Hangleton, Part 1. *SAC* 101, 54-181.

Holgate, M. S. 1927 Wantley Manor in the fourteenth century. *SNQ* 1, 47-8.

Holland, R. 2011 Personal communication (Bertram Adams buildings).

Hopkins, R. T. 1927 *Old English mills and inns*. London: Cecil Palmer.

Hudson, W. 1907 Assessment of the hundreds of Sussex to the King's Tax in 1334. *SAC* 50, 153-75.

Hudson, A. 1984 Volunteer soldiers in Sussex during the Revolutionary and Napoleonic Wars, 1793-1815. *SAC* 122, 165-81.

Hunnisett, R. F. 1957 Sussex coroners in the middle ages. *SAC* 95, 42-58.

Jones, F. undated *Marching with Thomas Skeel*. carmarthenshire.org.uk.

Kingsley, D. 1982 *Printed maps of Sussex 1575-1900*. Sussex Record Society, Vol 72.

King's Bench Controlment Roll 32, m. 45.

Ladurie. E. LeRoy 1978 *Montaillou: Cathars and Catholics in a French village*. Harmondsworth: Penguin Books.

Lambe, R. c.1914 *Incidents of my Life*. Unpublished MS notes.

Langton, J. and Morris, R. J. (ed) 1986 *Atlas of Industrializing Britain*. London: Methuen.

Lewes District Council 2011 *Health Profile*.

Lower, M. A. 1851 *The Chronicle of Battel Abbey, 1066-1176*. London: John Russell Smith.

Lower, M. A. 1860 The hospital of lepers at Seaford. *SAC* 12, 112-6.

Lower, M. A. 1868 *Note on Seaford, historical, antiquarian, anecdotal and descriptive*. Lewes: G. P. Bacon.

Lowerson, J. (ed) 1975 *An embryonic Brighton? Victorian and Edwardian Seaford*. Brighton: University of Sussex.

Mate, M. 1992 The economic and social roots of medieval popular rebellion: Sussex in 1450-1451. *Economic History Review* 45, 661-676.

Mate, M. 2006 *Trade and economic developments, 1450-1550: the experience of Kent, Surrey and Sussex*. Woodbridge: Boydell & Brewer.

National Archive: Sutton and Seaford. Documents SAS-M/1/331, 352, 354, 355, 356, 357, 358, 366, 367, 370, 372.

Newhaven and Seaford Sea Defences Act, 1898.

Nicklin, P. A. and Godfrey-Faussett, E. G. 1935 On the distribution of place-names in Sussex. *SAC* 76, 213-221.

Odam, J. 1999 *The Seaford story, 1000-2000 AD*. Seaford: SB Publications.

Page, W. (ed) 1905 *Victoria History of the County of Sussex*. Vol 1. London: Constable.

Palmere, Sir Thomas and Covert, Sir Walter 1587 *A survey of the defence of Sussex Coasts*.

Pettitt, F. W. 1949 *Memories of Seaford in the late 1870s and 80s*. Unpublished ms. in Seaford Museum

Renshaw, W. C. 1906 Notes from the Act Books of the Archdeaconry Court of Lewes. *SAC* 69, 47-65.

Ridley, K. H. 1984 *Schools in Seaford, East Sussex*. Unpublished BA dissertation, Durham University.

Robert Lambe Papers, Seaford Museum.

Robinson, T. 1822 *The common law of Kent* (3rd edition). London.

Roll of a Subsidy levied 13th Henry IV.

Russell, C. 2009 *An archaeological desk-based assessment of land and Bowden House School, Firle Road, Seaford*. Archaeology South-East, prepared for Warings Group.

Salzmann, L. F. 1901 *The history of the parish of Hailsham*. Lewes: Farncombe & Co.

Salzman, L. F. 1942 Sussex excommunicates. *SAC* 82, 124-140.

Salzman, L. F. 1943 The Hundred Rolls for Sussex. *SAC* 33, 35-54.

Sawyer, F. E. 1880 Proceedings of the Committee of Plundered Ministers relating to Sussex. *SAC* 30, 112-36.

Sawyer, F. E. 1887 Crown presentations to Sussex benefices. *SAC* 35, 179-88.

Seaford West Company & Mrs E. S. Lambe and Seaford Urban District Council 1913 *Heads of Agreement as to Firle Road*.

Searle, E. 1963 Hides, virgates and tenant settlement at Battle Abbey. *Economic History Review* 16, 290-300.

Simmons, H. 1878 A catalogue of drawings in the British Museum, relating to the county of Sussex. *SAC* 28, 148-79.

Simms, R. 2010 *Star Man: F. W. Thomas*. (website)

Skeel, T. 1815 *A true and corect accompt: the life of Thomas Skeel, Grenadier in the 40th Regt of Foot; with account of his travels through England and Wales, Ireland, Portugal, Spain, and France. Vol 1*. unpubd MS. Carmarthen Record Office

Sykes, E. 1946 *Newhaven-Seaford sea defences*. Paper for meeting of South Eastern District of the Institution of Municipal and County Engineers at Seaford, Sussex (27 Mar 1946).

Tate, W. E. 1949 Sussex inclosure acts and awards. *SAC* 88, 115-156.

Tattersall, J. F. 1927 Harpocrates, the god of silence. *Sussex Notes and Queries* 1, 184-5.

Thomas, G. 2010 *The later Anglo-Saxon settlement at Bishopstone: a downland manor in the making*. Council for British Archaeology Research Report 163.

Thorne, R. G. 1986 *The House of Commons 1790-1820*. History of Parliament Trust.

Torr, V. J. 1920 An Elizabethan return of the state of the diocese of Chichester. *SAC* 61, 92-124.

Valuation of the Rectories and Vicarages within the Rape of Lewes (1650).

Vincent, A. 2000 *Roman roads of Sussex*. Midhurst: Midhurst Press.

W. B. 1931 The Black Death in Sussex. *SNQ* 3, 124-5.

Williams, F. (undated) *Monk's Orchard*. Monograph.

Appendix A
The rectors of St Peter's, East Blatchington

1257-1293: Hamo de Warenne, the first of 61 known and named rectors
1294: William Peverell
1306: Thomas
1327-1340: Roger
1362-1366 Hugh de Ardern
1367: William Waryn
1368-1370: Richard de Flycham (exchanged)
1370-1371: Robert from Newtimber
1371-1375: William Hagham/Wagham (resigned)
1384: John Best (exchanged)
1384-1387: William Curteys
1387-1392: Roger atte Cote
1392-1398: William Mot
1398-1404: John de Depyng
1404-1420: William Stephen
1420-1442: John Fax
14? -1479: William Peyton (resigned)
1479-14? : John Dey
14? - 1486: John Clerke (resigned)
1486- ? : Ralph Scolay
?   -1520: John Prideaux (resigned)
1520-1521: Thomas Spyre (resigned)
1521-1543: John Person (died)
1543-1548: Thomas Deens/Deans (resigned)
1548-1550: Thomas Mason
1550-155?: Miles Airy or Milo Ayere.
155?-1555: John Durstan
1555-1559: ?
1559-1571: John James
1571-157? : Francis Cox
157?-1574: John Large
1574-1575: Robert Hide
1575-1578: John James
1578-1605: William Coell (died)
1605-1631: Robert Goffe (died)
1631-1635: Edward Fossbury
1635-1661: Nicholas Pope (died)
1662-1665: John Saxby (died)
1665-1680: John Cooke
1680-1690: Edward Wilson (deprived)
1690-1706: Benjamin Hyde/Hind (died)
1706-1722: William King

1722-1729: Thomas Knight (died)
1729-1730: Edward Walmsley (resigned)
1730-1734: John Goldwright (resigned)
1734-1742: Henry Lushington (resigned)
1742-1755: James Tattershall (resigned)
1755-1766: John Robson (died)
1766-1804: Samuel Topping (died)
1804-1843: John Lewis (died)
1844-1880: Robert Nathaniel Dennis (resigned)
1880-1915: Arthur John Richardson (resigned)
1915-1936: Henry Lancelot Martley (resigned)
1936-1938: Ernest Esdale Winter (resigned)
1938-1946: Percy Triquet Browning (resigned)
1946-1949: John Magnus Laing (died)
1949-1958: Cyril Kenwin Thorn (resigned)
1959-1973: Peter Westrope Wright (resigned)
1973-1983: Eric Charles Andrews (resigned)
1983-1995: Richard Simon Crittall (resigned)
1995-2004: Kenneth Yates (resigned)
2004-2011: Brian Robert Cook (resigned)
2011-   : Andrew Mayes

Appendix B
The lords of the manor of East Blatchington

1165	Robert Peverel
?	Walter Peverel
?	Thomas Peverel
? -1227	Robert Peverel II
1227- ?	Andrew Peverel I
?	Andrew Peverel II
?	Andrew Peverel III
? -1375	Andrew Peverel IV
1375-1379	John Brocas
1411	Richard Weyvils or Wyvill
?	The West family
?	The De La Warr family
?	The Jefferay family
? -1589	Sir Robert Sidney
1589-1593	Sir Thomas Sherley of Wiston
1593-1603	Edward Gage of Bentley & Edward Gage of Wormley Grange
1603-1627	John Gilbert
1627-1677	Nicholas Gilbert I
1678-1704	Thomas Gilbert
1704-1713	Nicholas Gilbert II
1717-1730	Colonel John Fermor
1730-1742	Sir Henry Fermor, Bart.
1742-1791	Rev John Sherley Fermor (or Boorder)
1791-1795	Thomas Harben
1795-1808	William Chambers
1808-1818	Barbara Chambers (m. Stephen Challen)
1818-1853	John King
1853-1877	Elizabeth King (m. Robert Dennis)
1877-1922	Robert Lambe

This is a tentative, provisional list only and the first half in particular may well need to be revised. At certain times, lordships of manors changed hands fairly rapidly and it is hard to trace all the trans-actions. On the two occasions when females inherited, the estate was held in trust for them; Barbara Chambers and Elizabeth King were 'beneficial' owners, entitled to live in the manor house and take rents from the estate, but not regarded as lords of the manor.

Index

Blatchington village, as it was in 1780.
Tracing from the Yeakell and Gardner map.
The Star Inn is missing, which seems an odd oversight.

The manor house has gone, but this remnant of Blatchington Court's eastern spinney is still on windbreak duty at the foot of Blatchington Hill, overlooking the Pond.
Robert Dennis called the two spinneys 'Mr King's trees'.

Books by Rodney Castleden

Classic Landforms of the Sussex Coast
The Wilmington Giant
The Stonehenge People
The Knossos Labyrinth
Minoans: Life in Bronze Age Crete
Book of British Dates
Neolithic Britain
The Making of Stonehenge
World History
The Cerne Giant
Knossos, Temple of the Goddess
Atlantis Destroyed
Out in the Cold: Ideas on Glaciation
The English Lake District
King Arthur: the Truth Behind the Legend
The Little Book of Kings and Queens
Ancient British Hill Figures
The History of World Events
Britain 3000 BC
The World's Most Evil People
Infamous Murderers
Serial Killers
Mycenaeans
People Who Changed the World
Events That Changed the World
English Castles
Castles of the Celtic Lands
The Attack on Troy
The Book of Saints
Assassinations and Conspiracies
Inventions That Changed the World
Natural Disasters that Changed the World
Great Unsolved Crimes
Conflicts That Changed the World
Discoveries That Changed the World
Witness to History
Encounters That Changed the World
Spree Killers: the Enigma of Mass Murder
The Bird Man of Blatchington